COLLECTION 14

Kristy and her friends love babysitting and when her mum can't find a babysitter for Kristy's little brother one day, Kristy has a great idea. Why doesn't she set up a babysitting club? That way parents can make a single phone call and reach a team of babysitting experts. And if one baby-sitter is already busy another one can take the job. So together with her friends, Claudia, Mary Anne and Stacey, Kristy starts THE BABYSITTERS CLUB. And although things don't *always* go according to plan, they have a lot of fun on the way!

Catch up with the very latest adventures of the Babysitters Club in these great new stories:

91 Claudia and the First Thanksgiving

92 Mallory's Christmas Wish

93 Mary Anne and the Memory Garden

94 Stacey McGill, Super Sitter

95 Kristy + Bart = ?

96 Abby's Lucky Thirteen

97 Claudia and the World's Cutest Baby

98 Dawn and Too Many Sitters

And coming soon. . .

99 Stacey's Broken Heart

The Babysitters Club

COLLECTION 14

Book 40
CLAUDIA AND THE
MIDDLE SCHOOL MYSTERY

Book 41
MARY ANNE vs. LOGAN

Book 42
JESSI AND THE
DANCE SCHOOL PHANTOM

Ann M. Martin

Hippo

Scholastic Children's Books,
Commonwealth House, 1–19 New Oxford Street,
London, WC1A 1NU, UK
A division of Scholastic Ltd
London ~ New York ~ Toronto ~ Sydney ~ Auckland ~
Mexico City ~ New Delhi ~ Hong Kong

Claudia and the Middle School Mystery
Mary Anne vs. Logan
Jessi and the Dance School Phantom
First published in the US by Scholastic Inc., 1991
First published in the UK by Scholastic Ltd, 1993

First published in this edition by Scholastic Ltd, 1999

ISBN 0 439 01226 0

Typeset by M Rules
Printed by Cox & Wyman Ltd, Reading, Berks.

1 2 3 4 5 6 7 8 9 10

CONTENTS

CLAUDIA AND THE MIDDLE SCHOOL MYSTERY

The author gratefully acknowledges
Ellen Miles
for her help in
preparing this manuscript.

1st CHAPTER

"So, if Gertrude used two thirds of a cup of chocolate to make eight biscuits, how much chocolate would be in each biscuit?" Janine asked.

I frowned. I bit my lip. I tapped my pencil against my front teeth. "Each biscuit would have. . ." Just then I *hated* Gertrude, whoever she was. Why did she have to make biscuits, anyway? And why did she have to measure out the chocolate? I'd just dump in as much as I had. I *love* chocolate. And I hate the name Gertrude.

Janine nodded at me encouragingly, smiling as if I'd already come up with the right answer.

I looked up at the picture hanging over my desk. Mimi, as a twelve-year-old, gave me her gentle smile. I looked down at the problem one more time. "It's got to be one twelfth." I said. "One twelfth of a cup in each?" Janine was grinning at me.

"You've got it, Claud!" she said. "I really think you understand it this time." She smiled some more. "Excellent!"

So now you know how much chocolate Gertrude put in each biscuit, and so do I, I suppose – at least this time. But you don't know who I am, or who Janine might be, or even who Mimi in the picture is.

I'm Claudia Kishi. I'm thirteen and I'm in the eighth grade at Stoneybrook Middle School. I have long black hair and almond-shaped eyes (I'm Japanese-American) and in case you haven't already worked it out, I'm not exactly what you would call a great scholar. In fact, the test I was studying for was in *remedial* maths. That's right. I can't seem to keep up with the rest of my class, at least in certain subjects. I try hard, but maybe not hard enough. The fact is, I'm just not interested in maths and science.

What *am* I interested in? I'll tell you. First on my list is art. I love drawing, painting, sculpting, making things out of papier-mâché, making collages, making jewellery . . . well, you get the idea.

Next, I love my family. We're pretty close. There's just Mum and Dad and Janine and me. My dad's an investment banker, my mum's a librarian and my sister, Janine, is a genius. I mean it! She's a junior at Stoneybrook High, but she's taking college courses already. It's, well, it's *interesting* to have a genius in the family. More about Janine later.

Mimi, the one in the picture, was my grandmother. (Of course, she wasn't yet my grandmother when that picture was taken.) She died not long ago, but I love that photo of her as a younger girl. She looked a lot like me back then.

I miss Mimi all the time. How can I explain how wonderful she was? Always calm, always gentle – that was Mimi. She understood me better than anyone else ever has. Sometimes I just can't believe that I'll really never see her again. But she'll always be in my heart, and just thinking of her and looking at her picture can make me feel close to her.

Now, where was I? Oh, right. Things that I like. Well, I love babysitting – so much so that I belong to a club called the Babysitters Club – but more about that later, too. I also love reading Nancy Drew mysteries, and I adore junk food. Hula Hoops, M&M's, Snickers bars – I never say no to any of them.

My parents, however, don't like me reading Nancy Drew books (they'd prefer it if I read "classics") and they *really* don't like me to eat junk food. "Proper nutrition is *important*. . ." You know the line.)

So I've learned to hide my secret vices. The Nancy Drew books get stuck under my mattress, or on the top shelf of my wardrobe, or underneath a pile of dirty clothes. The junk food gets stashed any where and everywhere – it's always turning up where I least expect it. Last night, for example, when I was looking for my favourite watercolour set, I found a bag of M&M's that I'd hidden months ago. (They were still tasty.)

On this night, though, I wasn't eating any junk food or reading any Nancy Drew books. I was studying for a big test, a huge test, a *killer* test. This maths test was going to count for a big part of my final grade. I just *had* to do well in it.

Janine was helping me study. It's sort of a rule in my family (my parents' idea) that somebody has to help me with my homework every night. Mimi used to be my favourite helper of all. She never got impatient with me, she never made me feel stupid, and even though she didn't often tell me so, I always knew that she was very, very proud of whatever I did.

Janine is a different story.

It's not that she's unkind or anything – but I just don't think she has any idea of what school is like for me. She *loves* school. She'd go to school eight days a week if she could. I don't think she's ever got any grade lower than an A–. And you should see the subjects she takes! I don't even understand the *names* of most of them – especially the computer ones.

And here she is, helping me try to understand how Gertrude measures chocolate – and why. She must think I'm so stupid. I know it's really nice of her to help me, but I really wish I didn't need her – or anyone's – help.

I looked back at my maths book. All those fractions were making me feel dizzy. Janine was being unusually patient. She knew this test was important to me.

"So how do you like Mr Zorzi, Claudia?" she asked. Mr Zorzi is my maths teacher – at least he is for now. My usual teacher is away for a few weeks, recovering from an operation, so we have Mr Zorzi as a long-term substitute.

"He's okay, I suppose. I've had him before. He knows it takes me a while to catch on to some of this stuff," I said, nodding towards my messy notebook.

Frankly, I never think too much about my teachers and whether I like them or not. I just do my best to get through most of my classes without making a complete fool of myself. Janine, however, just *loves* some of her teachers – and they all think she's brilliant.

Sometimes I get so tired of teachers asking me, "*Claudia Kishi?* Are you Janine's sister? Well, I know I can expect some wonderful work from you, if you're anything like Janine." Of course, they're always disappointed. Except my art teachers. Art is the one thing that I'm good at and Janine has no interest in.

"Okay, Claud. Let's try another one," Janine said. I tried to focus on the numbers in my maths book. I was getting tired. "Now, look," she said. "This is an improper fraction. But all we need to do is simplify, then multiply by the reciprocal. . ."

I blanked out for a minute. When Janine got that schoolteacher-ish tone in her voice, she could be hard to listen to. Besides, most of what she was saying sounded like gibberish to me. I know it was ungrateful, when she was being nice enough to take the time to help me study – but I just drifted off. I was thinking about this collage I'm working on, and wondering if there would be any good pictures in the new gardening magazine that my mum had brought home that day.

". . .and, by using cross-simplification we find that the train was actually travelling at forty-eight miles an hour, which is. . . Hey Claudia!" Janine snapped her fingers in front of my face. "Earth to Claudia, Earth to Claudia," she said. "Can you read me?"

"Oh, sorry, Janine," I said. "I was just—"

"You were daydreaming again," she said. "I know that look on your face." She frowned and pushed her glasses up – they'd slid down her nose while she was lecturing. "What were you thinking about?"

"Oh, nothing, really," I said. "Let's keep going. What about Problem Five?"

There was no way I was going to tell Janine what I'd been thinking about. I had finished planning my collage, and I'd started to ponder the very deep and important issue of . . . what I was going to wear to school the next day! If Janine only knew.

Janine couldn't care less about clothes – and that's just one more thing that makes us very different. Janine would be happy wearing the same white blouse, plaid skirt, red cardigan and flat shoes every day.

On the other hand, I am of the belief that "you are what you wear". (I'd rather think that than "you are what you eat". If that was true I'd be a Snickers bar or something.) Anyway, I love to dress in a way that some people here in Stoneybrook might call outrageous. For example, this is what I was thinking of wearing the next day:

Since I had the big test, I thought I'd start with my lucky earrings – the ones that look like a Princess's. They're huge (pretend) emeralds, surrounded by thousands of tiny (fake) diamonds. Then I thought I'd work downwards from there, wearing my new green-and-blue-tie-dyed T-shirt dress (the casualness of the dress would be an interesting contrast to those sophisticated earrings) over green leggings.

The only thing I hadn't decided on were the shoes – should I wear my old ballet slippers or the black leather high-tops I'd just got? I was having a hard time deciding.

But I wasn't about to ask Janine for her advice. If she had *any* idea of what I'd been thinking about – oh, my lord, I don't even want to imagine what she might say.

So I distracted her by showing off my mathematical brilliance. "Check out Problem Five, Janine," I said again. It was a word problem, about Jack and Jill renting a rowing boat and how much it would cost them if they rowed for two and a half hours. (Why I should care, I don't know – you wouldn't catch me out in some leaky old rowing boat even for five minutes.) I did some quick calculations and a bit of simple guessing. "The answer would be . . . let's see . . . four dollars and twenty-five cents, right?"

Janine looked at the problem for about two seconds, then beamed at me. "You really do understand, don't you, Claudia? I can see that you're not going to have any problems with this test."

"Right," I said. "No problems at all." I only wish I could have been as sure about it as she was.

2nd CHAPTER

When we'd finished going over all the problems, Janine gave me a few quick tips on test-taking in general. I have to admit that by then I was getting a bit tired of all this. But I nodded in all the right places, and soon Janine finished her little speech, wished me good luck with the test, and left my room.

"Thanks a lot, Janine!" I yelled after her. As soon as she had gone I turned on my radio. I hate studying when it's totally quiet, but Janine won't tolerate the radio when she's helping me. Then I turned my attention back to my desk. Time to tidy it up and then finish off the rest of my homework. I gave my maths book one more quick glance and then stuck it into my rucksack, along with my notebook.

The rest of my homework was easy compared to studying for that test. I raced through it. Then I put down my pencil, got up and stretched, and threw myself on to my bed. "Aaaahh!" I sighed. "All done." I rolled over and reached for the phone.

"Hi, Stace – it's Claud," I said, when my best friend, Stacey McGill, answered the phone at her house. I told Stacey all about my big maths test, and about how incredibly nervous I was about it. She tried to calm me down. (She's great at maths, just like Janine. She never gets nervous about tests.)

"C'mon, Claud," she said. "What about all that time we've spent going over everything?"

It was true. Stacey had been helping me with my maths all year, during study periods and sometimes even – when I was especially confused – during lunch.

"I know, Stace, but—"

"But nothing," she interrupted. "You know that material inside out. You're going to do a great job in that test. I guarantee it!"

This made me feel better, but I still wasn't convinced. I dropped the subject, and we talked for a while longer, about clothes, about a film we'd seen and about our club – the Babysitters Club.

"Just think, Claud," she said. "By the time we have our next meeting you'll have taken the test. It will all be over with."

She was right. We had a club meeting the next day after school. When we'd said goodbye and hung up, I thought about how lucky I was to have such a good friend. And even though Stacey's my *best* friend, I'm especially lucky because I've got a whole gang of other friends, too – the other members of our club.

Maybe I should tell you about them.

First off, there's Kristy Thomas. She's the chairman – and the founder – of the Babysitters Club. Kristy used to live on my street, and I've known her since I was about six months old. Now she lives on the other side of town with her "new" family.

Kristy's *original* family was pretty average – a mum, a dad, two big brothers (Sam and Charlie) and one little one (David Michael). But when David Michael was a baby (he's seven now), Kristy's dad just upped and left. I'm not even sure where he lives now – California, maybe? – but Kristy has hardly anything to do with him.

Kristy's mum is a pretty strong woman – I think Kristy takes after her in that way – and she held her family together for years. But then she was lucky enough to fall in love and get married again. And she didn't marry just anyone. She married Watson Brewer, one of Stoneybrook's millionaires. After that, Kristy and her family moved to the other side of town into Watson's mansion (yes, it really *is* a mansion) but, of course, Kristy remained chairman of our club.

So these days Kristy's family is anything but average. Besides being a millionaire, Watson is the father of two children from his first marriage – Karen, who's seven, and Andrew, who's four. They're at Watson's every other weekend. But even when they're not there, the house is pretty full.

Who else lives there? Well, there's Emily Michelle, the most adorable baby in the world. She's a two-year-old Vietnamese girl whom Kristy's mum and Watson adopted not long ago. Soon after Emily Michelle came, Nannie moved in, too. Nannie is Kristy's mother's mother, and she looks after Emily when nobody else is at home.

And as if that weren't enough, there's Boo-Boo and Shannon, too. No, they're not kids – they're pets. Boo-Boo is a grumpy, fat, old cat. (Watson would probably be cross if he heard me say that, but it's true!) And Shannon is a puppy who's going to turn into a gigantic dog one day – a Bernese Mountain dog, to be exact.

So Kristy's got a busy life at home. But I think she likes it like that. She's always doing two or three things at once and planning a fourth at the same time. She's a whirlwind with great ideas (like the one about starting our club). She's so busy that she doesn't care much about her looks – which, in fact, there's nothing wrong with. Kristy has brown hair and eyes, and a really friendly, open face. She's pretty, but she doesn't seem to want to bother with clothes, or make-up, or hair-dos, or any of that. She wears the same thing every day – trainers, jeans, a shirt and maybe a sweater, if it's cold. I suppose you'd have to call her a tomboy.

Kristy's only fault may be that she's got a bit of a big mouth. At times things just slip out of her mouth – but usually it's not a problem with the rest of us. We're used to it.

Even Mary Anne Spier isn't bothered by the blunt way Kristy can talk. And that's saying something, because Mary Anne is the most sensitive soul in the universe. Who's Mary Anne? She's the secretary of our club, and Kristy's best friend, which is pretty funny if you think about it – they're so different. Mary Anne is as quiet as Kristy is loud, and as shy as Kristy is outgoing.

They do look alike, though. Mary Anne's slightly taller than Kristy (Kristy's the shortest person in our class), but her hair and eyes are the same shade of brown as Kristy's.

However, Mary Anne's clothes are trendier than Kristy's, she's less of a talker (she's a great listener, in fact), and she's more of a romantic. Maybe that's why she's the only one in our club who's got a steady boyfriend. His name is Logan Bruno, he's incredibly cute, and he's *in* our club, believe it or not. (He's just an associate member, but I'll explain all about that later.)

Sometimes it amazes me that Mary Anne is *allowed* to have a boyfriend. I still think of her father as strict even though he's actually got a lot more relaxed recently. The thing is, Mary Anne's father brought her up on his own – her mother died when Mary Anne was just a tiny baby – and I suppose he thought that being very strict was best. But he got married again not too long ago, and that seems to have softened him up a bit. Actually, he was beginning to be less strict even before that – when he was just going out with his future wife.

And who *is* that wife? I thought you'd never ask. Mr Spier just happens to be married to the mother of another member of our club, Dawn Schafer. How did they meet? It's a strange story. Mrs Schafer and Mr Spier were high-school sweethearts, here in Stoneybrook. But Mrs Schafer went to live in California, and that's where she met and married Dawn's father. They had Dawn and her younger brother, Jeff, but later they got divorced. Then Mrs Schafer and Dawn and Jeff moved back to Stoneybrook, and it wasn't long before the high-school romance bloomed all over again! Isn't that great?

So now Mary Anne and Dawn are step-sisters – and also best friends. (Yes, Mary Anne has *two* best friends.) Mary Anne and her father and Tigger (that's Mary Anne's kitten) moved into Dawn's mother's house because it was bigger. Now they all live there happily, except for Jeff, who missed California and his father so much that he moved back there. Dawn misses them terribly, but she tries to visit the Californian part of her family whenever she can.

You'd know Dawn for a California girl the minute you saw her. She's absolutely gorgeous. Blonde? They don't come any blonder. Her clothes are great – casual, but stylish. She loves health food and the sun, and she's basically what I'd have to call "mellow". She knows her own mind – for example, she doesn't get tempted by all the great junk food I always have lying around.

One thing that *does* tempt Dawn is a mystery. And she also loves ghost stories. Her favourite ghost story, in fact, is the one about her own house! That's right – her house may be haunted. There's a secret passage in their old farmhouse, and one day I'm sure Dawn will catch the ghost that she believes lives there.

I don't think Stacey believes in the ghost. (That's Stacey McGill, my best friend.) She's blonde, and pretty, and very clever. Stacey grew up in New York City! But now she lives in Stoneybrook, with her mum. She and I became friends when she first moved here – probably because we both have the same taste in clothes – but now our friendship is much deeper. I was *crushed* when she moved back to the city (her dad's company transferred him) but it wasn't long before she'd moved back here again. Of course I was thrilled, even if the *reason* for her move wasn't very pleasant – it was because her parents had got divorced.

Stacey's coping with the divorce well – she visits her dad in the city as often as she can. And she and her mum are close.

Mr and Mrs McGill used to be quite overprotective of Stacey, because Stacey's got diabetes. That means that she has to be very careful about what she eats and when she eats it, or else her blood sugar gets all out of control and she can become extremely ill. It all has something to do with her pancreas, but the complete scientific story behind it is more than I can remember. (I almost failed biology.)

Stacey takes good care of herself, checking her own blood sugar and giving herself injections (ugh!) of insulin. She tries not to let the diabetes cramp her style, but lately I've noticed that she seems a bit tired and weak all the time. I hope she's okay.

The last but not least of my babysitting friends are Mallory Pike and Jessica (everyone calls her Jessi) Ramsey. They're younger than the rest of us (they're in the sixth grade) but they're pretty cool. They're best friends, and like most best friends they're different in some ways and alike in others.

This is how they're alike: They both love reading (especially horse stories), they both wish their parents would stop treating them like babies (eleven is a hard age), and they both come from close families.

This is how they're different: Mallory's family is *huge* – she has seven younger brothers and sisters. Jessi's family is smaller – just a little sister, Becca, and a baby brother, nicknamed Squirt – and also, they're black, while Mal and her family are white. Of course, Jessi's colour makes no difference to any of us, but there were plenty of people in Stoneybrook who felt otherwise, at least at first. Now I'd say that Jessi is pretty happily settled here. Another difference: Mallory loves to write and draw (she hopes to be a children's book author and illustrator one day) while Jessi's passion is ballet (she's a *really* good dancer and practises all the time).

So those are my friends. I'm pretty lucky to have every one of them. But I knew that the next day, during my maths class, it would be just me against good old Gertrude. I would be on my own.

3rd CHAPTER

"Okay, everyone," said Mr Zorzi, trying to be heard over the roar of everyone talking at once. "Let's get ready for this test." He stood at the front of the room with a stack of papers in his hands. "Books on the floor beside your desks."

Then he walked along the front row of desks, giving each person a pile of papers. "Pass them back, please." He folded his arms and watched as the tests were distributed. "This test will count for a large portion of your grade. But don't worry – I think all of you know the material. I'm sure you'll do well."

I looked down at the paper that had landed on my desk, and gulped. There were a lot of problems on it. Fractions and decimals were scattered like land mines all over the page.

I glanced up at Mr Zorzi. He saw me looking up and gave me a little smile. Then he pointed at the clock. I got the message – time to get started.

I focused on the first problem. It didn't seem to make any sense. I blinked and looked again. It still looked like nothing but a jumble of words and numbers. Oh, no! All of a sudden I felt dizzy. What was I going to do? There was no way I was going to make it through this test if I couldn't even make sense of the first problem.

Then I remembered something Janine had told me. "If you get nervous, Claudia, just take a few deep breaths." I did that. Now, what else had she said? I thought for a minute. Then I heard Janine's voice in my mind. "Remember, Claudia – you don't have to do the test in any special order. If the first question looks too hard, find one that you *can* do, and then you can always go back."

I looked down the page. There! Problem Six! I was sure I knew how to do that one. It only took a couple of minutes, and by the time I'd finished it, all the things I'd studied had come back to me. I went back up to Problem One and worked straight through the rest of the test.

I didn't work fast – I took my time and made sure I didn't make any "foolish mistakes", as Mr Zorzi calls them, like doing the whole problem right but then adding two and three and getting six.

When the bell rang, I nearly jumped out of my seat. I'd been concentrating so hard! I glanced over the problems one more time and then handed in my test. As I walked out of the room, I was grinning. I must have looked like an idiot, but I just felt so good. I had never felt like that after taking a test before. I *knew* I had done a good job. I was sure I'd get at least a B on the test – maybe even an A!

The rest of the day dragged, probably because I couldn't wait for it to be over. I was really looking forward to our club meeting that afternoon. I couldn't wait to tell Stacey and the others about how well I'd done in the test.

When I got home, I tried to work on my collage, but I felt too excited. By 5:15, it seemed as if I'd been waiting for ever for the meeting to start. I'd cleared up my room a little and put out some snacks – M&M's and crisps for me, Kristy, Mary Anne, Jessi and Mallory, and wholewheat crackers for Dawn and Stacey.

Finally I heard someone pounding up the stairs. (Nobody knocks on the front door or rings the bell when they come to meetings – they just let themselves in.) It was Kristy. Being chairman, she thinks it's important to be on time. She's almost always the first to arrive.

She sat down in the director's chair by my desk, put on her visor, and tucked a pencil behind her ear. She was ready for the meeting. "How's it going, Claud?" she asked.

I started to tell her about my test, but then I thought maybe I should wait until the others were here so I wouldn't have to tell everything twice.

I looked at Kristy in her chair and thought about all the other times I'd seen her sitting there. The Babysitters Club had been going strong for a long time, I realized. I thought back to how it had all begun.

Kristy got the idea for the club back at the beginning of the seventh grade. One night her mum was trying to get an after-school babysitter for David Michael (Kristy's little brother, remember?), which wasn't usually a problem, since most of the time either Kristy or Sam or Charlie would be able to sit for him. But anyway, that time, none of them could. And Mrs Thomas (she wasn't married to Watson yet) couldn't find a sitter, no matter how many phone calls she made. Kristy started thinking. Wouldn't it be a great service to parents if they could reach a whole group of babysitters with just one phone call?

And that's why we meet in my room every Monday, Wednesday and Friday from 5:30 to 6:00. Why my room? Because I'm the only one of us with my own phone. (I think that's why I got to be vice-chairman, too!) We couldn't tie up our parents' phones for all those times. During that half hour, parents call and arrange for our services. (They get our names from other parents, or from the leaflets we send out.) It's as simple as that.

Well, it's not *quite* that simple. It takes a lot of working out to know which of us is available for which jobs, and that's where Mary Anne comes in, as our secretary. She knows all our schedules – my art classes, Jessi's dance classes, Mallory's dental appointments – all of that. And she keeps track of it in the club record book. (The record book was Kristy's idea, too – she's into being "official" – and I must admit that it helps things run smoothly.) I don't know how Mary Anne does it, to tell you the truth. She's never made a single mistake!

The record book doesn't only have appointments in it. It also has all kinds of vital information like our clients' addresses and phone numbers, as well as detailed records on which kids have which allergies and which ones only eat peanut butter and bananas – stuff like that.

We also keep track of how much money we make, but that's Stacey's job. She's the club treasurer, mainly because she's such a maths whiz. It's lucky that she's not as sensitive as Mary Anne, because if she was, she might have a hard time with the worst part of her job: collecting subs. We all hate paying up, and when Monday (subs day) rolls round, we always whine and complain for a few minutes before finally parting with our money.

We always do pay up, though, because the subs are important. What do we use the money for? Well, club things. Like paying Kristy's brother Charlie to drive Kristy back and forth to BSC meetings – she lives too far away to walk or cycle like the rest of us. And for fun things, like pizza parties or food for club sleepovers.

We also use some of the money for our Kid-Kits, which are really just boxes that we've decorated so that they look pretty cool, then filled with all kinds of goodies for kids to play with. Books, toys, stickers, crayons – nothing special, but fun things that help to distract the kids on a rainy day. Guess who had the idea for Kid-Kits? Kristy, of course.

Anyway, Stacey does a great job of keeping track of our treasury. She also records how much we've earned on our jobs, though *that* money is ours to keep. It's just interesting to know how much we make overall.

You might be wondering what Dawn's job is in the club. Well, she's the alternate officer. That means if anyone else is ill or can't make it to a meeting, she fills in. She was treasurer for a while when Stacey had moved back to New York. And I think she's done everybody else's job at least once.

Mallory and Jessi don't really have jobs,

since they're junior officers. "Junior officer" means that they're not allowed to sit at night (except for their own brothers and sisters). But they get plenty of work in the afternoons and that helps free the rest of us for evening sitting jobs.

I've already told you a little about one of our associate members, Logan. We have another, Shannon Kilbourne, who lives in Kristy's neighbourhood. The associate members don't come to our meetings or sit on a regular basis, but they've helped us out of a tough spot more than once. It's rare that none of us can make time for a sitting job, but it does happen, and when it does, we're happy to have Shannon and Logan to call on.

There's one last thing I haven't told you about yet – maybe because it's my least favourite thing about the BSC. That's the club notebook. (Not the record book – this is different.) The club notebook is where we each have to write up about every job that we've had – who we sat for, what happened, etc. Not only do we have to write in it, but we also have to *read* it every week, so we know what went on when our friends were babysitting.

I won't even tell you whose idea the notebook was – I'm sure you've guessed. I don't mean to complain about it – it's actually a really good idea and it does help keep us informed about things. But it seems like a lot of work. And sometimes, I admit it, I'm a little embarrassed by how bad my spelling is. My friends never laugh at me, but I can guess what they must be thinking.

It's incredible to think back to the beginnings of the club and then look at it now. It's really a successful business! We're all such different people, yet somehow all of us have combined our talents and the club is the result.

Anyway, back to the meeting. Kristy cleared her throat loudly. I looked up and saw that, while I'd been lost in my thoughts, everyone else had drifted in. The meeting was about to begin.

I met Stacey's eyes as Kristy called the meeting to order. I smiled and gave her the thumbs-up sign. She raised her eyebrows and then tilted her head and smiled, as if to say, "See? I told you you'd do okay." Stacey and I have been close for so long now that we don't always need words to talk.

No sooner had Kristy started the meeting than the phone began to ring. Calls were coming in a mile a minute – everybody in Stoneybrook seemed to need a sitter that week. I was dying to tell my friends about the test, but it had to wait.

Finally, the calls slowed down. The meeting was almost over. The snacks I'd put out were all gone, so I rustled around in my favourite hiding places (like my hollowed-out book) and turned up some chocolate digestives.

"Time to celebrate!" I said. I told them about the test, and how I'd been so nervous at first. Then I told them how I ended up sailing through all the problems.

"Congratulations, Claud!" said Kristy. Stacey just looked at me with a big smile. Mary Anne was more cautious.

"Don't you think you should wait to celebrate until you get your test back?" she asked.

She was right, I knew it. But I'd know my grade the next day. And the exact grade I got didn't really matter, anyway. I just *knew* I'd done well. And it felt terrific.

4th CHAPTER

"As I promised, I have your tests marked and ready to return to you," said Mr Zorzi at the beginning of maths class the next day. "But I'm going to hand them out a little later in the lesson. We're starting on Chapter Twelve today, and we'll need to concentrate on the material."

Oh, no! I couldn't believe I was going to have to get through half the lesson without knowing my grade. How nerve-racking. I felt as if I was going to explode if I didn't know soon. I was sure I'd done well, but Mary Anne's comment had echoed in my mind all night. I knew she hadn't meant to upset me – and what she'd said was only common sense – but I just wouldn't feel at ease until I'd seen my grade.

Mr Zorzi had held back on returning our tests so that we would pay attention to the new material, but his plan certainly backfired when it came to me. I haven't got a clue about what he taught us for the rest of the class.

Finally (it seemed like *hours* later), Mr Zorzi finished telling us about ratios and proportions. My nails were bitten down as far as they could go. Mr Zorzi *strolled* to his desk (In my mind I was saying, "Come *on*, come *on*!"), picked up the pile of papers, and smiled at the class.

"With a few exceptions, I'm very proud of your performance in this test," he said. Then he passed out our tests.

"Put mine upside down, Mr Zorzi," called the kid next to me. "I don't want anybody to see my grade." About three other boys said the same thing. But I knew they weren't really as worried as they sounded. And of course, as soon as they got their papers back, they held them up and showed them to everybody.

The paper landed on my desk upside down. Closing my eyes and taking a deep breath, I turned it over. I opened my eyes. There was my grade, written in red ink at the top of the sheet. Ninety-four percent. An A–! I almost shouted out loud. I was so happy and so relieved. It hadn't all been in my mind – I really *had* done well.

"Let's go over the test quickly," said Mr Zorzi. "I want you all to look at Problem Three. Who got that right?"

Almost everybody raised their hands.

"How did you work that out, Heather?" asked Mr Zorzi. She answered, but I wasn't really listening. I just kept looking at that beautiful A– for the rest of the lesson.

Mr Zorzi worked quickly through the whole test. Finally, the bell rang, and everyone got up to leave. As I was gathering my books together, I heard Mr Zorzi speaking loudly over the noise we were all making. "Shawna Riverson and Claudia Kishi," he said, "please stop at my desk on your way out."

I decided that he must want to congratulate me on my especially high grade, and to tell me how proud he was that I'd studied so hard for the test. I couldn't really imagine why he wanted to talk to Shawna. After all, she almost always gets good grades. She's one of the best students in the class.

I walked up to Mr Zorzi's desk with a big smile on my face. Shawna was right beside me, looking bewildered. Mr Zorzi didn't return my smile. I stood there next to Shawna, waiting for Mr Zorzi to speak. He looked very stern.

"I'd like both of you to take out your test papers," he said. I didn't have to look far – I hadn't even put mine away. I had been planning to show it off to Stacey and the others. Shawna pulled hers out of a notebook.

"Put them side by side," said Mr Zorzi, "and tell me if you notice anything." I saw it straight away. We'd both got exactly the same grade – ninety-four percent. I said so to Mr Zorzi.

"That's right, Claudia," he said, still sounding pretty grim. "But there's something else." He pointed at my paper. "See Problem Five?" I looked where he was pointing. I'd got that one wrong.

"I think I understand what I did there, Mr Zorzi," I said. "I should have multiplied by the reciprocal instead of dividing, right?" Beside me, Shawna nodded as if she agreed.

"That's not the point, Claudia," he said. "Look at Shawna's paper." I did. And I realized something. She'd got the same question wrong – in exactly the same way.

Mr Zorzi went over our tests with us. We'd both only got three problems wrong, but we'd both done them wrong in the same way. I still didn't understand what Mr Zorzi was getting at, though. Maybe he thought we should be tutored together or something.

"Girls," he said, "the probability of this happening is virtually nil." He looked at each of us in turn. "Do you realize what this suggests to me?"

I turned to Shawna. For just a second, I saw something like fear in her eyes. Confused, I looked back at Mr Zorzi.

"One of you must have copied from the other," he said. He was looking straight at me!

Did you ever hear the expression "my blood ran cold"? Well, that's what happened to me. The second he said that, I felt as if there were icicles in my veins. I shivered. Then, just as suddenly, I felt hot all over, and I knew my face must have gone bright red. I just couldn't believe what Mr Zorzi was saying.

Shawna spoke up straight away. "Mr Zorzi, you're not my usual teacher, so you don't know me that well." I turned to look at her, feeling as if I was in the middle of a dream. Shawna went on. "If you did, you'd know that I would never cheat in a test." She sounded so sure of herself.

Mr Zorzi looked closely at her and then nodded. "You can go, Shawna," he said. She gathered her books together and left the room without looking at me.

I stood with my head down, trying to understand what was happening. I felt like such an idiot. Why couldn't I have spoken up like Shawna did? Of course, I knew right away that she *must* have copied my paper. I knew for sure that I hadn't cheated. But there was no way that Mr Zorzi – or any teacher, for that matter – would take my word against hers.

Shawna is a really good pupil – in everything but maths. But even in our remedial maths class, she usually gets the best grades. She always studies hard for tests. Shawna is also incredibly popular. She has a huge group of friends, she's in the Drama Club (and always gets the leading roles in their plays), and she's a member of the sports team. Miss Stoneybrook Middle School, that's Shawna.

And who was I? Good old Claudia "C-student" Kishi. Of course Mr Zorzi assumed *I* was the one who had cheated. Why shouldn't he? I stopped myself. Wait a minute. He shouldn't! So I wasn't the best pupil in the history of the world. I was honest, at least. I'd never even *thought* of cheating in a test!

"Mr Zorzi," I said. "I know this doesn't look good. But there must be some explanation! There's no way I would ever—"

But Mr Zorzi interrupted me. "Claudia," he said gently, "I've seen your record, and I know you must be tired of having to work so hard in order to get passing grades in your classes." He took off his glasses and rubbed his eyes. "But looking at somebody else's paper isn't the answer."

"But Mr Zorzi," I said. "I didn't—"

He held up his hand. "I'm sorry, Claudia, but I'm going to have to talk to the head teacher about this." He frowned. "Cheating is a serious matter."

As if I didn't know.

Mr Zorzi went on. "And he'll probably want to let your usual maths teacher know, just so that everyone can be aware of the incident."

I nodded miserably. I felt like a shipwreck victim, drifting away on a tiny rubber raft, helpless to do anything but watch as the ship tilted and then – *whooosh!* – went down.

But Mr Zorzi hadn't finished. "And, of course, the head teacher will be telephoning your parents."

The tiny rubber raft sprang a leak and sank. It was all over. I couldn't even begin to think about how my parents would react to a phone call like that.

Suddenly I felt very, very tired. I could see that there was no point in trying to say anything else to Mr Zorzi. He had his mind made up. He wasn't being mean about it or anything – I think just about any teacher would have acted the same way, dismissing Shawna and putting the blame on me. After all, why would Shawna cheat? She wasn't the one who got C's in all her subjects. "Claudia?" Mr Zorzi asked softly. I looked up. I'd been lost in a fog for a minute. "You can go now," he said.

I gathered my books to my chest. Then I glanced at my maths test, lying there on the desk. Obviously, I wasn't supposed to take it with me. Mr Zorzi needed it for evidence.

I walked out of the room without saying a word. I was in a complete daze. Somehow I found my way to my locker. I leaned against it for a moment with my eyes closed. I didn't feel like crying – I didn't feel anything at all. I was numb.

Finally, I opened my locker and put my maths book away. I never wanted to see it again.

I can't really remember much about the rest of the day – only that it was probably the worst one I've ever spent at school. And that includes the day I went back to school a few days after Mimi died, when everyone was afraid to speak to me. That was bad, but this was worse.

I spent my lunch hour in the girls' cloakroom, not wanting to see any of my friends. Luckily, I didn't have any classes with Stacey for the rest of the day. She would have taken one look at me and known something was wrong.

I knew I'd phone her that night and tell her all about it. After all, she was my best friend. And I could count on her to tell the others, so I wouldn't have to. I knew she'd be nice about it – supportive and all that – but boy, did I wish I didn't have to tell *anyone*. If only it had never happened.

What a day! I felt as if I had been on a roller coaster. I'd started off so excited, and here I was at the end of the day, feeling more miserable than I'd ever felt before. All I could think was: If this is what I get for studying, I may never open a book again.

5th CHAPTER

Tuesday

Excitement at the Pikes' this afternoon. As soon as I got there I could see that it was going to be a day to remember. Everything seemed kind of hectic. Not that it's ever calm at the Pikes'. But little did I know what "was about to transpire," as they say in those old-fashioned novels...

Stacey did have a pretty wild time at the Pikes' that afternoon. It was the same day I'd been accused of cheating, but luckily she didn't even know about that yet. She had enough on her hands as it was.

As Stacey said, it's never calm at the Pikes'. I told you that Mallory had a big family, but let me introduce them all just so you get the whole picture.

Mallory's the oldest. She's eleven and pretty quiet (at least in relation to the rest of the Pikes) and . . . well, I've already told you a lot about her. After Mal come the triplets – Byron, Adam and Jordan. They're ten. And if you think that one ten-year-old boy can be a noisy handful, you should try sitting for three at a time! Actually, Byron's pretty sensitive and a little calmer than the others – but Jordan and Adam make up for it by being extremely noisy.

Then, after the triplets, there's Vanessa. She's nine, and she thinks she's Emily Dickinson or something. She wants to be a poet and she goes around speaking in rhyme half the time. Then there's Nicky, who's eight. He longs to be old enough to play with the triplets, but unfortunately they leave him out of things too often. Most of the time, Nicky ends up hanging around with Margo. She's seven, and she's a pretty good kid. And then, finally, there's Claire, the baby of the family. She's five, and she seems to be in a permanent "silly" phase. She loves to play "pretend", and she generally refers to people as "silly-billy-goo-goos".

So this is what Stacey saw when she arrived at the Pikes': Mallory was dashing out of the door, trying to be on time for a sitting job of her own. She barely had time to say hello to Stacey. Mrs Pike was trying to round up Margo, Nicky and Vanessa for a shopping trip, but no sooner would she have all three of them in the car than one would jump out, claiming to have forgotten something that he or she desperately needed.

"Hi, Stacey," said Mrs Pike with a sigh. "Thanks for being on time. I know I must be mad to take all three of them clothes shopping at once, but at least it's better than taking everyone!"

Stacey tried for a moment (she told me later) to picture a shopping trip with all eight Pikes. The image was too horrible to think about. She smiled at Mrs Pike. "Why don't you just stay with the others, and I'll get Vanessa," she said.

She went into the house and found Vanessa in the living room, searching through a huge box of toys, games and other stuff. "Vanessa," she said, "your mother is waiting for you. Better get going!"

Vanessa looked up. "My green notebook I must find," she said, "for I have a special poem in mind."

"Not now, Vanessa," Stacey said, smiling. "Try to remember it, and you can write it down when you get back." She walked Vanessa out of the door and then waved as Mrs Pike backed down the drive.

Suddenly, Stacey sensed someone behind her. She turned, and saw *three* someones – the triplets. Each of them was making a different gruesome face. Claire stood nearby, giggling.

"Hey, you three!" said Stacey. "Nice faces! What if they stay that way?" They laughed, knowing that she was only teasing. Then, just as Stacey was about to suggest that they go outside to play since it was such a nice day (and since they seemed a little wound up), Adam announced that they were going to play baseball in the back garden.

"And *you* can't come!" he said to Claire, sticking out his tongue.

"I don't care, Adam-silly-billy-goo-goo," she answered. "Me and Stacey are going to play hopstotch."

"It's '*hopscotch*', you twit," said Jordan.

"Jordan," said Stacey. "Be nice!" But she knew he didn't really mean it. "Okay, have fun then," she said, waving them into the garden.

Then she turned to Claire. "Hopscotch?" she asked.

"Can we?" asked Claire. "Please? Margo *never* plays hopscotch with me any more."

"Of course, Claire," said Stacey. "Let's find some chalk."

They found some pink chalk in the toy box and went out to the drive to draw the board. Stacey started drawing the first three boxes, stacked on top of each other, then a fourth and fifth side-by-side stacked on top of them.

"No, Stacey!" said Claire. "You're not doing it right." She pointed at one of the lines Stacey had drawn, which *was* a little crooked.

Stacey tried to be patient. Claire always needed to have things done "just so", and sometimes it took a while before she was satisfied. "Okay," said Stacey. "Look, I'll draw that line like this, and then you can fill in the numbers. Can you make a one here and a two here?"

Claire's a pretty bright girl, and she knows her numbers really well. She and Stacey worked on the board for quite a while, Stacey drawing the boxes and Claire filling in the numbers. Finally, it was done.

They couldn't start to play, though – not until Claire had found a special "lucky" stone to throw down, and helped Stacey find just the right one, too. Then she went through an elaborate ritual to decide who got the first turn.

At last, the game began. Stacey threw down her stone and hopped. When she'd finished her turn (of course, she'd pretended to slip so that her turn wouldn't last for ever and Claire wouldn't get even more impatient than she already was), Claire threw down *her* stone. She didn't like where it landed, and she tried to get Stacey to let her throw again, but Stacey wouldn't let her. (Mean old Stacey!)

Then, Claire began to hop. Hop, hop . . . *CRASH!* Claire went tumbling over the neatly drawn squares. Stacey held her breath. Sometimes if you don't make a big fuss about a fall, the kid won't either. But then Claire began to bawl.

Stacey ran over to where she lay and took a look at the knee Claire was pointing to. This wasn't a false alarm. She'd grazed it pretty badly. And she'd grazed the other knee too – and one of her hands.

Stacey looked over to where the triplets were playing with a ball. They were so absorbed in their game that they'd barely noticed Claire crying. "Adam! Jordan! Byron!" Stacey yelled. "I'm taking Claire inside to clean her up. Don't go anywhere without telling me first, okay?" They nodded and kept on tossing the ball around.

Then Stacey scooped up Claire and took her inside. She washed the scrapes as gently as she could, while Claire gave her careful directions through her sobs. "Now put on some first-aid cream and then a bandage," said Claire. Stacey followed orders, rummaging in the medicine cabinet to find the first-aid cream.

Claire was so interested in the bandaging procedure that she'd begun to forget how much her hand and knees hurt. Her sobbing had slowed to a sniffle as Stacey applied the last bandage.

Just then, Stacey heard a loud *SMASH* from downstairs. "What—" she said. She realized immediately that the triplets had managed to break something. She ran down the stairs, Claire hobbling after her, and out of the door.

There were all three boys crowded around one of the basement windows. Their bat and a pile of gloves lay on the ground, but the ball was nowhere to be seen.

Stacey put her hands on her hips. "Okay, which one of the wrecking crew is responsible for this?" she asked. The triplets looked at each other, then looked back at Stacey. All three shrugged in unison.

"What's going on?" asked Stacey. "All I asked was which one of you did it."

The triplets shrugged again. Then Byron spoke up. "It's like this film we saw," he said. "*The Three Musketeers.* All for one. . ." he started, and then Jordan and Adam joined in, "and one for all!"

"We've decided to be like them. We'll never turn in a fellow triplet again!" said Jordan.

"Yeah!" said Adam. "We're a team."

Stacey rolled her eyes. Then she cleared up the broken glass. She made Claire and the triplets stand to one side – she didn't need any more injuries that afternoon.

When Mrs Pike got home, Stacey had to tell her what had happened. Mrs Pike rolled her eyes, too, when she heard about the Three Musketeers. Then she questioned the boys herself.

They still wouldn't tell which one of them had broken the window.

"You know, boys," she said, "ordinarily I'd let this go. But this is the *fourth* window you've broken in the last three months. This can't go on." She stopped to think. "Since you won't tell me who did it, I'm going to have to punish all three of you. You'll be grounded until you admit which one of you is the culprit. Also, none of you will get any pocket money until that window is paid for."

Stacey was sure that such a tough punishment would convince the triplets to abandon their pact, but they didn't give in. They just looked at each other silently, turned round, and headed for their room. Stacey watched them go, shaking her head. At least, she thought, you never got bored sitting for the Pikes!

6th CHAPTER

And what was *I* doing while Stacey was sitting at the Pikes'? Well, I was sitting, too. In my room, with the door closed. I wasn't doing homework. I wasn't listening to the radio. I wasn't working on my collage. I wasn't even reading Nancy Drew. And I wasn't eating the Hula Hoops that I'd hidden the day before in my sock drawer. I was just sitting.

I was thinking, too – or at least *trying* to think. I still couldn't believe what had happened in the maths lesson that day, and I hadn't decided what to do about it. I knew I was innocent, but what I didn't know was how to get everybody else to believe me.

I heard Janine come home, but I didn't call out to her. I wasn't ready to talk to anyone about my problem. Luckily, she didn't come upstairs to work on her computer, as she usually does. Instead, she started getting dinner ready in the kitchen. Good! That meant I could just keep on sitting.

A little while later I heard my mum come home. She and Janine were talking when the phone rang. Was this *the* call? Was the head teacher on the other end, telling my mother what a horrible person I was? I didn't even want to know. I stayed in my room.

Soon I heard my mum and Janine talking again. I couldn't make out what they were saying, but their voices sounded serious. Then my dad came home. I heard his footsteps go into the kitchen. More talking.

What would happen if I just stayed in my room for the rest of my life? I wouldn't go hungry for quite a while, with all the junk food I had hidden all over the place. And I could entertain myself by reading mysteries and working on art projects. The more I thought about it, the better the idea sounded. I nodded to myself. Yup, staying in my room was definitely the best plan.

"Claudia!" my mum called up the stairs. "Dinner!"

I didn't answer. I folded my arms and stayed where I was.

Five minutes later she called again. "Claudia, darling!" she said. "We're having tacos!"

Sure enough, I could smell the popcorn-y smell of tacos warming in the oven. Tacos are one of my favourite foods. I think it's because they're about as close to junk food as you can get when you're sitting around the table with your family. Mmm, a big crunchy taco filled with all that delicious spicy beef and then stuffed to the brim with toppings. . .

Once I'd started thinking about tacos, I couldn't stop. Suddenly I decided that staying in my room for the rest of my life might not be such a good idea after all. "Coming!" I yelled.

I slid into my seat at the table just as Janine brought in a big platter of tacos. On the table were a whole lot of little bowls filled with grated cheese, tomatoes, onions, lettuce, and sour cream. Yum! I took a taco and started to pile on the extras. Everybody else was busy doing the same.

Just as I was about to bite into the *very* stuffed, juicy, dripping mess I had created, my mum cleared her throat.

"Claudia, sweetheart," she said. "I got a call from your head teacher this afternoon."

I gulped. Suddenly the taco I was holding didn't look so tempting any more.

"Do you want to tell us what happened today?" she asked.

I looked down at my hands, which were now folded in my lap. The taco lay forgotten on my plate. I didn't know what to say.

"I – I don't know what to say," I said. "I didn't do it." I swallowed hard. All of a sudden I felt as if I was going to start bawling any minute.

"We'd like to believe you, Claud," said my father.

They'd *like* to believe me? Oh, no! Even my parents thought I was a cheat. I bit my lip to keep from crying. Then Janine spoke.

"I *do* believe her. There's no question about it. Claudia knew that material inside out." She was speaking very quickly. "I helped her study, remember?" She glanced at each of my parents in turn. "Besides, Claudia is *not* a cheat."

My parents exchanged a look. Then my mother got up and came around to where I was sitting. "I'm so sorry, darling. Janine's right. I don't know how I could have ever thought—" she said, as she hugged me tight. And I hugged her, trying hard to hold back my tears.

"You know," she said, as she walked back to her seat. "The head teacher didn't sound all that sure about it, either. He said he was just 'informing' us about the situation. I suppose it's all part of the procedure."

"I think we should go to your school and speak to the head teacher in person. Sort this whole thing out," said my dad.

That was the last thing I wanted. I knew that if they got involved, things might become even worse. I had to work out how to deal with this on my own. "No, Dad," I said. "Please. I can deal with it."

"But Claudia," said my mother, "the head teacher said that Mr Zorzi is going to have to give you an F in this test. What will that mean for your final grade?"

An F. I couldn't believe it. The one time I'd actually worked hard enough to earn an A–, fair and square – and I was going to end up with an F. "Don't worry, Mum," I said, sounding more sure of myself than I felt. "I'll work it out." Inside, though, *I* was worried. I'd have to get practically straight A's on every other maths test from here on, or I really might fail the class.

And I knew that if I failed maths, I might be forced to give up one of the most important things in my life – the Babysitters Club. There was no way my parents would continue to let me spend all that time on an "outside" activity if I was doing badly at school.

I picked up my taco and tried to finish it, but it tasted pretty much like sawdust. (Not that I've ever actually *eaten* sawdust, but you know what I mean.) My parents *said* they believed me, but I was getting a strange feeling from them. Were they a little suspicious? Did they have just the tiniest doubt about my honesty? Were they feeling . . . disappointed in me? I could hardly stand it.

Finally, dinner was over. I helped Janine clear the table, and then we cleared up the kitchen together. We weren't talking much, but I was giving her a lot of grateful looks. It's funny, Janine and I have definitely been through some rough times, but no matter what, she's my big sister. And there are times when that means everything.

When I'd finished drying the last pot, I headed for my room. I was still feeling very upset, and I needed some time to decide what to do. Janine followed me upstairs and into my room. I threw myself on the bed.

"Claudia," said Janine, "it'll be all right." She sat down at my desk. "Look, I'll be glad to help you with your maths for the rest of the year. If we work really hard, you won't fail the class, even if Mr Zorzi does give you that F."

"But Janine," I said. "It's so unfair. I got an A– in that test!"

Janine looked shocked. I suppose the head teacher hadn't told anybody what my actual grade had been. Then she gave me a big smile. "Congratulations, Claudia!" she said. "That's fantastic! I knew you could do it."

"I did it, all right," I muttered. "But Shawna ruined the whole thing."

"What?" asked Janine. "Who's Shawna?"

I explained everything to Janine, telling her all the details of what had happened at the end of maths class that day.

"But Claudia," Janine said, "why didn't you stick up for yourself?"

"I tried to," I wailed. "Mr Zorzi just didn't give me a chance. He's not a bad teacher – but I think he's making certain assumptions. He doesn't know me or Shawna that well."

Janine shook her head slowly. "What a mess," she said.

"I know," I answered. "And the worst thing is that I'm sure that Shawna must have cheated. But I can't work out *why* she did – and I have no way of proving it!"

"Think back," said Janine. "Try to remember the day of the test. Can you remember her looking at your paper?"

I closed my eyes and tried to concentrate. But no matter how hard I tried, I couldn't remember a thing about that day. (Except for what I wore. I can always remember what I was wearing on a given day. I had decided on the ballet slippers, in case you were wondering.)

"It's no use, Janine," I said. I felt so trapped. There just wasn't anything I could do about the horrible situation I was in.

"Don't you have any idea why Shawna might have cheated?" asked Janine.

"That's the weird thing," I said. "She's usually a pretty good pupil. Something strange is going on here."

"Yes, and you've got to try to get to the bottom of it," said Janine. "But where do you start?"

Janine and I talked for a little bit longer, but we couldn't decide on any plan of action except one: study, study, study. I'd just have to be a maths machine for a while. I accepted Janine's offer of help, but I can't say I was looking forward to the rest of the year.

Later, after I'd got into my pyjamas, I called Stacey and told her what had happened. I gave her just the bare facts – I was too tired to go into it much more than that She was incredibly nice about it all – that's why she's my best friend – but nothing she said could take away the awful feeling in the pit of my stomach.

As I went to bed that night, I thought about the day. The confrontation with Mr Zorzi was one of the most terrible things I'd ever been through. Being accused of cheating was humiliating. I also felt really awful about having my wonderful A– taken away from me. And I felt guilty about taking up so much of Janine's time so that she could tutor me.

But you know what was the worst part of the whole thing? The feeling that my parents were not *one hundred per cent absolutely, positively, definitely* convinced that I was telling the truth. *That* was what was making me feel so rotten.

7th CHAPTER

"I just can't believe that he would be so unfair!" said Jessi. She was sitting on the floor next to Mallory. They were both eating M&Ms.

"What gets me is the way he wouldn't listen to you." That was Stacey, who was sitting in my desk chair. It was clear that she'd already told everybody about my problem.

"Order!" Guess who said that? Right. Kristy. She was sitting in the director's chair, as usual, wearing her visor. And the clock next to my bed said 5:30. It was time for our club meeting to start.

"We've definitely got a problem on our hands," Kristy said. "But we need to take care of club business before we get into it."

We? I thought it was *my* problem. I should have known that my friends would want to help me out. And it felt good to know that everyone was on my side. I passed round a packet of Marshmallows as Kristy went through the club business. When she'd finished, she said, "Okay. Now, Claudia, why don't you tell us, in your own words, what happened yesterday."

In my own words? Whose words did she think I'd use? Kristy's funny sometimes, even when she doesn't mean to be. "Well," I began, "it all started just as the lesson had finished—"

Just then the phone rang. Kristy answered it and quickly arranged a job for Stacey with Charlotte Johanssen. I smiled at Stacey. Charlotte is her favourite kid to sit for.

Then I continued. "Mr Zorzi called me and Shawna up to his desk. I didn't know what was going on!"

The phone rang again. Mrs Braddock needed a sitter for Matt and Haley. Mary Anne checked the record book to see who was free that afternoon, and Jessi got the job. She's the best of all of us at sign language, so as long as she's free, she's usually the first choice to sit for them. Matt's deaf, but he's a pro at sign language. We've all learned a little.

"So, where was I?" I asked after the job had been arranged. I continued with my story, embellishing it with all the details I remembered. Even though I was interrupted three more times by phone calls, I finally got to the end of it.

"Why did Mr Zorzi have to be so horrible?" asked Mallory. She really looked upset.

Dawn looked upset, too. "He's just making assumptions, and that's not right," she said.

Then Mary Anne spoke up. Very softly, she said, "You know, Claud, if you *did* look at Shawna's paper, we'd stand by you anyway." I looked at her, amazed. I couldn't believe my ears. She went on. "If you did it, you should confess. You'll feel better, and we'll still be here for you."

The room was completely quiet for about five seconds. Everybody looked stunned. Then Kristy spoke up.

"Mary Anne, how *could* you? Of *course* Claudia didn't do it. You must be mad."

Mary Anne looked around the room. We were all glaring at her. She burst into tears. (I told you she was sensitive.)

I reached over and hugged her. "That's okay, Mary Anne. I know you were trying to be supportive. But I'd rather you just believed me," I said.

The tears were over almost as soon as they'd begun. "I do, Claud, I do!" she said. "I just wanted you to know that it wouldn't matter to any of us if—"

"Okay, Mary Anne, enough of that," interrupted Kristy. "Now, look," she went on. "Let's go over the whole thing again.

We've got to work out how to prove that Claud is innocent."

"Well, it's obvious that Shawna was the one who cheated," said Mallory. "So all we need to do is prove that."

"But why would Shawna cheat?" asked Stacey. "She always gets good grades. Why would she risk being caught?"

"Forget about Shawna for a minute," said Kristy. "What about Mr Zorzi? How can we convince him that it's wrong to consider Claudia guilty without proof?"

"My parents wanted to go to school and talk to the head teacher," I admitted. "But I wouldn't let them."

"No, I think it's best if we handle this ourselves," said Kristy. "Do you think Janine would have any ideas? She's such a genius – maybe *she* can work this out."

I shook my head, just as the phone rang again. Janine and I had been over it all already. If she hadn't thought of something last night. . .

Kristy put her hand over the mouthpiece of the phone. "Claud," she said. "Do you want to sit for the Perkinses on Friday? They asked especially for you."

That was nice of Kristy. Usually the jobs are given out very fairly, and we try not to let clients get too attached to any one sitter. I suppose this time Kristy thought I might need the distraction of sitting for Myriah and Gabbie and their baby sister, Laura Elizabeth.

"Okay," I said. "Sounds great."

Kristy finished with Mrs Perkins and hung up.

"You don't sound all that excited about the job," said Kristy.

"It's just that. . ." I started. I could hardly bring myself to say it. "I'm afraid that if I fail maths, my parents will make me give up the club."

A silence fell over the room.

"Okay, that's it," said Dawn. "We're going to get to the bottom of this. No way are we going to lose you!"

"Think, Claud," said Jessi. "Isn't there any way we can prove that Shawna cheated?"

"But that's just the thing," I said. "Maybe she didn't. Maybe Mr Zorzi was wrong. Maybe it was just a coincidence that we got the same problems wrong – in the same way."

Stacey was shaking her head. "No, Claud," she said. "He was right. It would have been one thing if you both just missed the same questions. But it's another thing entirely for you to have come up with exactly the same wrong answers. There's hardly any chance of that happening by coincidence."

"That's what Mr Zorzi told us," I said sadly. Stacey's such a maths whiz. If she said the same thing that Mr Zorzi did, it must be true.

"You know," said Dawn, as if she were thinking out loud, "Shawna and some of her friends are in my form. They've been acting a bit strangely lately."

"You're right!" said Mary Anne. (She's in the same form as Dawn.) "They've been passing notes a lot and acting as if they know it all."

"Boy, speaking of Shawna's friends, did you see Susan Taylor yesterday?" asked Dawn. "She's had another perm, and this one's really wild."

"I heard that her mother writes her a note to get out of classes when she has a hair appointment," said Kristy. "Can you imagine?"

"I know," said Stacey. "I told my mum about that. She said if I thought she'd do that for me I had 'another think coming'."

"Okay, everyone," said Mary Anne. She doesn't like gossiping as much as the rest of us do. She thinks it's unkind. "Let's get back to the problem. How are we going to prove that Shawna cheated and that Claudia is innocent?"

Everybody was quiet for a few minutes. Then the phone rang. I almost jumped out of my skin! This time Stacey took the call and arranged an afternoon job for Mallory, sitting for Jamie Newton while Mrs Newton took the baby (Lucy Jane) to the doctor.

I suppose Dawn had been thinking the whole time that Stacey was taking the call, because as soon as Stacey had hung up, she started to talk. "You know," she said, "Shawna's locker is right next to mine."

"So?" asked Kristy.

"Well, I'm just wondering. . ." said Dawn slowly. "Suppose one of those notes she and her friends keep passing said something incriminating about her cheating."

"And?" asked Kristy again. She usually thinks so fast. I could see that she was getting impatient with Dawn.

"Well, I happen to know Shawna's locker combination. There was a mix-up, and I had that locker for a couple of weeks when school started. Then we swapped."

"Dawn Schafer!" said Mary Anne in a shocked voice. "Are you saying that someone should *break into* Shawna's locker to look for a note?"

"It's a thought," said Dawn calmly.

"Well, I don't know about that," said Stacey. "That would be a bit like breaking the law or something, wouldn't it?"

"Not really," said Dawn. "We wouldn't be *stealing* anything. We'd just be looking for evidence."

"Don't you need a search warrant for that kind of thing?" asked Mallory.

"You've been watching too many detective programmes on TV," I answered. "Dawn's talking about looking for a note in a locker, not looking for a loaded pistol or something!" The idea was growing on me. "I think it might just work!"

"Well, we can think about it," said Kristy. "But there must be some other way – a safer way – to prove that Shawna cheated."

Kristy was probably right. But unfortunately, we hadn't come up with any brilliant ideas by the time that day's meeting was over.

8th CHAPTER

Thursday

Hey Mal, do me a favour.

What, Jessi?

Well, when I grow up, and I'm ready to have children, just remind me.

Remind you to what?

Remind me to never have triplets.

Right, Jessi.

I can't really blame Jessi for feeling a bit down on triplets. She'd had a bit of a rough afternoon with Adam, Jordan and Byron. Jessi had been right on time that afternoon for the job of helping Mal sit for her brothers and sisters. (Mrs Pike always insists on two sitters when all the Pike kids are at home, and that's fine with us. It would be almost impossible to watch all seven of them if you were alone!)

"The triplets are still grounded, Jessi," said Mrs Pike as she got her coat from the hall cupboard. "That means they aren't allowed out of the house. They don't have to stay in their room, but they can't go outside. And they aren't allowed to get or make any phone calls."

Jessi remembered the story that Stacey had written up in the club notebook. "You mean they still won't tell who broke the window?" she asked.

"That's right," said Mrs Pike. "I can't believe they're being so loyal to each other." She lowered her voice and went on. "I almost hate to keep punishing them – after all, that kind of loyalty is a good thing – but I have to be consistent with them. Anyway, it can't go on much longer."

Jessi nodded. She had already started to work out a plan. Maybe *she* could get the triplets to spill the beans!

"I've got to run," said Mrs Pike. "Mallory and the kids are in the kitchen, having a snack. Have a good afternoon!"

Jessi said goodbye to Mrs Pike and walked into the kitchen. The scene there was completely chaotic. Mallory was standing in the middle of the kitchen looking like a traffic warden who had lost control. Margo and Claire were sitting at the table, giggling as they peeled grapes and fed them to Nicky, who was acting like a film monster.

"Ummm," he said. "Delicious eyeballs. Norkon like eyeballs. Feed Norkon more!"

Vanessa was staring dreamily into the fridge, trying to decide on a snack. (The Pike kids are allowed to eat anything they want, by the way. Mr and Mrs Pike thought that if they argued over every bite of food that eight kids were eating, they'd have no time left to do anything else.)

"Carrot, apple, cottage cheese – which of these will truly please?" she rhymed.

"Vanessa, forget the poetry. Make up your mind and close the fridge door," Mallory said. "You know Mum doesn't like us standing there with the door open."

"*You know Mum doesn't like us standing there with the door open*," said Adam, mimicking Mallory.

"Oh, stop it," said Mallory. I could tell that she was feeling the effects of having had the triplets cooped up inside for a few days.

"*Oh, stop it,*" said all three triplets at once.

Mallory glared at the triplets, who were sitting on the work surface, eating peanut-butter-and-salami sandwiches and kicking their heels against the cabinet.

"Stop it. Now. And get down from there this minute!" said Mallory. She was losing her temper.

"*Stop it—*" began the triplets, but Jessi cut them off. This was getting out of hand.

"Come on, you three," she said. "That's enough."

I don't know why they listened to Jessi – maybe because she's not their big sister. But the triplets slid off the work surface and sat down at the table. Jessi and Mallory exchanged glances and Mallory gave a sigh of relief.

Just then, the phone rang. Vanessa grabbed it. "This is the Pikes'," she said. "Whom would you like?"

Honestly. When she gets started with that rhyming thing, there's no stopping her.

"It's for you, Adam," she said. "Somebody wants to know if you'd like to play baseball."

"*Would I!*" yelled Adam, reaching for the phone.

"Hold it, buddy!" said Mallory. "No way. Number one, you can't leave the house. Number two, you're not allowed to use the phone, remember?"

"Number three, you're a nerd," said Adam under his breath.

Mallory bristled and Jessi could see that she was on the verge of losing her temper completely.

"Mal," she said, "how about taking the younger kids outside to play? I'll stay inside with the triplets."

Mallory gave Jessi a grateful look. "Oh, that would be terrific," she said. "They've been like this for the last few days, and I just can't take it any more. They're like caged beasts or something!" Within minutes, she'd herded Nicky, Vanessa, Margo and Claire outside.

Jessi started to tidy up the kitchen, which looked as if a tornado had been through it, while the boys played in the living room. She could hear them talking as they looked through their baseball cards for the millionth time.

"Ave-day Infield-way," said Jordan. "E's-hay the oolest-cay."

"O-nay ay-way," cried Adam. "At-whay about-hay Al-cay Ipken-ray Unior-jay?"

Byron (who isn't as much into sports as the other two) spoke up. "I-hay ike-lay Agic-may Ohnson-jay."

The other two triplets sat in amazed silence for about two seconds. Then Jordan broke in "I-hay ike-lay Agic-may, oo-tay, ummy-day. Ut-baye-hay ays-play asket-ballbay!" He and Adam sniggered.

"Orget-fay about-hay ese-thay ards-cay. I'm-hay ick-say of-hay em-thay," said Adam. "Et's-lay eak-snay outside-hay!"

Jessi poked her head into the room. She was getting a bit tired of hearing Pig Latin, and she didn't like the way Jordan had spoken to his brother. Byron is sensitive, and his feelings get hurt easily. Besides, she wasn't about to let the triplets sneak out of the house.

"Ordan-jay, at-thay isn't-hay ery-vay ice-nay. Ell-tay our-yay other-bray ou're-yay orry-say or-fay alling-cay im-hay ummy-day!"

All three triplets stared at Jessi, gaping in disbelief. "You know how to speak Pig Latin?" asked Adam.

"Of course!" said Jessi. "I used to talk in Pig Latin all the time. Sometimes I get sick of it, though."

"We get a bit tired of it, too," admitted Adam. "But we've got to have a secret language for when we don't want anybody to understand us."

"Pig Latin's too common, though," said Jessi. "Lots of people know how to speak Pig Latin. Bop-u-top nop-o-bop-o-dop-yop kop-nop-o-wop-sop hop-o-wop top-o sop-pop-e-a-kop 'op-talk'."

"Whaaaat?" asked the triplets in unison.

"That's 'op-talk'," said Jessi.

"Teach us!" demanded Jordan.

"Yeah! Teach us!" said Adam and Byron.

"What do you say?" asked Jessi, teasing them.

"*Please?*" said the triplets.

Jessi sat down on the floor with the boys and told them about 'op-talk'. "It's simple," she said. "You just spell out each word, but you add 'op' after every consonant."

"What about the vowels?" asked Byron.

"You leave those alone," said Jessi. "So if you wanted to say, 'I want to go home' in 'op talk', you'd just say 'I wop-a-nop-top top-o gop-o—"

"Hop-o-mop-e!" yelled Adam. "I get it!"

Jordan was frowning slightly. "What about 'y'?" he asked.

"You treat 'y' as a consonant," said Jessi.

"O-kop-a-yop!" said Jordan. "Top-hop-i-sop i-sop gop-rop-e-a-top!"

"Say my name, Jessi!" said Byron. He still couldn't get the hang of it.

"Bop-yop-rop-o-nop!" said Jessi, Adam and Jordan all together. Then they burst out laughing. Byron's name sounded really funny.

"Do mine!" yelled Adam.

This time Byron joined in, too. "A-dopa-mop!" they yelled. The triplets dissolved in giggles. 'Op-talk' was a big hit.

Jessi sat back and let the triplets go at it. They were fast learners. After they'd done everybody's name, they started to plan how to best use 'op-talk' to annoy their parents. They decided to speak nothing but 'op-talk' at dinner that night, just to see what would happen.

Jessi was happy to see that the boys had forgotten, at least for a while, how tired they were of being in the house. They'd stopped playing up. Now they were just having fun. She thought this might be a good time to bring up the subject of the broken window. Maybe she could get them to tell her which one of them had been responsible.

"So, wouldn't you boys like to be able to go outside?" she asked. "All you have to do is tell me which one of you broke the window."

All three of them sat there silently.

"Come on," said Jessi. "It's not such a big deal. Do you want to be grounded for ever?"

Silence.

"Don't you want your pocket money back?" she asked.

The triplets ignored her.

Jessi thought for a moment. Maybe she could trick them into exposing the guilty party. She turned to Byron, and said, very casually, "Tell me, Byron. When you threw that ball through the window—"

"I didn't!" Byron said, without thinking.

"Aha!" cried Jessi.

"I didn't, either!" said Adam and Jordan at the same time.

That was it for Jessi. She sighed in frustration and let the triplets go back to practising 'op-talk'. If they were going to be so stubborn about it, she wasn't going to try to help any more. It wasn't *her* problem if they wanted to stay in until they were ninety-two years old.

9th CHAPTER

The next day at school, all my classes seemed to drag on for ever. I couldn't concentrate on what my teachers were saying; I just kept thinking about my problem and how to solve it.

Then it happened.

As I was heading for the canteen, I saw Shawna Riverson walking in front of me. Susan Taylor was with her, and so was another friend of theirs, this girl with wild red hair. Their heads were together, and they were talking in low voices as they walked. They were giggling, too. I followed them without really knowing why.

They started to go round the corner towards the canteen, but then Shawna stopped and gestured towards the girls' toilets. She walked in, and the other two followed her.

I stood outside the door for about thirty

seconds, trying to decide what Nancy Drew would do if she were in my shoes. Then I slowly pushed the door open and peeked inside.

There are four cubicles in those toilets. Three of them were occupied by Shawna and her friends. Quickly, before I could change my mind, I slipped into the fourth.

The toilet next to mine flushed then, and I heard someone walk over to the wash basins. The water ran for a minute. Then I heard a girl say, "Honestly, Shawna, you are so lucky." She was chewing gum loudly. That must be the one with the red hair, I thought.

"I know," said Shawna, who had just come out of *her* cubicle. "I still can't believe I got away with it." She giggled. "I just gave Mr Zorzi this incredibly sincere, honest look – and he let me go!"

I couldn't believe what I was hearing. Were they talking about what I thought they were talking about? I was suddenly terrified that they would find out I was eavesdropping on them. I held my breath and tried to get my heart to stop beating so loudly. I kept listening. This was exactly what I wanted to hear.

"And you know the best part?" asked Shawna. "I don't even have to feel guilty about it. It doesn't even matter to *her* that she's getting an F. You know what I mean?"

"Yeah, what's one more bad grade to Claudia Kishi?" asked Susan Taylor.

Oh, wow. I couldn't believe she'd said that! Suddenly, I was furious. How *dare* they talk about me like that? My face got all hot again, just as it had that day after the maths lesson. I felt tears welling up in my eyes.

I jumped up and started to open the door of my cubicle. I was going to give them the shock of their lives!

Then I stopped. I can't explain why – but I calmed down as quickly as I'd got worked up. It was as if I felt Nancy Drew herself tapping me on the shoulder and whispering in my ear. Maybe if I kept quiet, she was saying, I'd hear some more. And maybe what I heard would help me work out what to do next. I listened to Nancy's advice.

After all, the main thing was to prove my own innocence – not to Shawna, since she obviously already *knew* I was innocent – but to Mr Zorzi and to the head teacher.

I took a few deep breaths (very *quiet* deep breaths) and settled down to listen some more. I peered, carefully, through the crack between the cubicle and the door. Shawna and her friends were still standing there, looking in the mirror and talking while they brushed their hair and made what they seemed to think were film star faces. Susan Taylor pulled a tiny can of hairspray out of her bag and touched up her perfect perm.

"I wouldn't have done it unless I had to, you know," said Shawna. "I've never done it before."

"I know," said Susan. "But nobody could be expected to do everything you do *and* get good grades all the time."

"I just had too much going on," said Shawna. "There was that sketch I was directing for Drama Club, and that long paper for English—"

"Yeah, and then you had to help plan the sports rally on top of it all!" said the girl with red hair. "How were you going to find time to study for some stupid maths test, too? What are you supposed to be, Supergirl or something?"

I rolled my eyes. Was I supposed to feel sorry for Shawna? I mean, give me a break. She's the most popular girl in school! Of *course* she's too busy.

"I'd just decided it was all too perfect when I heard Claudia telling mousy Mary Anne Spier that her genius sister, Janine, was helping her study," said Shawna.

"Yeah, everybody knows what a boffin Janine is," answered Susan. "But who would ever suspect you of copying off Claudia Kishi's paper? It was the perfect crime." She giggled.

This was too much. Not only had she copied off me, but she'd planned the whole thing. And she sounded *proud* of herself.

Finally, after what seemed like hours, Shawna and her friends packed up their bags and left, letting the door slam shut behind them. I let out a big sigh and walked out of my cubicle. Staring at myself in the mirror, I shook my head. This was unbelievable.

I *flew* to the canteen to meet my friends. I couldn't wait to tell them what I'd overheard.

They were already sitting down and eating by the time I got there. I ran past the queue, too excited to eat. I threw myself down at the table and said, "You'll never guess what I've just heard."

I looked around the table at my friends. Mary Anne was sitting next to Logan. They had been talking quietly together, but they looked up at me as soon as I started to speak. Dawn put down her tofu in wholemeal bread sandwich (it looked disgusting) and turned to me, too. Kristy and Stacey were all ears. (Jessi and Mallory weren't there – the sixth-graders eat during another period.)

I turned, glancing over my shoulder, just to make sure that Shawna and her friends weren't standing behind me. Then I told the whole story from beginning to end.

Kristy got furious. "That . . . that *dirty rotten cheat*!" she spluttered.

Mary Anne felt sorry for me, I could tell. "That must have been horrible, to hear them saying those things about you," she said. "That's so unkind."

Stacey just gave me a sympathetic look. Then she smiled. "But Claud – now you've got proof, right?"

"I wish," I said. "But even though I know for sure now that Shawna cheated, I still can't prove it." I bit my lip and shook my head. "If I tried to tell that to Mr Zorzi, it would just be my word against Shawna's – and we know who *he'd* believe."

Logan nodded. "Claudia's right," he said. "So what do we do?" I suppose Mary Anne had filled him in on the details. It was nice to know that I had one more person on my side.

Dawn hadn't said anything yet, but just then she spoke up. "So Claud has solved the mystery of who really cheated – and why. Now we have to decide how to help Mr Zorzi and the head teacher solve the same mystery." She paused for a minute, then spoke again, in a lower voice. "We could always try what I thought of the other day," she said. "You know – we could check Shawna's locker."

I noticed that she wasn't using the term "break into" any more.

Mary Anne looked shocked. "Dawn!" she whispered, looking around the canteen. "Shhh! Don't talk about that here. Somebody might hear you and take you seriously."

"I am serious," said Dawn, more quietly. "I think it's our only chance."

"I don't believe you," said Mary Anne. "The whole idea is just unthinkable."

"I agree with Mary Anne," said Stacey quietly. "I'd do almost anything to help you to prove you're innocent, Claud." She looked over at me. "*Almost* anything. But not that. That's going too far."

I had to admit that Stacey was right, sort of. But what else could we do?

"Wait a minute," said Kristy. "Do you lot want Claud to have to give up the club?"

Stacey put her hand over her mouth. "Oh!" she said. "I wasn't thinking about that."

Mary Anne frowned. "Of course we don't want to lose Claudia. But there must be a better way of keeping her in the club."

Kristy sat up straight in her chair and pounded her fist on the table. "You know what Watson would say in a case like this? He'd say, 'Desperate times call for desperate measures!'"

I looked at her. What on earth was she talking about?

She must have seen that I was confused. "It just means that some things are emergencies, and that during an emergency you have to do things you might not otherwise do," she explained.

I nodded. I agreed completely. When I looked over at Stacey, she was nodding, too.

"You're right, Kristy," she said. "I think we should do it. And I'll be glad to help, if it means keeping Claudia in the club."

Dawn was grinning now.

Mary Anne was the only one of us who wasn't totally convinced. She still looked worried. "I think it's wrong," she said. "But if you have to do it, please be careful. Imagine what could happen if you got caught!"

10th CHAPTER

I didn't *want* to imagine what would happen if we got caught "checking" Shawna's locker – so I just didn't think about it. Instead, I joined my friends in planning exactly how to go about doing the deed.

The five of us spent the rest of lunch period talking about it. (Logan had left by then – I don't think he wanted to be involved in our plan.)

"I happen to know that the sports rally squad has got a meeting after school this afternoon – at three o'clock," I said. "Susan Taylor mentioned it when they were in the girls' toilets. She was worried that it would go past four o'clock and she'd miss the chance to go shopping with her mum."

"Is that all she ever does – shop and get perms?" asked Kristy.

"Seems like it," said Dawn. "Anyway, this meeting is perfect. By three o'clock, most of the other kids at school will have left – or else they'll be involved in some activity."

"But what about the teachers?" I asked, picturing Mr Zorzi strolling up behind me as I rummaged through Shawna's locker. "Won't they still be around?"

Dawn wasn't worried. "That's true, but they don't know whose locker is whose."

"Mr Kingbridge knows," said Mary Anne. "He knows every little thing about this school." (Mr Kingbridge is the deputy head teacher.)

"Oh, him," said Dawn. "He's half-blind." Mary Anne gasped, then giggled, covering her mouth with her hand. "Anyway," continued Dawn, "he'll just think I'm at my locker. All we have to do this afternoon is stand in front of Shawna's locker as if it were mine, and laugh and talk as we go through it for evidence."

Dawn was really into it. I was glad she'd decided that she would be the one to go through Shawna's locker. I still felt pretty uneasy about the whole thing, even if it *was* my only chance.

Mary Anne felt uneasy, too. "What if *Shawna* catches you?" she asked.

"She's going to be at practice, Mary Anne," said Kristy patiently. Mary Anne can be such a worrier.

"But what if she forgets something and comes back for it?" said Mary Anne.

Hmmmm. That made us all stop and think. Mary Anne had got a point. We certainly didn't want to be caught in the act by the owner of the locker.

"No problem," Stacey said after a minute. "I'll stand guard where the two corridors meet. If I see her coming, I'll warn you."

"Great!" said Dawn. "And don't forget to watch out for Susan Taylor and that redhead, too."

Just then, the bell rang. Lunch was over.

It's funny about time. Remember how I said that my morning lessons seemed to go on for ever? Well, that afternoon, when I really wasn't looking forward to school being over (I was *so* nervous about what we were going to do), my lessons flew by. Before I knew it, the last bell had rung.

I met my friends by my locker – we'd planned it that way. By then, Mallory and Jessi had heard about our plan. They were as excited as the rest of us.

"You two should go on home," said Dawn to Mal and Jessi. "If we get caught, we don't want you to be involved."

"That's right," I said. "Mary Anne, you should go, too. We'll tell you all about it later."

Stacey agreed with me. "Good plan," she said. "Kristy, you'd better leave with them too. The fewer of us that are involved, the better."

Once the four of them had left, it was just a matter of waiting until three o'clock rolled around. That sounds simple but it wasn't.

The minutes seemed to last for ever. At first, there were a lot of kids in the corridors. But after the school buses had left, the school grew quiet. Kids walked by themselves or in pairs, heading to things like Spanish Club or Football practice. We didn't see Shawna and her friends at all.

First we hung around my locker for a while. Then Stacey realized she'd forgotten her jacket, so we headed over to her locker. We got the jacket, but it still wasn't three o'clock.

The water fountain kept us busy for a couple of minutes – but how much water can you drink? I wasn't thirsty anyway. I was just a nervous wreck. This phrase kept going through my mind: "Breaking and Entering". That was what the newspaper called it when somebody got arrested for burglary. Was "Breaking and Entering" what we were planning?

After the water fountain, we headed for the girls' toilets. We didn't want to hang around in any one place too long, in case Mr Kingbridge noticed and got suspicious.

Being in the girls' toilets again made me remember all those nasty things Shawna and her friends had said about me. I got angry all over again, which was probably good – it kept me from being too nervous.

Finally, it was three o'clock. We stepped out into the corridor. It was empty. "Okay, this is it!" said Dawn. "Stacey, man your post."

"Don't you mean 'woman' my post?" said Stacey, giggling. Dawn rolled her eyes.

"Come on, Stacey. This is serious," she said. "Now don't forget – come running if you spot Shawna or any of her friends. Or Mr Kingbridge, for that matter!"

"Yes, sir!" said Stacey, giving Dawn a mock salute. Then she wished us luck and headed down the hall.

A few moments later, Dawn and I were standing in front of Shawna's locker. Dawn looked round and then bent over the combination lock. She twisted it a few times and tried the latch.

Whoosh! The locker opened and an avalanche of stuff fell out. Crumpled-up papers, stuffed notebooks, old chewed-up pens . . . and a picture of the most gorgeous guy I'd ever seen.

"Who's *that*?" I asked, grabbing it.

"Come on, Claud," said Dawn. "This is no time for boy-watching. Quick! Put it back before somebody comes."

She was right. I got down on the floor, grabbed a handful of papers, and shoved them back into the locker. Honestly, Shawna was a slob! I tried to check through the papers as I put them away, but nothing interesting was written on them.

"Check the shelf," said Dawn.

I nodded and stood on my tiptoes to see what was up there. "A swimming costume, a hairbrush, a copy of the school manual. . ." Pretty boring, I thought. "And what's this? Ugh! A gross, old, mouldy orange!" I pulled my hand away from it.

"Shhh!" said Dawn. "Who's coming?"

I listened and heard footsteps. They were coming closer. Dawn and I tried to act casual. "So, did you understand the homework for English?" I asked.

Dawn and I aren't even in the same English class, but I don't think the caretaker knew that. That's who was coming. He walked by, pushing a trolley. He didn't give us a second look.

"Okay, let's get serious," said Dawn. "Look for a note." She bent over and started rummaging around in the papers that covered the bottom of Shawna's locker.

For some reason, I looked at the inside of the locker door. Shawna had all the usual stuff – a mirror, some stickers, some posters of cute boys – but there, stuck in the vent – what was that? I pulled out a folded-up piece of pink paper. A note. "Dawn, listen to what this says," I said.

"'Congratulations on your A–. Who would have guessed that C.K.'s paper would have had so many right answers?'"

C.K. That was me. Evidence! I stuffed the note into my pocket, and Dawn slammed the locker shut. We ran down the hall, grabbed Stacey, and then collapsed against the wall, panting. Victory!

Then I had a terrible thought. The note wasn't worth a thing. If I showed it to Mr Zorzi or the head teacher, they'd want to know where I'd got it. And if I wouldn't tell them (which I couldn't), why should they believe that Shawna's friend even wrote it?

"Why don't you two go ahead," I said to Dawn and Stacey. "I've just remembered a book I need from my locker."

When they'd left, I ran back to Shawna's locker and stuck the note through the vent. It wasn't going to do me any good, and by putting it back I felt a little less guilty about what we'd done.

I also felt pretty low. Now we were really at a dead end. It looked as though I was just going to have to accept that F.

11th CHAPTER

"*You what?*" asked Dawn. "I can't believe you put that note back!"

It was lunchtime, the day after we'd broken into Shawna's locker. Dawn had been telling everybody the details of what we'd done and what we'd found. Then I confessed that I'd put the note back in the end.

"After all that!" said Stacey. "Oh, well, I suppose you're right. You couldn't really have used it for evidence without incriminating yourself."

"That's true," said Kristy. "But I wish I could have seen Shawna's face if you *had* confronted her with that note!" She shook her head.

Mary Anne looked at me and smiled. "You did the right thing, Claud," she said softly. "I'm really proud of you."

"*I* may have done the right thing," I said. "But Shawna didn't. And I still need to prove it." I frowned down at my disgusting-looking meat pie. "I just can't think of anything else to do, though. I'm stuck."

For a few minutes nobody said anything. It seemed as if we were *all* stuck. I felt miserable.

"And on top of everything else," I said, breaking the silence, "I've got another maths test coming up. What if I don't get an A in it?" I couldn't even think about what might happen if I started to fail maths.

"Don't worry, Claud," said Stacey. "I'll help you revise for it. You can get all A's if we work hard enough." She stopped to think for a moment. "But maybe you should ask Mr Zorzi if you can sit in a different seat on the day of the test. We wouldn't want the whole thing to start all over again."

She had a point. Shawna had done it once – why wouldn't she do it again? "Okay, you're right," I said. "I'll ask him. But we still haven't worked out how to prove that Shawna was the cheat instead of me."

"I've got it!" said Kristy. She'd been quiet for a few minutes, and she must have been thinking hard. "Remember how I accidentally got Cokie Gray to incriminate herself?"

"Yeah!" said Dawn. "That's right. Remember when she was pretending to be Kristy's mystery admirer? She finally gave herself away and admitted that she was the one sending all those weird notes."

"That's not the only time we caught Cokie out," said Mary Anne. "Remember when she was trying to make us believe that there was a bad-luck curse on me?"

"That's right," said Kristy, grinning. "She walked straight into our trap." She rubbed her hands together. "And if it worked on Cokie, it'll work on Shawna."

"Right!" said Stacey, beaming at me. "We'll just let Shawna prove her own guilt."

I nodded slowly. "Okay," I said. "I'll try anything at this point."

"Now all you have to do is work out how to set her up in front of Mr Zorzi," said Mary Anne, just as the bell rang. Lunch period was over.

The chalk screeched on the blackboard as Mr Zorzi drew a complicated-looking diagram. It was Monday and the maths lesson was just about to begin. I'd spent practically the whole weekend trying to think up traps for Shawna to fall into, but I hadn't come up with much. Still, I was pretty eager to get going.

I decided to start right away. My first idea was to try to nudge Shawna into confessing by using certain meaningful words – words that would let her know that I was "on to her", as they say in detective films.

"Oh!" I said, looking into my notebook. "I can't find my *copy* of that last handout." As I said the word *copy* I looked at Shawna. "Does anyone else have a *copy* I can borrow?" I asked. "I'd hate to *cheat* Mr Zorzi out of another one."

Shawna was looking back at me with a puzzled expression. Some of the other kids in class were giving me funny looks, too.

I hardly noticed their glances. I was enjoying this. "Can I just *steal* your *copy* for a minute, Shawna?" I said. "I really need it – and that's no *lie*."

I'd expected Shawna to break down and confess when she heard all those incriminating words. But she was looking at me as if I'd gone mad. "Of course you can borrow it," she said, bending over to search through her rucksack. "But I don't think we're going to need it today."

I was disappointed. Shawna didn't seem to be getting the messages I was sending her. I suppose she just didn't feel all that guilty about what she'd done. It wasn't going to be easy to make her crack.

"Here, Claudia," said Shawna, reaching over to give me the handout.

"Oh, never mind," I said.

"Claudia! Shawna!" said Mr Zorzi. "Are you ready to begin?" I'd been so involved in carrying out my plan to trap Shawna that I hadn't noticed him standing in front of the class, ready to begin.

“Yes, Mr Zorzi,” I said. Shawna was still sitting there with the paper in her hand. She raised her eyebrows at me and shook her head. Then she put the handout away.

“Yes, Mr Zorzi,” she echoed.

Oh, my lord. I’d really been expecting that plan to work. Maybe it would have, if I had been able to keep it up long enough. I hadn’t really come up with too many other ideas for trapping Shawna. What was I going to do next?

Mr Zorzi droned on about “whole numbers”. He wasn’t making a lot of sense – but then, I wasn’t paying that much attention to him. I was busy thinking.

How could I prove that Shawna had copied off my paper? First, I decided, I’d have to show that it was possible for her to read my answers from where she sat. But what was I going to do, give her an eye test?

Suddenly, out of nowhere, the answer popped into my mind. I thought of this bumper sticker I’d seen once on an old banger of a car on the motorway. “IF YOU CAN READ THIS, YOU’RE TOO CLOSE!” The sticker was printed in pretty small letters, so that you wouldn’t be able to read it unless you were right behind the other car.

I looked down at my notebook. So far I hadn’t taken any notes on Mr Zorzi’s lecture. Guess what I wrote across the page? I wrote it in letters about the same size as my ordinary writing, so it would make a good test of Shawna's vision. Here's what it said: "IF YOU CAN READ THIS, YOU ARE A CHEAT AND YOU MIGHT AS WELL ADMIT IT!"

I looked at it and almost burst out laughing. This *had* to work. Now I just had to wait for Shawna to notice what I'd written. When she read it (and I was sure she'd be able to) her face would go scarlet and she'd probably say something incriminating.

There was only one problem. Unlike me, Shawna *was* paying attention to Mr Zorzi. She was taking notes on everything he said. She had no reason to look over at me – or my paper.

I had to get her attention. First, I cleared my throat. "Ahem!" I said, loudly. She didn't look. I tapped my pen against my desk, hoping that she'd turn to see where the noise was coming from. She seemed absorbed in her note-taking.

"Psst . . . Shawna!" I whispered, as quietly as I could. She didn't seem to hear me.

I'd caught the attention of some of the other kids in the class, though. They were looking at me, watching to see what I would do next.

Desperate times call for desperate measures, I thought. I gave a *huge* yawn, stretching my arms over my head.

"Claudia Kishi!" said Mr Zorzi. "What on earth are you doing?"

Ooops. I'd got a bit carried away and forgotten where I was.

"Sorry, Mr Zorzi," I said, giving him my best smile.

"I suppose you know all about the whole numbers," said Mr Zorzi, "and you don't need to revise this material with the rest of us."

Yikes. That brought me back to earth. After all, even if I could prove that Shawna was guilty, I still needed to keep up with my lesson. And I wasn't doing a very good job of it that day.

"Yes, Mr Zorzi," I said without thinking. "I mean, no, Mr Zorzi," I said, correcting myself. "I'll pay attention. I'm sorry."

I heard some giggles behind me. I turned to see who was laughing, and saw one of the kids making the "she's nuts!" sign and pointing at me.

Better get a grip, Claud, I thought. My plans were not working out the way they were supposed to. I decided to give up and listen to Mr Zorzi instead. I might as well get *something* out of that day's class.

I turned to a fresh page in my notebook and then looked over at Shawna's desk to check on what notes she'd taken so far. Then it hit me. Of course! All I had to do to prove that she could read *my* paper was to prove that I could read *hers*.

I leaned over just a bit so I could see more clearly. She was scribbling away. I caught a few words: "So then he said, 'Well, I heard that Susan told Jason that you were going to ask me to the dance.' And so I said. . ."

Wow. Shawna wasn't taking notes on what Mr Zorzi was saying. All this time she'd been *writing* notes – to her friend!

And it looked like juicy stuff. I leaned over again to read some more. ". . .but Susan said that Jason said I had really nice hair. . ."

I was totally absorbed in what I was reading. I didn't even hear Mr Zorzi call my name this time, but he must have been trying to get my attention for quite a while. Just as I was getting to a really good part of Shawna's note, I felt a hand on my shoulder. I must have jumped about six feet straight up out of my seat.

"Claudia," said Mr Zorzi, shaking his head. I looked up at him with my mouth open. I couldn't think of a thing to say. I couldn't believe I had been caught in the act, doing what I'd been trying so hard to catch Shawna doing.

Just then, the bell rang. I was in luck – the maths lesson was over.

12th CHAPTER

Tuesday

Mal, your brillyunt. I can't beleive you got the tripplets "ungrounded."

Something had to be done. They were driving the rest of us absolutely batty.

I can see why. Ive never seen three boys in a werse mood. when I got too youre house, they dint even act glad to see me.

Try not to take it personally, Claudia. They were just so tired of being cooped up. But theyre definitely feeling better now!

Mallory and I were sitting for her brothers and sisters that afternoon and you can't imagine what a bad mood the triplets were in. They still wouldn't tell which of them had broken the window, and they were still grounded. They hadn't been outside, they hadn't seen their friends, and they weren't allowed to use the phone. When I reached the Pikes' house, they hardly even said hello.

Being grounded wasn't what was bothering the triplets – it was the fact that they weren't even earning any pocket money. And no pocket money meant no chocolate bars, no comics. . . "Not even a single piece of bubble gum!" Adam wailed, telling me about it.

I was sympathetic, but as babysitters we had to enforce Mrs Pike's rules. And the triplets weren't happy about that. They were sick of being inside, sick of Pig Latin, even sick of that "op-talk" Jessi had taught them – they were sick of just about everything. So I'll admit that I was pretty happy when Mallory suggested that I take the younger Pikes outside to play.

"I'll keep an eye on the triplets, Claud," she said. "I'm working on an idea that might solve the problem. And the problem *has* to be solved – or else I might go insane."

"Fine with me, Mal," I said. I rounded up the rest of the kids and headed outside. Then Mallory got to work on the triplets.

Adam, Jordan and Byron were lounging around the living room, listlessly playing with their Matchbox car collection. Mallory sat down and watched for a few minutes, ignoring the bored looks they gave her. By this time she'd got used to their foul mood.

"I've got an idea, boys," she said.

"Oh yeah?" asked Adam.

"So what?" asked Jordan.

"Big deal," said Byron.

"Oh, okay," said Mallory. "I suppose you don't want to hear how you might be able to get un-grounded and get your pocket money back. Fine with me!" And she got up to leave the room.

"Wait a minute!" said the boys at once. They begged her to tell them her idea.

"You know those reconstructions you see on the TV?" she asked. "Sometimes when they reconstruct the crime it suddenly becomes obvious that the seemingly innocent person was guilty all along."

The triplets nodded.

"Well, what if we reconstruct *this* crime?" Mal asked.

The triplets looked doubtful.

"It may be your only chance," said Mallory.

The triplets exchanged glances.

"How do we start?" asked Jordan.

Mallory told them that they should do everything possible to re-create the day that the window had been broken. "Think about that day. Try to remember everything about it," she said.

The triplets were quiet for a moment, thinking. Then they had a quick, hushed discussion. Adam turned to Mallory. "Wait here," he said. The boys ran upstairs, and when they came back down, Mallory burst out laughing. They'd changed into the same clothes they'd been wearing on the day the window had been broken!

"Okay, boys," she said. "Now I know Mum said you couldn't go outside, but I think this time we can make an exception to the rule. After all, how can we reconstruct the crime unless we're at the scene of the crime itself?"

The boys grabbed their baseball equipment and followed Mallory outside. "Whoops!" said Byron, when they'd reached the back garden. "Forgot my batting glove!" He ran back inside.

"He didn't *really* forget it," said Jordan. "He's just reconstructing. On the day the window broke, he really did forget his glove. So he's doing it again."

Mallory rolled her eyes. She could see that the triplets were going to take this very seriously. And she was right. They seemed to think that every single thing they'd done that day was important. Adam even remembered every knock-knock joke he'd told.

Finally, the boys got around to reconstructing what they'd each been doing when the ball went through the window. And, as Mallory told me later, she saw straight away whose fault it was – everybody's and nobody's.

What happened that day (as reconstructed by the triplets) was this: Jordan was pitching, Byron was batting and Adam was behind him, catching. (No one was fielding.)

Jordan pitched a pretty strong pitch, right up in the air and "outside". Byron swung at it, even though he should have let it go by. It bounced off his bat, and he saw that it was going towards the house. He shouted to Adam to catch it, but Adam misjudged the direction of the ball and ran the wrong way. Then the ball crashed through the basement window. And you know the rest of the story.

Mallory said she was relieved to have finally found out what had happened – and she said the triplets seemed happy to let the story out. They'd kept it quiet for so long.

She and the triplets joined me and the younger Pikes, and we played together in the garden until Mrs Pike came home. As soon as she pulled into the drive, Mallory ran to her.

The triplets performed their reconstruction again, this time in front of all their brothers and sisters *and* their mother. Nobody had to explain anything to Mrs Pike – she saw straight away that the accident hadn't really been anybody's fault.

"Adam," she said. "Byron. Jordan!" They gathered around her. "You are now officially 'ungrounded'!" The triplets cheered and slapped each other's hands. Then they turned to Mallory.

"Thanks, Mal!" shouted Byron.

"You saved us!" said Adam.

"You're the greatest!" said Jordan, hugging Mal so tightly that her face turned red. The reconstruction had been a success.

That night, after dinner, I went into Janine's room and asked her if she had time to talk. She turned off her computer immediately and listened while I told her about *everything* that had been going on at school.

I told her about the conversation I'd overheard in the girls' toilets. I told her about how Dawn and I had "checked" Shawna's locker. I even told her about the silly tricks I'd used to try to get Shawna to break down and confess.

Janine listened to everything I said without making comments. All she said was "Yes?" and "Then what happened?" She was being really understanding about it, and I was glad.

Then I told her what Mallory had done with the triplets that day. She laughed at first, but then she started nodding, as if she understood completely.

"So do you think it would work for me?" I asked her hopefully.

“Would *what* work, Claud?” she asked. I suppose she hadn’t followed my train of thought.

“A reconstruction!” I said. I was excited. It seemed like a great idea to me. “We get Mr Zorzi to let me and Shawna reconstruct taking the test! Then he’ll see straight away what happened that day.”

“Slow down, Claud,” said Janine. “You’re forgetting something very obvious here. All Shawna would have to do is pretend not to cheat!”

I felt so stupid. How could I have missed that? There was no way Shawna would incriminate herself in a reconstruction. She’d had no problem lying to Mr Zorzi in the first place. And I had to admit she was a good actress. She’d convinced him straight away that she was innocent.

What a stupid idea that reconstruction had been. It was becoming obvious to me by now that I’d never be able to prove my innocence.

“This has been really hard on you, hasn’t it, Claudia?” Janine asked me gently.

I looked at her and nodded, gulping back my tears.

“Don’t worry,” she said. “Shawna’s not going to get away with making you look a cheat.”

Janine was smiling secretly, as if she was working something out. But I was sure that even Janine couldn’t solve my problem. I shrugged. "It doesn't really matter any more," I said.

Then I told Janine that I was going to bed, and we said good night. Or at least *I* said good night. Janine looked as if she were off in some other world. I doubt that she even noticed when I left. She was just sitting there, smiling to herself.

13th CHAPTER

"It doesn't really matter any more." That's what I'd said to Janine, and that's what I had to make myself believe. Maybe I could do a really good job of acting as if I didn't care about being accused of cheating. If I convinced everybody else that it didn't matter any more, maybe I would start to believe it, too. I would simply put the whole thing behind me.

I practised my new attitude as I washed my face and brushed my teeth. It doesn't matter! I don't care! It doesn't matter! I don't care! I said to myself over and over again.

I kept on saying it as I changed into my pyjamas and got into bed. It doesn't matter! I don't care! And before I knew it, I'd fallen asleep.

I woke up early and lay in bed thinking about what to wear to school. What outfit could I wear to best express my new attitude? I decided that somebody who felt the way I did (or at least the way I *wanted to* feel) would dress pretty wildly.

I decided to do a Miss Frizzle.

Do you know who Miss Frizzle is? She's a character in this great kids' series – the Magic School Bus books. Miss Frizzle is a wacky teacher who takes her class on amazing class trips – like, would you believe, inside the human body!

Anyway, you must be wondering what this has to do with what I was going to wear. Well, here's the thing. Miss Frizzle is *the wildest dresser* I have ever seen! She always wears these coordinated outfits. In *Inside the Human Body*, she wears a dress with eyes and ears and noses all over it. And her shoes have – you guessed it – tongues! In another book, she wears a dress with a caterpillar design – and on her shoes are butterflies instead of bows.

I love the way Miss Frizzle dresses.

I decided that my theme for the day would be The Sea. I put on a blue skirt with brightly coloured tropical fish printed all over it. Then I put on a green blouse. I thought that could represent seaweed or something. I pulled my hair into a ponytail, over to one side, and I pinned it with a starfish hairslide I made last summer.

"Claudia!" my mum called up the stairs. "You're going to be late!"

I ran to my wardrobe and pulled out a pair of shoes. They're the plastic kind called "jellies" that I'd decorated with stickers of seahorses and shells. I looked at myself in the mirror as I slid the shoes on. Was it too much? I shook my head. I looked great. I looked like someone who didn't care about what grade she got for a stupid maths test.

I ran downstairs for breakfast, and Mum gave me a big smile. "Interesting outfit, darling," she said. My parents are pretty good about letting me dress the way I want.

I laughed and talked all through breakfast. Janine gave me a couple of strange looks. She must have thought I was pretty weird, after the dejected way I'd left her room the night before. But she didn't know that this was the New, Improved Claud. The Claud who didn't care.

I had a good day at school – the best day I'd had in quite a while. I paid attention in all my classes and even put up my hand a few times when I thought I knew the answer. My teachers seemed happy with my performance.

So did my friends.

At lunch, everybody wanted to know how I'd made the hairslide and where I'd got the skirt. I felt pretty good. I sat with my friends and we talked about everything *but* tests, or maths, or cheating.

At one point Kristy started to tell us a story about something Shawna Riverson had done during her English class that morning. Stacey shot her a Look, and Kristy stopped talking. I'm lucky to have such a sensitive best friend.

Nobody would ever have guessed that the girl in the wild outfit – the one who laughed and gossiped with her friends – cared *anything* about her grades.

By the end of the day I was exhausted. I knew I'd done a great job of convincing everybody that "it didn't matter" – but had I convinced myself? Not really. I still had this ache inside. I hated the fact that I'd been accused of cheating, and I hated the idea that there would be an F on my record where there should have been an A–.

When the last bell rang, I went to my locker and got my stuff together. I didn't have a sitting job that afternoon, so I was planning to spend some time working on a collage.

I headed out of the door, deep in thought. Then, out of the corner of my eye, I saw someone go by in the opposite direction. Janine! I did a double take. Then I ran after her. "What are *you* doing here?" I asked.

"I decided it was time to do something about this awful situation," she said. "I always had a good relationship with the head teacher when I was at Stoneybrook Middle School. He might remember me."

Remember her! Teachers and head teachers never forget Janine. They'll hold her up as an example of a model pupil for the next fifty years.

"I know you didn't cheat, Claudia. And I'm going to talk to the head teacher about that test," she went on.

I couldn't believe it. All I wanted was for everybody to *forget* about the whole thing.

"I thought I told you to stay out of this!" I said to Janine angrily.

"No," said Janine solemnly, "you told Mum and Dad to stay out of it. You never said *I* couldn't help."

"But what are you going to tell him?" I asked. I didn't want the head teacher to know everything that had happened since the day of the test. If he did, I could be in even deeper trouble.

"Don't worry," said Janine. "I'm only going to tell him about how hard you studied, and how well you were prepared for the test. I won't say a word about the conversation you overheard in the girls' toilets."

"And you won't tell him about Shawna's locker, will you?" I asked.

"Claudia," said Janine, "of course I won't."

We'd been walking as we talked, and by then we'd reached the door of the head teacher's office. Suddenly, I felt hopeful. Janine seemed so determined. Maybe this wasn't such a bad idea after all. I smiled at Janine and whispered into her ear. "Thanks!" I said.

She opened the door and disappeared inside. The door closed behind her.

I stood in the hall and waited, feeling incredibly nervous. The school was pretty quiet by then, and I could hear the clock above the door ticking past the minutes. Once in a while I smiled as someone I knew walked by on his way to team practice.

The halls became completely silent. How long had Janine been in the office? I looked at the clock, but the minute hand had hardly moved. Then I heard footsteps. I looked up to see Mr Zorzi coming down the hall.

He nodded to me when he saw me. I couldn't meet his eyes. I watched as he walked into the head teacher's office. What was going on in there? I was dying to know.

Just then, the door to the office opened wide. I saw the head teacher standing there, smiling at me. "Won't you come in, Claudia?" he asked.

I looked down at my shoes. Oh, my lord! Suddenly I felt a bit silly in my wild outfit. I'd never have worn it if I'd known I'd end up in the head teacher's office.

I took a deep breath and smiled back at him. Then I walked into his office. Mr Zorzi and Janine were sitting there chatting as if they were the best of friends.

"Please sit down, Claudia," said the head teacher. I looked round and saw a chair next to Janine. I slipped into it. I sat up straight and folded my hands in my lap, trying to look more like a nice, normal eighth-grader and less like someone ready for a trip to the ocean bed.

Janine smiled at me, as if to say that everything was going to be all right. I gave her a weak smile in return.

"Claudia," said the head teacher. "Janine tells me that you studied very hard for your maths test last week."

I nodded. I didn't trust my voice.

"And she says that she's sure you knew the material," he continued.

I nodded again. Janine had always been more sure of that than I was myself!

"How did you feel when you took the test that day?" he asked.

I cleared my throat. "I – I felt good," I answered. "I felt I had done well in the test. I felt all that studying had been worthwhile."

Janine nodded encouragingly.

"And you're willing to sit here and tell all of us that you absolutely did not take even one little peep at anyone else's paper?" The head teacher looked closely at me.

"That's right," I answered in a steady voice. "I did not cheat."

"Well," said the head teacher, "I always think everybody deserves a chance to prove his or her innocence. Innocent until proven guilty – that's the basis of our criminal justice system, isn't it, Mr Zorzi?"

Mr Zorzi nodded, smiling at me.

The head teacher went on. "I'd like you and Janine to leave Mr Zorzi and me alone now," he said. "We'll work out a way for you to get a fair trial. He'll let you know tomorrow what it will be." He looked at Janine, and then at me. "Is that satisfactory?"

Janine nodded and smiled. "Oh, yes. That's wonderful!" She stood up. "Thank you so much," she said.

I just sat there, stunned. Janine's plan had worked. I was going to get a chance to prove I hadn't cheated!

14th CHAPTER

I would probably still be sitting in the head teacher's office, in a state of total shock, if Janine hadn't grabbed my hand and dragged me home. I just couldn't believe that Janine had convinced the head teacher and Mr Zorzi to give me another chance.

"Why not?" asked Janine, when I said this to her later that night. "You *deserve* a second chance."

Was this the same Janine that I'd argued with all those years? She was acting like the best big sister I could ever hope for. "So what do you think they'll decide?" I asked her. "I mean, what will I have to do to prove I didn't cheat?"

"I can't be sure," answered Janine. "But I would imagine that you're going to have to convince Mr Zorzi that you really *do* know that material."

"I'm nervous," I confessed.

"There's no logical reason for you to feel nervous," said Janine. "But we can go over a few problems if you'd like."

I got out my maths book, and we studied for about five minutes. Straight away I could see that I did remember the material. In fact, it was so familiar by now that it was almost boring. I was ready to stop before long, and I realized that Janine was missing valuable time on her computer.

"Janine, I think I'm ready," I said. "Thanks so much for what you did today."

"That's all right, Claudia," she said. "Nobody gets away with calling my little sister a cheat."

Janine is A-OK.

I finished off my homework and then worked on my collage. It was almost finished. I'd decided to give it to Janine as a thankyou present. Then I phoned Stacey.

"You'll never believe where I was at three-fifteen this afternoon," I said when she answered the phone. I could picture her, standing in the kitchen. If we talked for a while she'd probably stretch the phone cord down the hall and into the big coat cupboard. That's the only way she can get any privacy during her phone calls. I know I'm incredibly lucky to have a phone in my own room.

"Where were you?" she asked. "Not looking through Shawna's locker again, I hope!"

"No way!" I had to laugh. How could we have done that? We were lucky that we didn't get caught. I told Stacey all about the scene in the head teacher's office.

"Weren't you scared?" she asked.

"Are you kidding?" I answered. "I was shaking like a leaf. But it was worth it."

"What do you think they'll make you do?" she asked. I told her that it didn't matter. As long as they gave me a second chance, there was no way I was going to blow it.

We talked for a while longer. When it was time to get off the phone, she said something that reminded me of what she'd said on that fateful night before that maths test. "Just think, Claud. By the time we have our next meeting, this will all be over."

She was right. We had a Babysitters Club meeting the next afternoon. I hoped I'd have good news for everyone by then.

I wore my lucky earrings to school the next day. Even though I felt pretty confident, I thought it wouldn't hurt to have a little extra good luck.

I made a point of arriving at the maths lesson a little early, so I could find out what Mr Zorzi and the head teacher had decided. When I walked into his room, Mr Zorzi was marking papers at his desk.

"Claudia," he said. "I'm glad you're here early. This is what we've decided. During the lesson today, you're going to take the test again."

I took a deep breath and nodded. "Okay," I said. "I'm ready."

"The test isn't exactly the same," Mr Zorzi went on. "It covers similar material, but the questions are different." He led me to a desk at the back of the room. "The rest of the class will be studying in small groups today, so if you work with your sister tonight you won't fall behind."

I sat down at the desk and looked around me. No other desks were close by. Good! I didn't want there to be any doubt in anybody's mind that I could have cheated in *this* test.

The rest of the kids in my class were drifting in by now. I got a couple of curious looks, but I ignored them. (I couldn't help noticing that Shawna looked as if she was *dying* to know what I was up to.) I started to work on the test.

This time, I wasn't nearly as tense. Once again there were questions that looked harder and questions that looked easier; I just started with the easier ones and worked my way through the test. When I had finished, I checked my answers. Then I walked up to Mr Zorzi's desk and handed the paper to him. There was still time left in the period, so he said he'd check it straight away.

I sat down at my usual desk and started studying. I wasn't exactly nervous, but I'll admit that the numbers and symbols on the page weren't making much sense to me. Once in a while I looked up to see whether Mr Zorzi had finished marking my test.

Just before the bell rang, Mr Zorzi called me to his desk. I crossed my fingers as I went to the front of the room.

"You know, Claudia," said Mr Zorzi, looking up at me as I stood in front of his desk. "I'm not just a teacher – I also help coach the boys' basketball team. And I believe that taking a test is like playing a game. You can either win the game, or you can lose it." He looked at me to see if I was following his little speech. "If you lose," he continued, "it just means you need more practice."

What was he trying to tell me? I wished he would get to the point.

"Good news, Claudia!" he said smiling. "You've won the game this time. You did even better on this test than on the first one. You only got two answers wrong."

Wow! I'd done it! All right!

"I owe you an apology, Claudia," said Mr Zorzi. "I'm sorry that I accused you of cheating. I've learned a lesson from this."

"That's okay, Mr Zorzi," I said. "As long as you believe me now." I was impressed that he had apologized so directly.

Then the bell rang and everybody got up to leave. "Just a minute," said Mr Zorzi. "Shawna Riverson, please come to my desk.

Uh-oh. I stood to one side. I thought I had a right to hear what happened next.

"Shawna," said Mr Zorzi. "Claudia has just retaken the test she was accused of cheating in, and she's passed it with flying colours."

Shawna looked at me for a second, and then back at him "Yeah?" she asked. "So what?"

"I believe she's demonstrated that she did not, in fact, cheat in the test," said Mr Zorzi. "I'm going to have to ask you to prove the same thing."

Shawna turned white.

"You don't have to stay late today," he said. "You may take the test tomorrow morning during registration."

Wait a minute, I thought. That didn't seem fair. That would mean that Shawna would have time to study for the test. But it turned out that it didn't matter.

"I – I can't!" said Shawna. Now her face was red.

"What do you mean?" asked Mr Zorzi. "Aren't you going to be at school tomorrow?"

"No!" said Shawna. "I mean, yes – I'm going to be at school. But I can't take the test." She rubbed her hands together anxiously.

"Shawna, what are you saying?" asked Mr Zorzi.

"I can't take it because I don't know the work. I don't know it, and even if I studied all night I wouldn't pass the test." Shawna looked as if she was about to cry. "I did it! I copied off Claudia's paper!"

My mouth dropped open. I never expected her to actually confess.

Mr Zorzi's mouth was open, too. Just for a moment. "Why, Shawna?" he asked. "Why did you cheat?"

She told him the story – how she'd stretched herself too thin with her activities and clubs and all. "So I just didn't think there was any other way," she finished.

"And you let me believe that Claudia was the one who had cheated?" Mr Zorzi asked, frowning. "I think you owe her an apology."

Shawna looked at me and mumbled something I barely heard. I didn't care. I'd done it! I'd stuck this thing out and I'd proved my innocence. With Janine's help, the mystery had been solved. Now everybody would know who the real villain was. I felt as if a tremendous weight had fallen from my shoulders.

Shawna, the cheat, was in tears. I almost felt sorry for her. Almost.

Mr Zorzi sent her straight to the head teacher's office, and I found out later that she got suspended for two days. And, she got an F in that test. Poor, poor Shawna.

That's what Kristy said when I finished telling the story in the canteen. "Poor, poor Shawna."

"I *knew* everything would work out," said Mary Anne.

Stacey just smiled and gave me the thumbs-up sign.

I felt terrific.

15th CHAPTER

It was later that same day. I'd been in my room all afternoon, putting the finishing touches to my collage. I hummed along to the radio as I worked, and occasionally I burst into song. (I'm tone deaf, but as long as I'm sure nobody's around to hear me, I love singing at the top of my voice.) I was in a *great* mood.

I hadn't looked at the clock for a while, so I was totally amazed when I saw the time. It was 5:29 – and Kristy hadn't shown up for our meeting yet. Kristy's always so punctual. I couldn't believe she wasn't already sitting in the director's chair.

I shrugged, turned up the radio, and went back to my collage. I knew everybody would start to straggle in within a few minutes.

Just as I was in the middle of belting out a really romantic love song, the door to my room flew open.

"SURPRISE!"

I almost jumped out of my skin. What a shock! There were all my friends, and Janine, crowded around my door. They were loaded down with bags of crisps and huge bottles of lemonade. Jessi was holding a platter of chocolate chip cookies. All of them were grinning at me.

I grinned back. "What's going on?" I asked.

"We wanted to do something special for you," said Mallory.

"We're proud of you," added Stacey. "You really stuck it out!"

"And Kristy had the idea to make this meeting a kind of party," said Dawn. "What do you think?"

What did I think? I was overwhelmed. It's not very often that Kristy bends the rules and changes the form of a club meeting.

"I think it's terrific!" I said. "And I think you are the best friends in the world."

Then I saw Janine. She was hanging back shyly, trying to blend into the woodwork. She must have felt out of place. "And Janine is the best sister in the *universe*," I said, gesturing to her. "C'mon in, Janine. I've got something for you."

I grabbed the collage and held it behind my back for a minute. "I wanted to give you something to show you how grateful I am for all your help," I said.

"Oh, Claud," she said. "You don't have to do that! I enjoy helping you study."

"Well, even if you do, I know you've got lots of other things you could use that time for," I said. "And anyway, it's not just the study help. If you hadn't talked to the head teacher for me, I might never have had a second chance with that test." I showed her the collage. "I'd like you to have this," I said.

Janine looked at it and smiled. "It's beautiful," she said. She held it up for everyone else to see. "Thank you, Claudia," she said. "I'll hang it in my room with pride."

Just then, the phone rang. I'd totally forgotten that this was our usual meeting time! Kristy took the call.

"Babysitters Club," she said. "Oh, hi, Mrs Pike." She listened for a moment. "Oh, of course," she said. "I'll call you straight back."

"Mrs Pike needs a sitter for the younger kids on Saturday afternoon," said Kristy. "She said she and Mr Pike are taking the triplets to a film matinée, to celebrate their ungrounding."

"They're going to take them out for ice cream, afterwards," said Mallory. "I think she feels pretty bad about how long they were stuck inside. I'd watch Nicky and my sisters myself," she went on, "but Jessi and I are going shopping on Saturday."

Mary Anne looked in the record book to see who was free, and Stacey got the job. After Kristy had called Mrs Pike back, Mal filled us in on the rest of the story about the triplets.

"You wouldn't believe how happy they are to be free again," she said. "They're actually acting human – it's a pleasure to be around them."

"Are they going to get their pocket money back?" asked Stacey.

"Well," answered Mallory, "my parents realized that if the boys had to give up their pocket money until the window was paid off, they'd be broke until they went to college.

The Pike kids get a pretty small amount of pocket money – I suppose because there are so many of them.

"So Dad made a deal with the boys," continued Mal. "They're going to work off their debt by doing chores around the house. You know, raking leaves, cleaning out the basement – that kind of stuff."

"That's great!" said Dawn.

"Yeah, they're pretty thrilled about it," said Mal. "Now they can get back into some serious baseball-card collecting."

(The triplets don't collect baseball cards like some boys do – as investments. They just collect the cards of players they really like. That way, it doesn't cost as much – and they're just as happy.)

"That's good news, Mal," I said. "I'm glad everything's settled, for them *and* for me."

"That's right," said Mary Anne. "We've got a lot to celebrate. By the way, did Mr Zorzi tell you what your grade would officially be?"

I smiled. "Yes, it's true sports fans," I said, pretending to speak into a microphone. "Claudia Kishi will go down in the record books for this one. She really earned that A–!"

"All *right*, Claud!" said Dawn

"I'd like to propose a toast," said Kristy. Everybody scrambled to make sure they had some lemonade. (Dawn and Stacey were drinking plain old mineral water.) Kristy held up her cup. "To Claudia," she said. "Congratulations! Nancy Drew would be proud of you. You solved the mystery and you passed the test!"

"Yea!" yelled Jessi and Mallory together.

"Congratulations, Claud!" said Stacey.

Everybody clinked their cups together (or *pretended* to clink them; plastic doesn't clink very well) and grinned at me.

I was blushing. "Okay, everyone," I said. "Let's get down to some serious pigging out!" I opened up the crisps and passed round the cookies.

"Claudia," said Janine. "There's just one thing I want to ask you."

"Yes?" I said.

"Aren't you glad that Jessi made these biscuits – instead of Gertrude?"

I laughed. Then I explained the joke to my friends, and we all fell about laughing. That day's meeting was one of the best we've ever had.

At dinner that night, Janine told my parents what had been going on. They'd already heard that I'd got my A– back, but they didn't know the details. (Janine didn't tell them *everything*, for which I'm grateful.)

"Claudia, darling," said my mother. "I'm so proud of you! You really stood your ground."

"Well," I said. "I don't want you to be disappointed in me. I knew I had to make sure my record was clear."

"Your record is *always* clear with us," said my father.

"I was worried that if I didn't do well in maths you would make me give up the Babysitters Club," I confessed quietly.

"Oh, Claudia," said my mother. "From now on, just make sure you let us know when you need help. Janine," she went on, "can you please give me a hand in the kitchen for a moment?"

The two of them disappeared into the kitchen, carrying our empty plates. My father jumped up from the table and went to the hall cupboard. When he came back, he was holding his camera.

I couldn't work out what was going on. Then my mother and Janine reappeared Janine was carrying a huge cake, with pink roses all over it. My dad started taking pictures as they walked towards the table.

"What's that for?" I asked. Had I forgotten somebody's birthday?

"Look at it, Claud!" said Janine. "Read what it says!"

I looked more closely at the writing covering the cake. CONGRATULATIONS, CLAUDIA! it said. What a shock! In our family, it's usually Janine who gets the cakes and has fusses made over her – whenever she wins another prize or award. But this time, the cake was for me.

I looked round the table at the faces of my sister, my mother, and my father. They were proud of me! And, I had to admit it – I was pretty proud of myself.

The Babysitters Club

MARY ANNE vs. LOGAN

This book is in honour of
Olivia Connett Swomley.

1st CHAPTER

"How do I look?" I asked.

"Look? You look fine," replied Dawn. "Anyway, you're only going to be babysitting for Jenny. What's the big deal?"

"I don't know. I suppose Mrs Prezzioso is the big deal. You know how she's always dressed. And how she always dresses Jenny."

"Yeah. They always look like they're entering a mother-daughter beauty contest."

Dawn and I giggled. Dawn is not only one of my two best friends; she's also my stepsister. It was a Friday night and I was getting ready to sit for Jenny. Dawn was perched on a chair in my room.

"You know what?" I went on. "Mrs P has only got worse since she found out she's going to have another baby."

"I can't believe that *we* know what the baby is going to be, and the rest of the

BSC members don't. They don't even want to know, Mary Anne."

"They want to be surprised, that's all," I said.

(BSC stands for the Babysitters Club. Dawn and I and a group of our friends belong to it. I'll tell you about it later.)

Who am I? I'm Mary Anne Spier. I live in an old (*very* old) farmhouse with Dawn, my father and Dawn's mother. In case you're wondering, Dawn and I have been friends longer than we've been stepsisters. After our parents got married, Dad and I and my kitten, Tigger, moved into Dawn's house. That's because it's bigger than my old house was. Since we're pretty new at being a family, I call Dawn's mother Sharon, and Dawn calls my father Richard. That feels more comfortable than Mum and Dad. All things considered, our family is coming together pretty well. We have our tough times (what family doesn't?), but the good times are getting to be more frequent, and they last longer.

Let's see. I have brown hair, brown eyes and a boyfriend! His name is Logan Bruno. Sometimes it's hard for me to believe I have a boyfriend. That's for two reasons: 1. I'm really shy. I bet I'm the shyest eighth-grader at Stoneybrook Middle School. 2. For a while now, Logan and I haven't been getting on all that well. We've hit a few rough patches. There was the time when Dawn, Claudia (another BSC member), and four kids went on a sailing trip and got stranded on a little island off the coast. (It's a long story.) Practically everyone here in Stoneybrook, Connecticut, was looking for them or worrying about them. (I was a worrier. I wanted to be a searcher, but I have very fair skin, so I can't stay out in the sun too long.) Anyway, just before the sailing accident, Logan and I had a row. It was a big one, but it was over the smallest thing. I learned something from that row. I learned that Logan and I don't always trust each other. And I learned that Logan can't always be counted on in a crisis. He wasn't there when I needed him the most. I thought he could forget about our row while our friends were lost at sea. But he couldn't, or didn't, until just before the end of the crisis.

We did make up after that, but it hasn't been our only argument. We had a pretty good one during another crisis – when Tigger was missing. Tigger is *little*! He's just a bundle of soft, grey, tiger-striped fur and a lot of purrs. He could have been in big trouble (although it turned out he wasn't). So while he was missing, I was scared to death – and Logan and I weren't getting on.

Logan and I have had some other difficult times, too. This is hard to believe, since everything was so great when we first met and realized we liked each other. For one thing, I couldn't fathom that a boy even liked me. I was shy, mousy Mary Anne. And Logan was drop-dead handsome. He looks exactly like my favourite star, Cam Geary. And he's from Louisville, Kentucky, and he has a wonderful Southern drawl. Everyone loves the way he sounds. Yet Logan chose *me* for his girlfriend. We've given each other presents, gone to school dances together, and been out on dates. Logan was with me the day I chose Tigger at the animal shelter.

So Logan and I started off with a great relationship. But lately he's been a little pushy. At least, that's the way it seems to me. Sometimes I wonder if I'm falling out of love with Logan, but I don't think so. Not over a few tiffs and misunderstandings.

"So, anyway," I said to my stepsister, "do I look nice enough for Her Royal Highness?"

"Like a real princess," Dawn answered, even though I was just wearing jeans and a new baggy sweater. "Go and find your crown and you'll be all ready."

I laughed. Then I checked my watch. "I'd better get going," I said. "I'm supposed to be there in twenty minutes."

The phone rang then, and Dawn said, "I'll get it. You find your crown."

I was looking for my shoes when Dawn called, "Mary Anne! It's for you!"

"Okay!" I called back. I dashed into our parents' bedroom, where Dawn was standing, holding the phone out to me. "Thanks," I told her. I took the receiver, and Dawn immediately left the room. That was a sure sign that Logan was on the other end of the line. If any of our other friends had called, Dawn would have hung around to see what was going on. But she respects my privacy where Logan and I are concerned.

"Hello?" I said.

Sure enough, the voice that returned my hello belonged to Logan. "Hi, it's me."

"Oh, hi," I said. "I can only talk for a couple of minutes. I'm on my way to the Prezziosos' to sit for Jenny."

"Can't I talk you into going to see a film instead?"

"Right now? No. I really can't." I hated to disappoint Logan, but I had a responsibility as a babysitter.

"Aw, come on. You and I are a couple, Mary Anne," said Logan.

"I know we're a couple," I replied, "but . . . um. . ." I tried to explain what I was thinking. I couldn't. I have trouble expressing myself sometimes. And when I do show that I'm angry or upset, I usually start to cry – which was not going to help this situation.

When I didn't finish my sentence, Logan said, "Well, is Dawn free to sit tonight?"

"You mean, to take over at the Prezziosos' so I can go out with you?"

"Yeah."

"Logan, I can't send Dawn on my sitting job," I said, my voice trembling.

"You mean you won't come to the cinema with me?" Logan sounded confused.

"Well . . . no."

"Okay," said Logan uncertainly.

"I've got to go," I said in a rush. "I'm going to be late. I'll talk to you tomorrow."

We hung up then, and I had to force myself not to cry. I concentrated on Jenny. That was my job. I could think about Logan another time.

I left the house in a hurry then, and ran all the way to the Prezziosos'. (They live nearby, and it was still light outside.) I made it just in time.

Mr and Mrs P left pretty quickly, so soon I was alone with Jenny. When her parents had left, Jenny held out her wrist and said, "Look. Mummy's bought me a watch! I can't tell the time yet, but a watch is a very grown-up thing to have. That's what Mummy said. She's bought me some other things, too. Want to see?"

"Okay," I replied.

I followed Jenny upstairs to her bedroom. Jenny, as usual, was dressed up to the nines. That's what my friend Kristy's stepfather would say, meaning that Jenny was very dressed up (even though it was just an ordinary old day). Mrs P *loves* to dress up Jenny and herself. That's what Dawn meant when she said they look like contestants in a mother-daughter beauty contest. They look like that most of the time.

Jenny took my hand and pulled me into her room. "Here," she said, heading for her dressing table. "Mummy got me some more grown-up things. Clip-on earrings, and look – trainers with *laces*. Mummy says big girls learn how to tie their shoes."

"Wow, that's great, Jenny!" I exclaimed, looking at her old plimsolls, which fastened with Velcro straps and were pretty tatty compared to her new trainers.

The phone rang then, so I said, "Come on, Jenny. Race you to the telephone."

Giggling, we ran down to the kitchen.

Guess who was on the phone? Logan.

"Logan, I'm – I'm busy now," I said.

"O*kay*."

We hung up, and I felt stung, but Jenny was my responsibility, so we went back to her room.

"Your mum has certainly been buying you a lot of presents, Jen," I ventured. I was making every effort not to think about Logan.

"Yup. They're big-girl things. Mummy says the baby won't know how to do anything for itself." (Apparently even Jenny didn't know whether she would have a little sister or a little brother.) "So Mummy will be busy, and I'll have to be a big girl."

Since Jenny didn't look too happy about this, I said, "You're very lucky – new shoes, earrings – and all because of the baby."

"Yeah. Mummy wants to make sure I'll like that baby."

Whoa. Had Jenny just said what I thought she'd said? It sounded as if she *knew* she was being bribed to get along with the new baby. Mrs P certainly had an interesting method for dealing with sibling rivalry.

Jenny showed me two more things that her mother had bought for her. Then I helped her to brush her teeth, wash her face, and finally climb into bed. After just a few pages of Babar, Jenny's eyes began to close, so we said goodnight. I turned out her light, and then I tiptoed out of her room, leaving the door open just a crack.

The phone rang immediately. I raced downstairs and picked it up.

It was guess who.

"Jenny asleep yet?" asked Logan.

"Yup. She fell asleep pretty quickly."

"Oh. Well, just checking to see how the job is going."

"It's *fine*."

"O*kay*."

Twenty minutes later, the phone rang again. I knew I should be professional and say, "Hello, Prezziosos' residence." Instead I said, "Hi, Logan."

"You knew it was me?" He sounded surprised.

"I just had this feeling."

"Jenny still asleep?"

"Yes."

"So. How about a date? There must be one evening when you're not babysitting."

I hesitated.

"Just tell me when you're free," said Logan.

I told him I'd be free the next night.

"Great. We'll see a film and grab a pizza. It's all arranged."

All arranged by Logan, I couldn't help thinking. What had happened to me in our relationship?

2nd CHAPTER

I must be the world's biggest wimp. It wasn't that I didn't want to go to see a film with Logan. It was that I felt I'd let myself get talked into it. Logan was trying so hard. Why did he need to do that? Had he always been like that? I tried to remember. I didn't think so. Then again, when two people are having problems, it's hard to tell who has changed. Usually, I supposed, they both had. So how had *I* changed? Was I more independent than I used to be? Was I sending Logan mixed signals? Maybe. I wanted to be with him – but I didn't want to lose myself in him.

There was just one thing to do – phone a friend and talk about it. As a babysitter, I knew the call would have to be short. (It's not a good idea to tie up a client's phone line with personal calls. The parents might be trying to phone to check on things.) So I would have to choose just the right person to talk to – someone who knows about boys. I consider all the girls in the Babysitters Club my friends, and Dawn and Kristy Thomas are my best friends. However, Claudia Kishi and Stacey McGill definitely know the most about boys. I tried Stacey first. Her line was engaged. So I phoned Claudia on her private phone.

I complained to her for about five minutes.

Claud listened patiently, but she didn't have any suggestions. That was okay. I'd wanted a solution, but I knew the problem was mine, and I would have to work it out for myself. Anyway, I was glad about one thing. I was glad that I had so many friends – so many people I could talk to. And that's due mostly to the Babysitters Club, which is more of a business than a club. My friends and I babysit for children in our neighbourhoods. We earn a lot of money doing this and we're good at it. I suppose it's because we all love children so much. We're the kind of sitters who really get involved with the children we look after.

Let me tell you about my friends, the BSC members. I'll start with Kristy Thomas, for two reasons. One, she's my oldest friend in the world. (I mean, we're the same age, but we've known each other since we were born.) Two, Kristy had the idea for the BSC, organized it, and got it running. That's just the way Kristy is. She's a doer, an organizer, and she's got a head full of ideas – which she usually carries out. She's also got a big mouth. I don't mean that she blabs on and on and won't stop talking. I mean that she doesn't always think before she speaks. If something pops into her head, she says it. Occasionally, she hurts people's feelings, although she never means to.

Kristy is part of the most unusual family I know. She used to be part of an ordinary family – a mother, a father, two older brothers, and a baby brother named David Michael. Then, shortly after David Michael was born, Mr Thomas walked out on his family. He just *left* them. Kristy and I lived next door to each other then (and across the road from Claudia), so I know how hard this was for her family. But Mrs Thomas pulled things together quickly. She got a good job and she managed to support her family. Then, when Kristy and I were twelve and in the seventh grade, Mrs Thomas began to get serious about Watson Brewer, a man she'd been going out with. Watson (most of us refer to him as Watson because that's what Kristy calls him) just happens to be a millionaire. He lives in a mansion on the other side of town in a much wealthier neighbourhood than the one Kristy and I lived in. And at the end of school last year, he and Mrs Thomas decided to get married. So they did!

Watson moved the Thomases out of their cramped house and into his huge one. You'd think Kristy would have just *died* to be living in a mansion with bedrooms galore and a rich stepfather, but she wasn't too happy at first. I think that was just because there were too many changes in her life. Not only did she acquire a stepfather and move out of the house in which she'd grown up, but she acquired some other family members, too.

First of all, Watson has got two kids – Karen, who's seven, and Andrew, who's almost five. Kristy didn't want to like them, but she couldn't help it. They're too adorable. Now she's wild about them. And she even complains that she doesn't see them enough. (Karen and Andrew only live with their father every other weekend and for two weeks during the summer.) Then, after Watson and Kristy's mother had been married for a while, they adopted a two-year-old girl from Vietnam. They called her Emily Michelle. And talk about adorable, well, Emily is right up there with Karen and Andrew. When Emily was adopted, *another* member joined the Thomas/Brewer household. That was Nannie, Kristy's grandmother. She moved in to help with Emily while Watson and Kristy's mum are at work, and to help run the household. Everyone loves Nannie. She's very special.

Back to Kristy. Kristy has brown hair and brown eyes. She and I look sort of alike.

We're both short, although I'm taller than Kristy. And Kristy doesn't need to wear a bra yet, which bothers her. She's a tomboy, and she started a softball team for kids in the neighbourhood. The name of her team is Kristy's Krushers. Kristy has a boyfriend, too, although she won't admit it often. He's Bart, the coach of a rival softball team!

It's hard to tell you about Kristy without telling you about me. I suppose that's because she's one of my best friends, and because we have a lot in common. In other ways, we're very different, though. (Maybe there's something to the saying that opposites attract.) Anyway, you already know a little about me: that I've got brown hair and brown eyes, and I'm short; that I have a stepmother, and a stepsister called Dawn, who's my other best friend; and that I have a kitten called Tigger, and a boyfriend called Logan with whom I'm having some problems at the moment.

Here are some other things about me. I'm *extremely* shy and sensitive (that's where Kristy and I are opposites), I'm romantic, and I cry easily. My dad brought me up after my mother died. That was when I was quite young. Dad was very strict. He made up lots of rules, such as I wasn't allowed to ride my bike into town, even when all of my friends were allowed to. He even chose all my clothes and made me wear my hair in plaits. I looked like a real baby at the beginning of the seventh grade. Kristy didn't mind that. She isn't – and never has been – interested in clothes. (She just wears jeans and things.) But *I* was interested in dressing more stylishly (or at least not like a first-grader), and I wanted my hair *out* of plaits. Well, sometime during the seventh grade, I was able to prove to my dad that I wasn't a baby, and he started giving in to me. He relaxed the rules, allowed me to wear my hair loose, and even allowed me to choose my own clothes. (I am *not* allowed to get my ears pierced, though. But that's okay. I'm not sure I want holes punched through my ears. Besides, Kristy doesn't have pierced ears, either.)

So that's me.

Now, just as it was hard to tell you about Kristy without telling you about me, it's hard to tell you about me without telling you about Dawn, since she's my stepsister. For starters, Dawn is *gorgeous*. She has long, pale blonde hair and sparkly blue eyes. Dawn is our California girl. She grew up just outside LA, and lived there until her parents got divorced. After the divorce, Mrs Schafer (Dawn's mother) moved Dawn and Dawn's younger brother, Jeff, all the way to Stoneybrook. That's because Mrs Schafer grew up here and her parents still live here. Of course, the move was difficult for Dawn and Jeff. They switched from a warm climate to a cold one (cold in the winter, anyway), and they had to leave all their friends behind. Dawn adjusted to this pretty well, but Jeff never did, and after a while, he moved back to California to live with Mr Schafer. This isn't an ideal situation, but it's the way things are. Dawn and Jeff frequently fly across the country to visit the other half of their family.

I think one of the reasons Dawn adjusted to the move so well is because she's an individualist. She's independent and usually doesn't care what people think about her. She eats what she wants (health food) and dresses the way she likes. (My friends and I think of Dawn's style as California casual.) Dawn loves mysteries and reading ghost stories, so you can imagine how delighted she was to find that the old farmhouse her mother had bought came complete with a secret passage. The passage leads from Dawn's bedroom (the entrance is concealed in the panelling) to the barn on our property, and it was part of the Underground Railroad long, long ago. Guess what? The passage may even be *haunted*!

Here's how Dawn and I got to be stepsisters. First we became friends (right after Dawn moved to Connecticut), then we realized that my father and Dawn's mother had gone to Stoneybrook High together, and then, by looking through their old yearbooks, we discovered that they had been in love. We found out that they wanted to get married, but Dawn's grandparents didn't think my dad was good enough for their daughter, so they sent Sharon off to college in California. That's where Sharon met Mr Schafer, and where they married and had Dawn and Jeff. Anyway, when Dawn and I realized that our parents had been in love, we were quick to get them back together. They had an on-again, off-again romance for a while, but finally they got married. The rest is Schafer/Spier history.

Claudia Kishi, another BSC member, is the one I spoke to on the phone when I felt as if I was wimping out with Logan. Although Claudia grew up with Kristy and me, she's always been more mature than we have. She wears the trendiest clothes you can imagine, and she is *so cool.* A typical Claudia outfit might be black leggings, a baggy black-and-white shirt-dress, low black shoes and big wild earrings for her pierced ears. This outfit would be particularly striking on Claud because of her looks. She's as gorgeous as Dawn, but in a different way. Claudia is Japanese-American. She's got silky, jet-black hair; dark, dark, almond-shaped eyes; and a creamy complexion. The fact that her complexion is flawless comes as a great surprise to everyone, since Claud is the biggest junk-food addict we've ever known. If it tastes good and is bad for you, Claud likes it. Of course, her parents don't approve of the habit, so Claudia has to hide her junk food. She's got it stashed all over her bedroom – in drawers, under pillows, behind books on her shelves. It's amazing.

Poor Claud. She's got another habit her parents don't approve of – she reads Nancy Drew books. So she has to hide her books, too. The reason her parents don't approve of Nancy Drew is that they feel Claud should be reading something more challenging. *I* think she should be allowed to read what she wants to read. If she didn't read her mysteries, she wouldn't read anything at all. Claud isn't a great pupil. She's *bright,* but she does poorly at school, especially at maths, reading and spelling. Her teachers say she doesn't apply herself, but if I were Claud, I'd be pretty nervous about school. That's because Claud has to follow in the footsteps of her older sister, Janine, who's a real genius. Janine is at high school, but she takes courses at the local community college. And she is always winning awards for her school work. Luckily, Claudia has one big talent. She is an artist. She can do just about anything – paint, sketch, sculpt, even make jewellery. She makes a lot of her own jewellery, and sometimes makes jewellery for other people.

Claudia's best friend is Stacey McGill. Like Dawn, Stacey is a newcomer to Stoneybrook. She and her parents moved here from New York City just before Stacey was to begin the seventh grade. Stacey had grown up in New York (she is *so* lucky) and she's as sophisticated as Claudia, which may be why they get along so well. Stacey also wears super-trendy clothes – layers on layers, hats, scarves, cowboy boots, that sort of thing. And she's allowed to have her blonde hair permed and she likes wearing nail polish, usually with sparkles in it.

Stacey may seem glamorous, but her life has definitely *not* been that way. Stacey's had a tough time, with both her family and her health. Stacey had moved to Stoneybrook because the company her father works for had transferred his job to Stamford, which is a city not far away. The McGills had been here for less than a year when the company transferred Mr McGill *back* to New York. We were all sad to see Stacey leave (Claudia was especially sad), but then something traumatic happened. Stacey's parents decided to get a divorce. Even worse, Mr McGill wanted to stay in New York with his job, while Mrs McGill wanted to return to Stoneybrook. So Stacey had to decide whether to live in the city in which she'd grown up or to move back to Stoneybrook with her mum. Luckily for Claud and all us BSC members, Stacey chose Connecticut, but she still visits her father pretty frequently. Going back and forth between Connecticut and New York is not always easy, though.

As for Stacey's health, she's got an illness called diabetes, and she has a severe form of it. (She said something recently about being a "brittle" diabetic, but I don't know what that is.) Anyway, when someone has diabetes, it means that a gland in the body, the pancreas, stops making something called insulin. Insulin breaks down sugar in the blood. Without insulin, a person's blood sugar level gets all out of control and he (or she) could even go into a diabetic coma, which is very dangerous. So poor Stacey has to *inject* herself with insulin (ugh, *ugh*, UGH!) every day, and stay on a strict diet. On her diet she can eat practically no sweets, and she has to count her calories to make sure she consumes the proper number – without fail. Stacey has been looking thin lately and feeling tired. Sometimes we worry about her.

The last two members of the BSC are younger than Dawn, Kristy, Stacey, Claudia and me. Their names are Mallory Pike and Jessi Ramsey, and they're both eleven and in the sixth grade. They're also best friends, and like most friends they have some things in common, yet in many ways are very different. Here are the ways in which they're different.

Mallory comes from a *huge* family. She has seven brothers and sisters! And three of them are identical triplets (boys). Jessi comes from a more normal-sized family.

She has a younger sister and a baby brother. (Mal and Jessi each live with both of their parents, and Jessi's Aunt Cecelia lives at the Ramseys' house too.)

Jessi is thinking of becoming a professional ballet dancer one day, while Mal is pretty sure she's going to write and illustrate children's books after she goes to college. Boy, you should see Jessi dance. She's *really* talented. She dances *en pointe* (that means *on toe*), she goes to lessons at a special ballet school in Stamford, *and* she's danced lead parts in lots of productions before big audiences. Mallory is talented, too, but she's more private about her stories and drawings. We don't get to see many of them, but when we do, we're impressed.

One last difference between Jessi and Mal – Jessi is black (with long, long dancer's legs, and beautiful eyes), and Mal is white (and not feeling very pretty these days. She wears glasses and a brace, and has unruly red hair).

Here are the ways in which Mal and Jessi are similar:

They both like reading, especially horse stories by Marguerite Henry. And they're both the oldest kid in their family but feel that their parents treat them like babies. For instance, the Pikes absolutely will not allow Mallory to wear contact lenses instead of glasses. However, in a recent parent-daughter breakthrough, Mal and Jessi convinced their parents to allow them to have their ears pierced. So that was something. Maybe contact lenses for Mallory will come next.

I feel really grateful to have so many good friends. If there were such a thing, I think the BSC members would be the Seven Musketeers. Oh, of course, we've had our arguments and fights, but we're usually there for each other, through thick and thin. And we're pretty understanding of each other.

3rd CHAPTER

"What is *that*?" I asked, looking horrified.

Claudia looked pretty horrified herself.

The two of us were in her room, along with Dawn and Mallory, waiting for a meeting of the BSC to begin, and I had just pointed to something. It was a large, sticky-looking brown stain on Claudia's bedspread, and it was only partially covered by the quilt folded at the end of the bed.

"Oh, lord," said Claudia, examining it. Then she leaned over and smelled it.

"Ugh!" exclaimed Mal. "How can you do that?"

But Claudia looked relieved. "It's only chocolate," she said. "I hid a Mars Bar under the quilt. I suppose it got a bit warm in there."

"What are your parents going to say when they see it?" asked Dawn.

Claudia shrugged. She pulled the quilt over the stain to hide it. "I'll worry about that another time."

Claudia flopped on to her bed and leaned against the wall. She was looking especially acute that day. (*Acute* means *cool.* My friends and I make up words all the time, and only we know what they mean. *Distant* and *dibble* also mean *cool.*) Claud was wearing an over-sized raspberry-coloured shirt, a short black skirt, and black leggings (the layered look). On her feet were black cowboy boots, and dangling from an earcuff was a huge collection of beads and stones. (Claud does have pierced ears, but the holes were empty.)

I settled myself in my usual spot on Claud's bed (beside Claud), but only after she had covered up the chocolate stain. Compared to Claudia, I looked like a complete nerd, even though I was wearing one of my better outfits: blue printed trousers that were wide on top but narrowed to cuffs at the ankles, and a short-cropped T-shirt with the sleeves rolled up and this acute picture of a cactus wearing a cowboy boot.

Kristy came thundering up the stairs and into Claud's room then. (There's no mistaking when Kristy is on her way to club headquarters.) "Where is everybody?" she asked immediately. "It's already five twenty-five."

"They'll be here," replied Claud calmly.

And Claud was right. By 5:29, we were

all in our places. Dawn and Claudia and I were sitting in a row on Claud's bed; Jessi and Mal were cross-legged on the floor, leaning against the bed; Stacey was straddling Claud's desk chair backwards; and Kristy – our chairman – was sitting in a director's chair, wearing a visor, a pencil stuck over one ear.

She looked almost regal, even though she was just wearing blue jeans, a poloneck and her trainers.

As soon as the numbers on Claud's digital alarm clock changed from 5:29 to 5:30, Kristy said loudly, "Okay. Come to order!"

Kristy, being the chairman, gets to lead the meetings. Anyway, the original idea for the Babysitters Club was hers. A year or so ago, when Kristy still lived across the street from Claud, and before Mrs Thomas had married Watson Brewer, Kristy and her older brothers took turns babysitting for David Michael after school. They didn't mind that arrangement, but of course a day came when all three of them knew they were going to be busy after school, so they wouldn't be able to take care of their little brother. That night, Kristy sat around eating pizza for dinner and watching as her mother made call after call, trying to find someone to look after David Michael the following afternoon. And that was how Kristy got her big idea to form a babysitting club. If a parent could make one call and reach several sitters at once, it would save time for the parent and also pretty much guarantee him or her a sitter. Someone was bound to be free.

Kristy told her idea to Claudia and me, and we thought it was great. We also thought a fourth member might be a good idea. Three people didn't seem like quite enough. So Claud mentioned that she was getting to be friends with Stacey McGill, a new girl at school. When we found out that Stacey had done a lot of babysitting in New York, we invited her to join the club.

Now we had a sitting business – but no one knew about it. We decided to advertise. We told everyone we could think of about the club. We passed out leaflets. We even put an advert in the paper. Our advert and the leaflets told parents that they could reach us on Monday, Wednesday and Friday afternoons from five-thirty until six at Claudia's house.

Well, at our first meeting, everything went perfectly. We got job calls straight away. And the business just kept growing. By the middle of the seventh grade we had too much business and realized we needed a fifth member. Dawn had just moved here from California then, and she and I were already friends. So Dawn joined the club. Then Stacey had to leave, so we replaced her with both Jessi and Mal. And *then* Stacey returned. Of course, we let her back in the club. Now the club has seven main members (there are two other members who don't come to meetings, but I'll tell you about them later), and we think seven is plenty. Claudia's room is getting pretty crowded!

Everyone in the BSC has a title. For instance, as I've mentioned before, Kristy is the chairman. This is not only because she thought up the business in the first place, but because she gets good ideas and really knows how to run a club (even if she does get bossy sometimes). Kristy makes us keep a club notebook. In the notebook, each of us writes up every single job she goes on. Then, once a week, we're responsible for reading the notebook to see what happened while our friends were sitting. None of us really likes writing up jobs (except maybe Mallory), but we have to admit that finding out how the other sitters solved problems, and what's going on with the kids we sit for, is pretty helpful.

Kristy also decided that we should have a record book in which we keep lists of our clients, their names, addresses, phone numbers, the rates they pay, etc. Also, we keep a record of any money we earn, and in the appointment pages we keep track of when our sitting jobs are.

Another one of Kristy's great ideas was for each of us to make a Kid-Kit. A Kid-Kit is an ordinary cardboard box that you decorate to look cheerful and pretty and fill with things kids will like, such as our old games, toys, and books, as well as new things that have to be replaced from time to time, like art materials, and colouring and sticker books. Then we can bring the Kid-Kits on sitting jobs if we want to. (They're especially handy on rainy days.) Kids love them, so their parents are happy, which means our customers will call the BSC again, which means more sitting jobs for us!

The vice-chairman of the club is Claudia. Since she has her own phone and personal phone number, we use Claudia's bedroom for our headquarters. And since we therefore descend on her three times a week, use her phone and eat her junk food, we felt it was only fair that Claud be our vice-chairman.

I am the club secretary, and I'm responsible for keeping the record book up-to-date and in order. I'm also responsible for scheduling every single sitting job. There are a lot of details involved here, but I'm good at details. Besides, Kristy thinks I have the neatest handwriting of any of us.

Our treasurer is Stacey. She's a real maths brain. *Her* job is to collect our weekly subs, put the money in the treasury (a manila envelope), and hand out money when it's needed – for instance, to buy refills for the Kid-Kits, to help pay Claud's phone bills, and to pay Charlie for driving Kristy to and from meetings now that she lives on the other side of town. Stacey also records the money we earn. (This is just for our interest. We don't pool our earnings and then divide it up. The money each of us makes is ours to keep.)

Dawn is the alternate officer of the BSC. That means that she can take over the job of anyone who misses a meeting. She knows the responsibilities of everyone in the club. That way we'll never have to go without a secretary, a treasurer, or anything. Dawn is like an understudy in a play, or a substitute teacher.

Mal and Jessi are our junior officers. This simply means that they're younger than the rest of us, and aren't allowed to sit at night unless they're watching their own brothers and sisters. They can babysit after school or at weekends though, which is good because it frees us older club members for evening jobs.

Can you believe it? Even with *seven* members of the BSC, people sometimes call and offer us a job that none of us can take. That's because we're so busy. Apart from babysitting and homework, most of us have other activities or responsibilities. Jessi goes to ballet lessons, Claud goes to art classes, Mallory has appointments with the orthodontist. . . When we realized that there were going to be occasional times when we'd have to disappoint a client and tell him or her that nobody in the BSC was free to sit, we signed on two associate members. The associate members don't come to meetings, but they are good backups (also good babysitters). They're people we can call on in an emergency. One is Shannon Kilbourne, a friend of Kristy's (she lives in Kristy's neighbourhood) and the other is . . . Logan Bruno!

Our club is very efficient (thanks mostly to Kristy), and it's businesslike and professional, which is why it's successful.

I am proud to be a member of the BSC.

When Kristy said, "Come to order!" the rest of us sat up a bit straighter. We paid attention to our chairman.

"Okay," Kristy went on. "It's Monday, subs day. Hand it over."

Most of us groaned as we reached into our pockets for money. Stacey, however, passed around the treasury with a gleam in her eye. She *loves* collecting money. (But she hates parting with it. She makes a big drama out of withdrawing funds from the treasury each time any of us needs to replace an item in the Kid-Kit or something.)

When the subs had been collected, Kristy said, "Any club business?"

We shook our heads. Things were running smoothly.

"How's Mrs Prezzioso?" Kristy wanted to know.

"She's fine," I replied. "She's going to have—"

"Don't tell us what the baby's going to be!" shrieked Jessi.

"I wasn't going to. I was just going to say that she's going to have the baby soon. In a few weeks, I think. But she's the same old Mrs P."

The phone rang then, and Dawn answered it. "Hello, Babysitters Club. . . Oh, hi, Mr Ohdner. . . Friday night?. . . Okay. I'll check and call you straight back." Dawn hung up the phone and turned to me. "Mr Ohdner needs a sitter next Friday night from seven until about ten-thirty. Who's free?"

I checked the appointment pages in the record book. "Let's see. You're free, Kristy, and so are you, Stace," I said.

"You take the job," Kristy said to Stacey. "You live much nearer to the Ohdners than I do. Besides, Andrew and Karen will be with us that night. I want to spend some time with them."

That's how we usually handle job calls – no squabbling over who gets one if several of us are free. We know there will be other jobs.

Dawn phoned Mr Ohdner back to tell him that Stacey would be sitting on Friday.

As soon as she'd hung up the phone, it rang again. Then two more times. The meeting was pretty busy. One of the last calls to come in was from Mr Prezzioso, Jenny's father. He hardly ever calls, so Jessi was surprised when she picked up the phone. "It's *Mister* Prezzioso," she mouthed to the rest of us. Then she went back to the phone call. She was saying, "Three of us? . . . Well, we don't usually take on jobs like that, but this sounds like fun. Let me check with the others and call you straight back. . . You're at *work*? Oh, that makes sense." Jessi jotted down a phone number, said goodbye to Mr P, and hung up.

"What was that all about?" asked Kristy.

"Mr Prezzioso," Jessi said, "is planning a surprise baby party for Mrs P. He wants three of us to give him a hand that day – one to watch Jenny, and two to decorate the house while Mrs P is out for lunch or something, and also to serve food, clear up, and things like that.'

"Well, I think we should take the job," said Kristy. "The Prezziosos are good clients, and besides, there is *some* babysitting involved." She turned to me. "Are three of us free that day?"

Jessi gave me the date and time of the party. I checked the appointment pages. Claudia, Stacey and I were free, so we took the job.

When the meeting was over, Kristy announced, "Good one, everyone!" and sent us all home.

4th CHAPTER

Ahhh.

I had been looking forward to this for a *long* time. It was a snowy Saturday afternoon, and I had already finished my weekend homework. I didn't have a babysitting job or anything to do. I mean, anything I *had* to do. In other words, I was free, free, free. And with the snow falling outside, I felt that this was the perfect afternoon to do cosy indoor things. Let's see. I could work on the sweater I was knitting. Or I could start a present for the Prezzioso baby – maybe a knitted blanket, or a hat and booties.

Or I could read.

That was what I really wanted to do. Dad had built a fire in the living-room fireplace, and I was just dying to lie in front of it and read *Wuthering Heights* again. I'd read it about three times, but *Wuthering Heights* is like *To Kill a Mockingbird*. You simply can't read it often enough. In fact, I think both books get better every time you read them.

So I found my copy of *Wuthering Heights*, grabbed the quilt off my bed, and ran downstairs. Then I sat in front of the fire, the quilt around my shoulders, and began the book once more. "1801. I have just returned from a visit to my landlord. . ." As soon as I read those words I was transplanted from our living room to old England, the moors, Heathcliff, Cathy and romance.

The house was quiet except for the crackling fire. Dawn had gone over to Claudia's to learn how to make jewellery (she likes beaded jewellery), Dad was in the study doing some work (he's a lawyer) and Sharon was running errands.

I was really content.

I had been enjoying the book, the fire, and the quiet for about ten minutes when the doorbell rang. I sighed, then called, "Dad, I'll get it!" and walked reluctantly to the front door.

I peeped through one of the side windows. Guess who was standing on our steps?

Logan.

He hadn't said anything about coming over that day. At least, I didn't think he had.

I opened the door.

"Surprise!" said Logan, grinning, except that with his gentle accent it sounded more like he'd said, "Supprazz!"

I just stood there. Half of my mind was back in 1801 with Heathcliff and Cathy and the moors. The other half was trying to work out what Logan was doing here.

After a few seconds, Logan said, "Aren't you going to let me in?"

"Oh! Oh, yes, of course." I stepped aside.

Logan came into our front hall, but he didn't bother to take off his coat. "Let's go out," he said. "It's a perfect snowy day in the park. Bring your ice skates." (Logan's skates were slung over his shoulder.) When I didn't say anything straight away, Logan went on. "I know you're free. Dawn told me you were looking forward to this afternoon."

"I – I was."

"So come on," said Logan. "Ice-skating, a walk in the snow. . ."

I looked over my shoulder at the fire and my open book. Then I looked back at Logan. He seemed so excited and happy. He added that he had planned a romantic afternoon, just for us.

How could I turn him down?

I couldn't. "Dad?" I called. "Logan's here. We're going to go to the park for a few hours, okay?"

"Okay," replied my father.

So I found my skates, wrapped up warmly, and set off with Logan. I had to admit that walking through the light snow that was falling *was* nice. Romantic, too.

The walk to the park took about ten minutes, and Logan talked most of the way there. That was okay with me. I didn't feel much like talking.

When we reached the park, my body still half at home by the fire, Logan said, "Boy, it's crowded today."

Stoneybrook's little park *was* crowded. It was colourful, too. Kids wearing bright skiing jackets were playing everywhere. They looked like confetti against the sharp, white snow.

"Now, I've got everything planned," Logan informed me. "Ice-skating first."

"Okay," I replied, beginning to feel even better about the afternoon.

Logan and I sat next to each other on a bench by the frozen pond. Laughing, I laced up Logan's skates for him, while he laced up mine. Then we tottered arm-in-arm to the edge of the pond and stepped gingerly on to the ice. In a flash, Logan was flying me around the pond, holding tightly to my hand. Or maybe *I* was gripping *his*. I'm not a good skater. In fact, unlike Kristy the tomboy, I'm no good at sports at all.

I think something is wrong with my coordination.

"Logan!" I said, gasping. "Slow down!"

"Oh, you want a leisurely turn around the ice? That's a good idea. Then everyone can see what a great couple we make."

Logan dropped my hand, and we linked arms again. We skated round and round. Sometimes we had to dodge little kids, and twice I almost fell over, but still, skating was pleasant. . . Until my toes began to freeze.

I skated slower and slower. I could barely feel my feet.

"Mary Anne?" said Logan questioningly.

"Can we stop now?" I asked. "My toes are—"

"Okay. I'm tired of skating, too," said Logan.

Whew! What a relief.

Logan and I glided back to the bench, untied our laces, and pulled our skates off. "Ahh," I said, rubbing each foot between my hands. A little feeling began to come back. I wriggled my toes. That was more like it.

As soon as I'd put my boots on, Logan jumped up, skates slung over his shoulder again. "Next we're going to be kids!" he exclaimed. "Look over there."

I turned in the direction that Logan was pointing and saw a group of children building a snowman.

We didn't know any of them, but Logan trotted over anyway, and I followed him.

"Need a little help with that?" Logan asked two girls who were valiantly trying to lift the snowman's head on to his body.

The girls looked up at Logan. "Okay!" they said.

Logan plopped the head on to the body.

"Thanks! Will you help us find some sticks and pebbles and things so we can finish our snowman? We want him to look just right."

"Of course," Logan replied. "Come on, Mary Anne."

Logan wandered happily around the park, looking for twigs. I limped after him. Once again my feet were starting to freeze. "Logan, I'm—"

But Logan didn't hear me. He was too busy putting a face on the snowman. When the snowman was finally finished, Logan grabbed my hand and pulled me to a quiet area of the park. I could hardly move. You need your toes for balance, and I couldn't feel mine.

"Let's make snow angels," Logan said, and flopped face-up on to the snow.

"Logan—"

"Come on. We're kids again today, remember?"

"But Logan, I'm *cold.*"

"Oh. Well, let's go over to the snack bar and get some hot chocolate. My treat."

I hobbled to the snack bar and allowed Logan to buy two hot chocolates with whipped cream on top. He carried them to a bench and handed me one of the steaming cups. I had taken my mittens off, and for a moment, I just held the cup, trying to warm my hands.

By now, my feet weren't the only frozen parts of my body. The rest of me was pretty cold, too. In fact, my teeth were chattering which made drinking quite an interesting experience.

We finished our hot chocolates and then walked slowly through the park. Logan kept admiring the white-frosted tree branches, the mounds of snow that were actually buried bushes, and icicles that hung from unlikely places. Once, we saw a robin fly from one tree to another, a splash of red against the grey sky.

Even I was enchanted by that and let out an "Ooh."

Logan looked at me happily.

I think he was going to tell me something, but I just had to say, "Logan, I'm really sorry, but I'm *freezing*."

"You can't be *too* cold, Mary Anne. I don't feel cold." (Logan wasn't even wearing his gloves.)

Why couldn't I feel cold? I *was* cold. I get cold easily.

Logan was heading for the pond again. "One more time on the ice?" he said.

The *ice?* No, no, no. . .

It was time to speak up – and be forceful. This was not going to be easy. I have trouble being forceful with anyone. But since my body was turning into an iceberg, I said, "Logan, can we go home *now*? I really am freezing."

Logan took a long hard look at me. At last he said, "O*kay*," in a sort of huffy voice, and marched towards the park entrance, leaving me to follow him.

All I could do was sigh.

5th CHAPTER

Saturday

I may be thirteen, but I still get excited about Valentine's Day, just like I did when I was little. So I was pretty happy today when I was left in charge of my younger brothers and sisters and discovered that David Michael wanted to make valentines for the kids in his class. That was a fun project.

But I had a problem on my hands, too: Karen. She and Andrew are here for the weekend, and Karen has a "boyfriend" she's arguing with. She said they were going to get married, but now the wedding is off. Karen was mopey, so I tried to talk to her, control Andrew, who was being pesty (not like himself at all), and oversee David Michael-- and Emily, who likes anything involving glue and glitter. Especially glue.

Straight after lunch on Saturday, Kristy's grandmother was picked up by some friends who were taking her to the cinema, Watson and Kristy's mum left to go shopping in a nearby town, Charlie went off somewhere in the Junk Bucket (his car), and Sam headed for school to attend a special meeting.

So Kristy babysat for David Michael, Emily, Andrew and Karen. David Michael and Andrew were wound up. The day was grey and drizzly, so they'd been cooped up all morning and had no chance of going out in the afternoon, either. They ran screaming through the house. They could make a circle by starting in the front hall, tearing through the dining room, into the kitchen, through another hallway, through the living room, and back to the front hall. They looked as if they were chasing each other, but Kristy couldn't tell who was chasing whom. Sometimes Andrew was just in front of David Michael, and sometimes it was the other way around. Neither of them was tagging or tackling the other. Kristy supposed they were just having a let-your-energy-out however-you-can chase.

The chase had been going on for about five minutes when Emily joined in. She's a bit unsteady on her legs, so she couldn't keep up with the boys very well, but she can scream along with the best of them. And she followed the circle that her brothers were making through the house. She chugged along, giggling, while David Michael and Andrew kept passing her. The "chase" reminded Kristy of that story about the tortoise and the hare.

Ordinarily, Kristy would have put a stop to the running around. (It was the kind of indoor activity that could lead to tears, or to a knocked-over-and-broken something.) But the kids were having so much fun that Kristy let them carry on for a while. Besides, she was worried about Karen.

Karen had been sitting on the bottom step of the stairs since before everyone had left. Her chin was resting in her hands, and she seemed oblivious to the three children who kept roaring by her. She just sat, looking thoughtful. No, Kristy decided. Not thoughtful, sad. Karen looked really sad.

"Karen?" said Kristy.

Karen didn't answer. She didn't move, except for her eyes. She looked up at Kristy. And her eyes seemed to say, "Everything in my life is wrong".

"Come on, Karen," said Kristy, reaching for one of Karen's hands. "Let's have a talk. We'll go into the study, so we can escape your brothers and sister."

Karen stood up wordlessly and let Kristy lead her into the study. Kristy pushed the door closed – but not all the way. She needed to keep her ears open for the other kids.

"So what's going on?" Kristy asked Karen. "I've hardly ever seen you look like this."

"Like what?" asked Karen. She was curled into a tight ball at one end of the sofa. Kristy was sitting at the other end, but Karen wouldn't look at her.

"As sad as a rain cloud," Kristy replied, trying to get a smile out of Karen.

No such luck. All Karen replied was, "I *feel* as sad as a rain cloud."

"Why?" asked Kristy. "What's wrong?"

Karen shrugged. Then tears filled her eyes. "It's Ricky," she finally managed to say.

"Ricky Torres?" asked Kristy, who tries to keep up with Karen and Andrew's lives, even though she doesn't see them very often.

Karen nodded miserably. Her eyes were red, but no tears had fallen.

"Is he teasing you again?" Kristy demanded.

Karen shook her head. "It's much worse than that."

"What then?"

"Ricky and I were supposed to get married. He asked me, and everything. I even have a ring for him. But we had an argument and now we're not talking to each other."

"What was the argument about?" Kristy wanted to know.

Karen squirmed. "It was a bit silly, I suppose."

"Most arguments start out like that," Kristy told her sister.

At that moment, she and Karen heard a thud. In less than a second (well, maybe I'm exaggerating) Kristy had flung open the door to the study and was racing along the kids' chase route. She was relieved not to hear tears.

"What happened?" she called.

"Emily lost control," David Michael called back. "She slipped on a rug and fell, but she's okay."

Kristy had reached the living room by then and saw Andrew helping Emily to her feet. Emily was smiling. "More!" she cried.

Kristy smiled, too, but had to say, "Sorry. *No* more. No more of this game, Emily. Or for you two, either," she added, looking at Andrew and David Michael.

"Aww," said Andrew.

"Bullfrogs," said David Michael. Then he added, "What are we going to do now?"

"Well," Kristy began thoughtfully, "a certain day is coming up."

A pause. Then, "Valentine's Day!" shrieked David Michael.

"How about making cards for the kids in your class?" suggested Kristy.

"Okay," said David Michael.

But Andrew said, "I've already made cards. Karen and I made them with Mummy. We made a lot."

"Maybe you could help Emily, then," said Kristy. "She's never made a valentine before. I'm sure she'd have fun if you worked with her."

So it was settled. Kristy spread newspapers over the kitchen table and got out the box of art materials that are kept in the study. (By the way, Kristy walked into the study, loaded up the materials, left – and Karen never budged. She was still a little ball in the corner of the sofa.)

Kristy left Karen there. They would finish their talk later. She put the art materials on the kitchen table, and let David Michael, Andrew and Emily get to work.

David Michael immediately reached for red construction paper and the pair of safety scissors. He cut out a heart, took a black felt-tipped marker, and wrote on the heart:

HAPPY VALENTINE'S DAY TO YOU!
HAPPY VALENTINE'S DAY TO YOU!
YOU LOOK LIKE A MONKEY,
AND YOU SMELL LIKE ONE, TOO.

"David Michael!" exclaimed Kristy. "Who are you giving *that* to?"

"Blair D'Angelo. He's a bully. He teases all the girls." David Michael paused. Then he went on. "Hmm. Maybe I'd better not sign this one."

Kristy just shook her head. Then she went back to the study to try to coax Karen out. "Come into the kitchen with the rest of us," she said. "I know you've already made valentines, but I need to keep an eye on the others, especially Emily, and I want to talk to you, too."

Karen heaved a great sigh and then got up. She followed Kristy into the kitchen. Since the boys and Emily were working on one side of the table, Kristy pulled the empty bench a little away, for privacy, and then straddled one end. Karen sat facing her. Now Kristy could keep an eye on the card-makers and talk to Karen at the same time.

"Okay," Kristy began. "What was your stupid argument about?"

"My row with Ricky? Well. . ." Karen looked down at her hands. "Everyone in our class got invited to Pamela Harding's birthday party. And you know she doesn't like Hannie or Nancy or me or Ricky – or most of the kids. But her parents made her invite the whole class, and *our* parents made us go to the party. *But*," Karen continued, "Ricky and I decided to do nasty things to Pamela to ruin the party. Ricky even said he would give Pamela a snake for a present. "But he didn't. He didn't do one nasty thing. He gave her a really nice present. And he even smiled at Pamela."

"Maybe you're a bit jealous," said Kristy gently.

"Maybe. I don't know. Anyway, we stopped talking to each other, and then Ricky poured ink on a drawing I was making. He did it *on purpose.* So I put some old chewing gum in his desk, and . . . everything's awful. I suppose we won't be getting married now. But I don't know for sure, because we aren't speaking."

"That's hard," said Kristy. "You must feel pretty bad. But you know what? These things have a way of resolving themselves."

"What?" said Karen.

"I mean, they have a way of working themselves out."

"Oh." Karen stared off into space.

"Andrew, cut it out!" David Michael cried suddenly.

Kristy looked up in time to see Andrew dropping glitter into David Michael's hair. David Michael was frantically brushing it out.

"You look cool!" Andrew was saying. "You're a punk rocker!"

"Andrew," said Kristy. "I don't think David Michael likes what you're doing. Besides – look at Emily. She could do with some help." Emily was having a bit of trouble with the glue. Somehow she had unscrewed the cap. Glue was everywhere, but mostly on her hands – and anywhere she touched. At the moment, she was brushing her hair out of her eyes, so her face and hair were gluey.

"Uh-oh," muttered Kristy. This was a job for her, not for Andrew. "Bath time, Emily," said Kristy.

"NO!" cried Emily.

"I am *so* sad," said Karen.

"You're a monkey-face, David Michael!" exclaimed Andrew.

"Shut up," David Michael replied.

"In this house, we do not say 'shut up'," Kristy reminded her brother.

"But Andrew called me a monkey-face."

"Okay, okay." Kristy led Emily to the sink. "I'll wash you off here for now," she told her. "Andrew, please stop pestering your brother. David Michael, calm down. You've made five valentines already, and four of them are gorgeous, so keep going. Karen, why don't you find a book and I'll read to you two in the kitchen while David Michael and Emily work on their cards."

Karen heaved a great sigh as if Kristy had just asked her to clean the whole house. Then she stood up slowly, left the kitchen, and after ten minutes returned with a copy of *The Dead Bird*.

"Couldn't you have found something more cheerful?" asked Kristy.

"No," Karen answered, and sighed again.

Kristy almost smiled. The trials and tribulations of being seven, she thought. She began to read the story, and the rest of the afternoon passed uneventfully.

6th CHAPTER

"Hello? I'm home!" I called.

It was a Friday night and I'd just returned from a date with Logan. We had planned to eat dinner at a coffee shop in town and then go to the cinema. I had told Dad and Sharon that I would be home at about eleven.

It was ten minutes to nine.

The date had *not* gone well.

When we reached the coffee shop, we were shown to a table. (*That* was okay.) Then we had opened our menus and looked and looked. The menus were huge, but I chose my meal fairly quickly. I already knew what I wanted. I'd been wanting it all afternoon – a grilled cheese-and-tomato sandwich and a vanilla milkshake.

Soon Logan closed his menu, and straight away a waiter materialized. "What can I do for you?" he asked with a smile.

I opened my mouth to give my order, but before I could make a sound, Logan said, "I'll have the cheeseburger deluxe and a large Coke, and my friend will have the same."

I just looked at Logan. It's true that I often order a cheeseburger and a Coke, but that wasn't what I wanted today. Too late. The waiter had scribbled down the order and left.

"Logan," I said, "that, um, wasn't what I wanted."

"No? Sorry. Maybe we can get the waiter back."

"That's okay," I mumbled, which got dinner off to an awkward start. We didn't talk much during it.

But afterwards, Logan perked up a little. He looked at his watch, rubbed his hands together, and announced, "All *right!* Time to go and see *Halloween, Part Three.*"

"*Halloween?*"

"Yeah. I know it's been out for a while, but I haven't seen it, and it's playing just around the corner. I hope you haven't seen it, Mary Anne."

"No, I haven't . . . I thought we were going to see *The Music Man.* It's playing at the oldies theatre."

"*The Music Man* is a kids' film," Logan informed me.

"But the *Halloween* films are so horrible."

"So what do you want to do?"

"I – I suppose I want to go home," I replied.

Logan glared at me. Then he stood up and stomped off to the pay phone to phone his parents and ask one of them to pick us up.

So we didn't see a film, and that was why I arrived home at ten to nine instead of at eleven. That was also why I wasn't in a particularly good mood, and possibly why I was tired.

Logan was wearing me out.

Dad was the only one who answered when I announced that I'd returned. "Mary Anne? Is that you? You're home early. Come and talk to me. I'm in the study."

I walked into the study and flopped into an armchair. "Where are Sharon and Dawn?" I asked. "Have they gone out?"

"They've just gone to the grocery shop. They'll be back soon. Actually I'm glad you and I have a few moments alone together. I want to talk to you."

Ordinarily those awful words ("I want to talk to you") would have set me on edge right away. They never mean anything good. But my mind was still on my "date" with Logan. Nothing could be worse than this evening, I thought.

So I said simply, "Okay."

Dad cleared his throat. (He's not good at having talks.) "Well," he began, "I think you and Logan are getting – I mean, that you and Logan are spending too much time together."

I nodded.

"I'm not *worried* about you. I'm just concerned because you're not around very often, and . . . I miss you." (I knew those words were difficult for Dad to say.) "Also, you don't seem terribly happy lately. And you got a C in your last English test. That's not like you."

"I know," I said.

"So I think that you and Logan should cut back on the amount of time you spend together. I know this is hard for you to hear, but this is the way it's going to be. If necessary, we can decide on exactly how many hours you and Logan may spend together every week."

"No," I said. "We don't need to do that. I *have* been seeing too much of Logan. I'm tired. And I can't believe I got a C in that test. You're right, Dad."

My father looked so taken aback that I laughed.

"I'm *right*?! When are parents ever right?" Dad teased me.

"Hardly ever," I replied. "This is just one of those rare times."

It was Dad's turn to laugh.

"I'll phone Logan tonight and talk to him," I told Dad. "I—"

But we heard the back door open then.

Sharon and Dawn had come home. Our talk was over. I think Dad and I both felt relieved.

"Hey," said Dawn when she saw me. "You're home early. What happened?"

"Let's go upstairs and talk," I replied. (I caught Dad and Sharon raising their eyebrows at each other.)

Dawn followed me into my bedroom and sat in the armchair while I lay on my stomach on the bed.

"So what happened?" Dawn asked again.

"The date was a flop," I said simply.

Dawn frowned.

I told her about ordering dinner and about the film and everything. Then I went on. "When I came home, Dad wanted to have a talk with me."

"Oh," said Dawn. "Did Mum and I interrupt something?"

"Not really," I replied. "We'd finished talking."

"What did your dad want to talk to you about?"

"Logan and me. He thinks we're spending too much time together."

"Uh-oh. What's he going to do?"

"Nothing. I agreed with him."

"You *did*?"

"Yeah. Something's wrong between Logan and me. I'm . . . just not always happy when I'm with him. I feel as if he's taking over my life. I feel as if I'm not Mary Anne any more. I'm not whole. Logan's taken over part of me."

"Has he *taken* over part of you, or have you *let* him take over part of you?" Dawn asked wisely.

She's so clever.

"I suppose I let him," I admitted. "I could have stood up for myself, but I didn't. I mean, I usually don't. Not really."

"So what are you going to do about this?"

My answer was ready. "I'm going to phone Logan – now – and tell him we have to cool things for a while. I need the time apart from him to think. Then when we've got ourselves together, we can pick up our relationship again. It will be hard to do, but I think it will be good for us."

"Whoa," said Dawn. "I never thought I'd hear you say that. Somehow I pictured you and Logan going steady through high school, then college, and finally getting married. After that, you'd have two children. Well, two or three. And—"

"Dawn!" I exclaimed. "Stop! First of all, I just want some time apart, not a break-up. Second, I'm only thirteen. And Logan is the first boy I've ever been serious about. Did you really think we were going to get married?"

"Yes. And I'd be your bridesmaid . . . wouldn't I?"

"I don't know. Yes. I mean, I hadn't exactly planned our wedding. I was planning on graduating from the eighth grade first."

Dawn smiled. Then she stood up. "I'll leave you alone so you can phone Logan," she said. "Use the phone in Mum and your father's room. For privacy. I'll be in my bedroom if you need me."

"Okay." I felt shaky. Dawn left, and I went into Dad and Sharon's room. I closed the door. Straight away I thought, I could stop now if I wanted to. I don't *have* to phone Logan.

But I phoned him anyway. Without even hesitating. I just picked up the receiver and punched the buttons.

Logan answered the phone. "Hi!" he said, when he heard my voice. He probably thought I was calling to apologize. He sounded as if he would accept my apology.

"Logan," I began, "this isn't going to be easy for me to say, but I'm calling—"

"To apologize, right?"

"Well, not really," I told him. "I'm calling because I think we need to cool down our relationship a little. I think—"

Logan interrupted me again. "Cool down our relationship? *Why?*"

"I'm going to tell you, if you'll, um, if you'll just let me talk."

"All right, all right."

"I think we've been seeing too much of each other," I said. "I feel as if you're

– you're taking over my life. You plan everything for us. You always want to be with me – and I *do* like being with you – but, I don't know. I suppose I feel as if you don't understand me very well any more. . ." I trailed off.

There was a pause. Then Logan said, "Okay," in an odd-sounding voice.

"Let's try cooling things down for a few weeks," I went on, my voice beginning to quiver. (I just couldn't believe what I was doing.) "Then when we've had some time apart, we'll pick things up again."

"Okay."

"Well . . . goodbye."

"Goodbye. Goodnight," said Logan.

I hung up. Then I burst into tears.

I cried for a long time.

7th CHAPTER

Clangs, bangs, shouts.

It was Monday. Another week at Stoneybrook Middle School was beginning. I wondered what would happen that day. It was the first time I'd have the chance to see Logan since I'd phoned him and told him we needed to cool down our relationship.

Would he respect what I'd said? Or would he be waiting at my locker as usual, but this time full of apologies and questions?

I approached my locker hesitantly.

"Mary Anne?" asked Dawn, who was walking with me. "Are you okay? You look funny. Sort of faraway."

"I was thinking about—" And at that moment I saw him.

Logan.

He was striding down the hall towards me. My locker was in between us. So he was going to wait for me after all.

Logan and I drew closer and closer and. . .

Logan walked right past Dawn and me. He didn't smile or say hello. He didn't even look at us. That was painful. But I told myself that what I was doing was meant to save our relationship.

"Mary Anne? Are you okay?" Dawn asked again.

"Yeah," I replied.

"Logan just ignored us."

"I know. I suppose I told him to."

Dawn gave me a rueful smile, then left. I spun the dial on my locker. I half expected to see a note stuck through the vent at the top of the door. Logan and I were always leaving notes for each other that way. Maybe Logan had got to school early, stuck a note in my locker, and then avoided looking at me because he knew he shouldn't have done that.

But there was no note.

That morning we had an assembly. I think it was about our school's dress code, but I wasn't paying much attention. Logan was sitting a row in front of me and four seats down. I had a perfect view of him. And if he turned his head slightly to the left, he had a pretty good view of me, too.

But we only glanced at each other once. And that was only because somebody near us dropped a book on the floor. As we looked round to see what had happened, our eyes met. Then we both faced the front again.

Needless to say, Logan didn't sit with Dawn, Kristy, Stacey, Claudia and me at lunch that day. (Jessi and Mal eat during another period, as they're in a different grade.) Not that Logan *al*ways sits at our table, but he usually does. And for the past several weeks he hadn't missed a day. He would move as close to me as he could get without actually sitting in my food. Sometimes he would feed me titbits of his lunch, which was romantic, but embarrassing.

Anyway, the five of us sat at our usual table that Monday. When we had got settled, Kristy looked round. The first thing she said was, "Where's Logan, Mary Anne? Shouldn't he be in your lap?"

"He does not," I replied testily, "sit in my lap."

"*Sor*ry," said Kristy. "But really. Where is he? In the library or somewhere?"

I glanced at Dawn. She was the only one who knew what was going on between Logan and me. I knew I would tell the rest of my friends soon, because we don't usually keep secrets from each other. But I didn't feel like telling them right now.

"Oh, Logan's off with the boys," I said to Kristy. "He needs boy-talk, a break from us girls." I scanned the canteen. "See? There he is with Pete and Austin and Trevor and everyone."

Nobody questioned this. We ate, we talked about how bad the food was, we wondered how Jenny Prezzioso would react when the baby was born. Then lunch was over.

Whew.

By the end of the day, I felt drained. But working out relationships, I told myself, is not easy.

As I approached my locker after the last bell that afternoon, I could see Logan waiting for me. At least, I assumed he was at my locker. It was hard to tell since both walls are lined with lockers.

I began to walk more slowly. What was I going to say to Logan? What was he going to say to me? Maybe he'd thought things over and had decided we should break up. Noooo. I didn't want that.

When I finally reached my locker, feeling as if I were walking underwater, I dared to look into Logan's eyes. He looked into mine.

"I just wanted to say hi," he said very seriously.

"Oh. Hi," I replied.

"See ya," said Logan, and walked off.

I stared after him. Well, that was better. We were speaking to each other, and I'd been expecting to do that. I do not consider the silent treatment to be a form of cooling off.

At home that night, while Dawn and I were supposed to be doing our homework, I couldn't concentrate on anything – except Logan. In my history book, William Penn's face turned into Logan's. The romance story in our English text turned into a story about Logan and me.

"This is ridiculous," I said aloud.

"Mary Anne?" called Dawn from her room.

"Yeah? Can I come in? I need to talk."

"Of course. I'm ready for a break."

I walked down the landing, into Dawn's room, and sat on her bed. Dawn turned round in her desk chair.

"It's Logan, isn't it," she said. (It was a statement, not a question.)

I nodded.

"Are you having second thoughts about what you said to him?"

"I don't know. I can't stop thinking about him, about us."

"You did what you thought was right," Dawn told me. "You stood up for yourself."

"I suppose. . ."

"Mary *Anne*," said Dawn, "remember how you've been feeling lately – as if Logan's too pushy, always taking charge, not listening to you? You don't want to go back to that again, do you?"

"No. But I miss Logan."

"My mum missed my dad at first, just after the divorce. But she knew she'd done the right thing."

"I wish," I said, "that 'cooling off' didn't hurt so much."

8th CHAPTER

Tuesday

I sat for Jenny P today. She's going through a rough time with this new baby business. You lot should know two things about Jenny right now: 1. She knows exactly what her mother is doing (bribing her) to make her feel good about the baby. 2. Jenny does NOT want to be a big sister. She wants to stay an only child. (Well, she didn't exactly say that, but that's what she meant.) I had a talk with her about brothers and sisters, but I'm not sure how much she got out of it.

Who could be a better expert on brothers and sisters than Mallory? She's got more of them than any other member of the BSC. (Although Kristy comes close, having six.) So I was glad that Mal had at least one sitting job with Jenny before the baby was born.

Mrs Prezzioso left Jenny and Mal at about four o'clock to go to a lecture on childbirth at the hospital. Just like when I had sat for Jenny, the first thing she did after her mother left was take Mal's hand and say, "Want to come up to my room and see my new things from Mummy?"

More new things? I wondered as I read Mal's notebook entry. Or was it the same new stuff she'd shown me?

Nope. It was *more* new things.

"See? Mummy got me this letters-and-numbers learning machine. Big girls have to start learning hard things because they'll be going to school soon. And she got me a workbook. Oh, and this doll. I'll tell you about the doll later. Want to see my new grown-up clothes?" Jenny went on.

"Okay," replied Mallory.

Jenny opened her wardrobe door and pushed some coat hangers to one side. "Here's a new dress. Here's another new dress. And here is a *very* grown-up outfit." Jenny pointed to a pink plaid pinafore dress over a white cotton blouse. "And this hat" (a pink straw hat with a white ribbon round it), "and these shoes" (pink ballet slippers), "go with the outfit."

Mal nodded. "Beautiful," she said. She paused. Then she asked, "What were you going to tell me about your new doll?"

Jenny scowled. "The doll is different from the other new things. Mummy buys me those new things so I won't be annoyed about the baby. But the doll is for this. Come on." Jenny picked up the doll and left her room. Mal followed her. They walked across the landing to the room next to Jenny's.

"This is the baby's room," Jenny informed Mal.

"It's very pretty," said Mal politely, looking at the cheerful yellow-and-white room. A white rug covered the floor. Yellow-and-white striped curtains hung at the windows. The walls had been painted a pale, pale yellow, and around the walls ran a frieze of parading ducks and lambs. The Prezziosos were ready for the baby. The cot was made up (some stuffed animals already sat in it); the changing table was equipped with nappies, powder, Baby-Wipes and more; and a yellow duck lamp sat on the dresser. Everything looked brand-new, except for the cot.

As if she had read Mal's mind, Jenny said, "That used to be *my* cot."

Mal wasn't sure what to say to that, but it didn't matter. Jenny didn't seem to expect an answer. She had marched over to the cot, expertly pulled the side down, and placed her new doll on the mattress.

"Mummy," said Jenny, "is teaching me to change my doll's nappy and give it a bottle."

"It?" repeated Mal. "Isn't your doll a girl or a boy?"

"Not yet," replied Jenny.

Mal let that one go by. She said, "Show me what you've learned so far."

"Okay," said Jenny grimly. She moved the doll from the cot to the changing table. Then, steadying the doll with one hand, she reached for a disposable nappy. And *then*, as if she'd done it a thousand times before, she cleaned her doll with a Baby-Wipe, shook some powder on it, and then peeled off the tabs on the nappy and fastened it securely to her "baby".

"Wow! Very nice," said Mal. "Soon you'll be ready to be a babysitter yourself. Maybe you can join the Babysitters Club."

Jenny didn't even crack a smile. "I'll be busy with our baby," she said. "Anyway, look. See how you give a bottle to a baby?" Jenny sat in a rocking chair, held the doll carefully, and pretended to feed it. "Then you burp the baby," she went on. Jenny put the doll to her shoulder, patted its back, and said, "Burp!"

Mal smiled. "Terrific!"

"I told you I could do it. Mummy makes me practise every day."

"Oh."

With that, Jenny stood up, walked out of the baby's room, and down the landing towards hers. But instead of going into her room, she just tossed the doll through the doorway as she went by.

"Can we have a snack?" asked Jenny as she headed downstairs.

"Okay," said Mal. "Let's make peanut butter sandwiches."

"Yum!" was Jenny's reply.

Mal got out paper plates, napkins, two plastic knives, a jar of peanut butter and some bread. Also a bottle of orange juice.

Jenny and Mal ate in silence at first. Then Mal asked, "So how do you feel about becoming a big girl?"

"I already am a big girl," replied Jenny.

Mal smiled. "That's true. You are a big girl. I suppose I meant how does it feel to know you're going to be a big sister?"

"Yucky." Jenny was spreading peanut butter on a cracker. She didn't look at Mal.

"Yucky? How come?"

"Because of what I just showed you. The baby is going to need lots of help. Mummy and Daddy will probably spend all their time with the baby. The baby won't know how to feed itself or anything.

Mummy will have to feed it, and carry it around, and change its nappies, and – I don't know. Lots of things."

"But," said Mal, trying to create a bright spot in what Jenny saw as her dark future, "babies sleep a lot. You'll be able to spend plenty of time with your mum and dad when the baby's asleep."

"I suppose. . ."

"You know, I have *seven* brothers and sisters," Mal pointed out.

"I know. I'm sorry."

"No, it's great!" exclaimed Mal.

"How can it be?"

"For lots of reasons. There's always somebody around to talk to or play with. And I *like* looking after my younger brothers and sisters. I feel grown-up and important. I can teach them things. *And* – guess what being the oldest means?"

"What?" asked Jenny.

"It means you get to do things first. I'm the only girl in my family with pierced ears. Vanessa and Margo and Claire will have to wait a few years before they get theirs pierced."

Jenny looked interested.

"Also, think of all the things you can do that the baby *won't* be able to do. You can ride your tricycle. You can play games. You can look at books. You can go into the back garden to swing and slide. The baby won't be able to do that. The baby will be stuck, dependent on your mum or dad to carry it around."

"And, I can talk," added Jenny.

"That's right," said Mal. "You can say, 'Mummy, I'm hungry'. Or, 'Mummy, I'm tired'. When the baby wants something, all it will be able to do is cry. Then your parents will have to *guess* what it wants."

Jenny was silent for a moment. Finally she said, "Mallory? Do you *really* like having brothers and sisters?"

"I really do. When they're babies, I can take care of them. When they grow up, they become my friends. I'm never lonely."

"After the baby, you and I will be a bit alike," said Jenny.

"We will?" Mal asked.

"Yup. We'll both be the oldest in our families. And we're both girls."

"That's right!" said Mal. "Maybe we should form a Big Sisters Club."

Jenny smiled this time, but she didn't look deliriously happy. In fact, her smile faded and she stared into space, saying nothing.

"Jenny? What are you thinking about?" Mal wanted to know.

Jenny sighed. "Oh, the baby. I know I'll be able to do more things and have more fun than the baby. But some things are going to change."

"That's true," Mal agreed.

"I'm used to having Mummy and Daddy all to myself. Now I won't be so important. The baby will be here, and it will be important, too."

"Oh, Jen," said Mal, suddenly feeling sympathetic. "You'll be just as important as you were before."

Jenny looked unconvinced. And Mal thought she knew why. Mal didn't remember ever having been the only child. She'd been just a year old when the triplets had been born. But Jenny had been the centre of attention for *four years*. Now she was going to lose that position.

It would be hard for anybody.

9th CHAPTER

"Mary Anne! You look—" Kristy started to say something, but thought better of it. For once, she controlled her big mouth.

I had a pretty good idea how I looked, though: awful. It was a Monday afternoon, just before a club meeting, so my friends had seen me at school a few hours earlier. I hadn't looked great then (I hadn't been sleeping well), but I couldn't possibly have looked as horrible as I did by 5:20. That was because I'd spent most of the afternoon crying. I'd been home alone. (Dad and Sharon were at work; Dawn was babysitting.) And I'd been thinking about what Logan and I were going through. I'd started to cry and couldn't stop. Now my nose was red and my face was blotchy, I also had dark circles under my eyes.

"I know," I said to Kristy. "I look like my own evil twin."

Kristy laughed. "You don't look *that* bad. But something is wrong, isn't it, Mary Anne? Are you in trouble?"

I shook my head.

"Do you want to talk about it?"

"Not yet," I replied. "We might as well wait until everyone else gets here. Then I won't have to tell the story five times."

"Okay." Kristy settled herself in the director's chair and adjusted her visor. She was ready for the meeting.

I sat on Claud's bed.

We waited.

By five-thirty, everyone had arrived, and Kristy called our meeting to order. We got club business out of the way, and then waited for the phone to ring. When it didn't, Kristy looked at me with raised eyebrows. The others then glanced from Kristy to me. I could almost hear them wondering what was going on.

I cleared my throat. "Um, you must all have noticed that Logan hasn't been sitting at our lunch table recently."

My friends nodded curiously, except for Dawn, who knew the story already. And Stacey said, "You haven't exactly been yourself, either."

"I know," I replied. "Well, the thing is, I told Logan that I wanted to cool off our relationship a little." I looked down at my shoes. "I didn't know how hard that would be, but I *had* to do it. Logan was getting to be – I mean, I felt as if he was taking over my life. Or taking something away from it. So I told him I wanted to cool things off, and well, we haven't spoken in days."

"I noticed that he hasn't been hanging around your locker," said Kristy.

I nodded. "He hasn't phoned or anything. When I said 'cool off' I didn't mean 'break up', but I think Logan took it that way."

Jessi gasped.

"What is it? What's wrong?" asked the rest of us.

"I can't believe you two are breaking up. It seems as though you've been a couple practically for ever," said Jessi.

'*I* thought they were going to *be* a couple for ever," said Dawn. "I thought they'd go through school together, then get married, then have kids—"

Dawn stopped talking when Stacey cleared her throat loudly.

I was crying. As usual.

"Oh, Mary Anne, I'm sorry," said Dawn, leaning over to give me a hug.

"That's okay. Almost anything makes me cry these days." I sniffed.

The phone rang then, and we arranged for a sitter at the Perkinses'.

When business was over, Stacey said quietly, "Separation is never easy. Remember when I thought I was in love with that lifeguard? Boy, was I hurt when I found out he had a girlfriend."

"But then Toby came along," I reminded her.

"And then we had to separate when the holiday was over and we left the beach."

"And I had to separate from Alex, Toby's cousin, remember? That hurt, too," I said.

"But then *Logan* came along."

"And now we're. . ."

I couldn't finish my sentence, so Claudia said, "Well, I fell in love with Will at camp, and then we had to leave each other when camp was over. And then I fell in love with Terry in California, and *we* had to separate."

"Ow, ow, ow!" said Jessi. (We looked at her as if she were mad.) "All this separating," she explained. "All this hurting. Ouch!"

We laughed. Then Claudia continued, "I fell in love when we were on the cruise through the Bahamas. How come we always fall in love when we're on holiday and the relationship can't last?"

"Logan's here, though," I said.

"And maybe your relationship *will* last," Mal pointed out.

"I hope so."

I looked around the room then at all the sombre faces, and was glad when the phone rang again. We needed something to lighten the atmosphere.

And the call certainly did lighten the atmosphere. That was because the caller was Karen, Kristy's little stepsister. "Just a sec," said Dawn, who'd answered the phone. "I'll hand you over to Kristy."

Dawn handed the phone to our chairman, whispering, "It's Karen."

Kristy smiled. "Hi, Karen. What's up? . . . You want to hire a babysitter?"

My friends and I looked at each other, amused. We were even more amused to hear Kristy say, as gently as possible, "We don't usually sit for stuffed animals. Haven't Moosie and Goosie stayed by themselves lots of times before?" (Moosie and Goosie are identical stuffed cats. Karen keeps Moosie at her father's house, and Goosie at her mother's house.) There was a pause. Then, "Why don't you introduce them to some of Andrew's animals?" we heard Kristy suggest.

Kristy and Karen talked for a few more minutes before hanging up the phone. When the receiver had been replaced, Kristy burst out laughing. "Can you believe it?" she asked. "Karen's suddenly decided that Moosie and Goosie get lonely when they're at home alone. So she wanted to hire us as sitters. She offered to pay us fifteen cents an hour."

The rest of us couldn't help giggling.

"I suggested that she introduce them to some other stuffed animals," Kristy continued.

"That was nice," said Jessi, grinning.

"Thanks," said Kristy. "I try to be

sensitive to Karen and Andrew. They've been through separations like the rest of us – and they're a lot younger."

Another job call and then another came in. When we'd finished dealing with them, I said, "You know what? I don't know if Jenny realizes it, but in a way she's anticipating a separation from her parents when the baby comes. She knows she won't be the centre of attention any more."

"Poor Jenny," said Kristy sincerely. (Generally, Kristy doesn't like Jenny.)

Something occurred to me then. "Hey, you lot," I said, "I've just thought of something. Okay, so we've been talking about all these separations. But you know what the difference is with Logan and me? I'm *choosing* to leave him. He isn't leaving me. In a way, I have control over this situation. I can—"

The phone rang, and this time I answered it. Guess who was calling?

"*Logan?*" I exclaimed.

"Hi," he said. "I've got business to discuss with you." (He *did* sound businesslike.) "I need a sitter for Kerry and Hunter" (they're Logan's younger sister and brother) "on Valentine's Day. It's a Friday night. Mum and Dad are going out, and now so am I. Kerry and Hunter asked if you'd be their sitter, Mary Anne. I know that's not club policy, but they miss you."

"I'll get back to you," I told him brusquely, and hung up the phone.

I looked at my friends in shock and amazement, and told them what Logan had just told me. Everybody was saying, "Go ahead and take the job," or things like that, but all I could think was, who was Logan going out with on Valentine's Day? Had he found another girlfriend? And did I really want to go over there and see him leave the house with some new girl?

But then I remembered Logan saying that Hunter and Kerry missed me. I didn't want to disappoint them. Besides, as a professional businesswoman, I shouldn't let my emotions get in the way of my job.

So I phoned Logan back and told him that I would sit that night.

"Great," he said. "Thanks, Mary Anne."

"You're welcome."

"See ya."

"See ya. . . Bye."

I tried to imagine Logan's girlfriend. She was probably the opposite of me – tall, blonde, not shy, self-assured. Maybe *that* was what had gone wrong in our relationship. I was so shy that Logan felt he *had* to take over for me.

Oh, well. I began to look forward to Valentine's Day in the same way I look forward to a trip to the dentist.

10th CHAPTER

"Da-da. Ma-ma. Goo-goo."

I closed my eyes for a moment. Jenny was giving me a headache. It was a Saturday evening, and I was looking after her from six until ten. And she was pretending she was a baby. She was driving me mad.

I looked at my watch. It was only 6:45.

I sighed. Not only was Jenny driving me mad, but I was driving myself mad. I couldn't stop thinking about Logan. I kept imagining his new girlfriend. But that was all I *could* do – imagine. I hadn't seen him with the girlfriend yet. Not at school, not in town, not anywhere.

So my imagination was running wild. Now not only was the girl tall, blonde, not shy, and very self-assured, but she was *extremely* bright; had a lovely, romantic name like Olivia; and was embarking on a promising singing career. Sometimes Logan would go to the recording studios with her. Maybe one day he would be "discovered" at the studios. (He *is* awfully handsome.) Then he would become an actor and, after college, he and Olivia would go to Hollywood and make it big.

"Ma-ma," said Jenny again. She patted my knee. She'd been crawling around the living room, but now she was sitting on the floor, sucking her thumb.

"Yes, Jenny?" I said. (I was getting low on patience.)

"Not Jenny! Baby. Me baby."

"Okay, baby. What do you want?" I tried to concentrate on her instead of on Logan and Olivia.

"Wet. Baby wet." When I didn't respond straight away (I mean, what was I supposed to say?), Jenny tugged on my jeans. "BABY WET!" she screamed. "NAPPY!"

"Okay." I pretended to reach for a nappy, then fasten it on Jenny.

"NO! Real nappy."

"Jenny, I'm not going to put a nappy on you," I said. "That's silly."

Jenny got on her hands and knees again, and crawled frantically out of the living room. I could hear her going upstairs. A few minutes later she crawled back to me (I was daydreaming about Logan again) with a nappy in her mouth.

"Put nappy on baby," she demanded.

"You do *not* need a nappy," I replied.

"You're a big girl. You're toilet trained now."

"NO! Not a big girl. Me baby."

"I know. You've already told me."

"PUT NAPPY ON!"

"Jenny," I said with as much patience as I could muster, "I am not going to put a nappy on you."

"Oka-ay," said Jenny, switching to a singsong, four-year-old voice.

"Thank you," I replied, not realizing that I should have paid more attention to that change in her voice. "Now would you please go back to the baby's room and put the nappy where it belongs?"

"Oka-ay," said Jenny again.

She stood up and marched out of the room. And I went back to Logan and Olivia. They were living in Hollywood with a mansion and a swimming pool and maybe a tennis court. Once or twice a month, Olivia would throw a huge party for their glamorous friends, and Logan would often say to her, "What a wonderful hostess you are, dear. Mary Anne could never have done anything like this."

It was at this point that I heard a thump from upstairs. I realized that Jenny should have been back long ago from returning the nappy. What was I doing? Certainly not being a responsible babysitter, I thought, as I dashed up the stairs.

"Jenny?" I called.

No answer.

I peeped into her room. It was neat . . . and empty.

So I ran down the hall to the baby's room.

I couldn't believe what I saw.

It was an absolute wreck. Everything on the changing table had been swept off and was scattered across the floor. Everything in the cot had been thrown out. Stuffed animals and bedding had been flung from one side of the room to the other. The drawers in the dressing table had been opened and clothing was draped over the animals and nappies. Jenny was now attempting to scale the dressing table – I suppose in the hope of attacking the yellow duck lamp.

She had trashed the baby's room.

"Stop it!" I cried.

Jenny stumbled and fell to the floor. But she didn't cry. She had landed on nappies and a pile of clothes.

"What on earth do you think you're doing?" I demanded.

"I hate the baby," was Jenny's reply.

"Well, I'm sorry, kiddo," I said, "but the baby is coming whether you like it or not. And whether you mess up the room or not. There are going to be some things in life" (Oh, no, I sounded like my father!) "that you can't change. The baby is one of them. Now I want this room cleared up *right now.*"

Jenny looked at me, eyes as big as basketballs. (I suppose I'd never spoken to her in that tone of voice.) Then, wordlessly, she began to put things back in the cot, on the changing table, in the chest of drawers.

I helped her, especially with the clothes. Jenny wasn't a very good folder yet. And as we worked (in silence) I got an idea.

When the room looked the way it should (the way I remembered it looking), I turned to Jenny and said, "Okay, baby. What about a bottle?"

Jenny's face changed from sullen to surprised and then to pleased. "Me baby?"

"Yes, you baby. Let's go downstairs. I'll make you something to drink before bedtime. How's that?"

"Da-da-da-da-da-da!" exclaimed Jenny. She crawled out of the baby's room and followed me down the hall. When we reached the top of the steps, I bent over and scooped Jenny into my arms.

"Hey!" she cried. "What are you doing?"

"I'm carrying you downstairs."

"But I can go down by myself."

"Not if you're a baby," I told her. "You might fall."

"Oh."

I carried Jenny all the way into the kitchen and sat her in the high chair that the Prezziosos had been storing in their basement, but which now stood in a corner of the kitchen.

"Hey!" said Jenny again. "I can't fit in here."

But she could, even though it was a tight squeeze. And I said, "This is where babies eat. And you're a baby, remember?"

"Yeah. . ." said Jenny slowly.

"All right. Now I'll make you something nice to drink." I took a carton of milk out of the fridge and started to pour it into a pan.

"What's that?" Jenny called from the high chair.

"Milk," I told her.

"I don't like milk. I want juice."

"But babies drink milk. . . And they drink it warm."

Jenny practically gagged at the idea of warm milk. Then she said, "I don't want a drink after all. I mean – Da-da-da. No milk for baby."

She had caught me just before I poured the milk into the pan. "Are you sure?" I asked her. "Because it's almost bedtime."

"No it isn't. I get to stay up lots later than this."

"Babies don't," I reminded her. "They need lots of sleep. They go to bed straight after supper and don't get up until the morning. Unless they're hungry and need another bottle of warm milk in the middle of the night."

Jenny appeared stumped. Clearly, the "game" was not going the way she wanted.

She tried another tactic. "Baby hungry. Want snack."

"Oh. Okay," I replied. I found the cereal and plopped a handful of cornflakes on to the tray of the high chair.

Jenny glanced from the cereal to me. "Want toast," she said.

"Not for babies." (How many times had I said that in the last ten minutes?)

"Not for babies?" repeated Jenny.

"No way. Babies can't eat toast."

Again, Jenny looked stumped. Finally she said, "Goo goo. No snack. Snack over." She tried to disengage herself from the high chair, but I lifted her out – and carried her towards the door.

"Where we go?" asked the baby Jenny.

"Nighty-night time," I replied.

"You mean I'm really going to bed?"

"Yes. In the cot."

"But I'm too big for the cot." Jenny paused. Then she said, "Mary Anne? I'm tired of this game. I don't want to be a baby any more."

"Are you sure?" I asked her. "You're missing out on all sorts of good things. Warm milk, a nice cot to sleep in. . ."

Jenny wriggled out of my arms. "I'm sure," she said. "I want to watch TV. And before I go to sleep tonight – *in my own bed* – I want orange juice and biscuits."

"Okay," I replied. "Well, it certainly is

nice to have Jenny back. You're much more fun than a baby."

Jenny smiled. "I feel a bit sorry for babies," she informed me.

11th CHAPTER

At 11:45 on a Saturday morning, the phone rang. Even though I'd been sitting by the phone for fifteen minutes, *waiting* for it to ring, I jumped. Then I picked up the receiver and, trying to sound calm, said, "Hello?"

"It's time," said a man's voice.

I couldn't control myself any longer. "You mean she's just left? Great! I'll call Stacey and Claudia. We'll get there as soon as we can. See ya!" I depressed the button on the phone, then let it up and immediately dialled Claud's number. When she answered her phone, I said, "All clear! Go to the Prezziosos' right now!"

"Okay!" cried Claudia. "Stacey's here with me. We're ready to leave."

"Great. I'll see you in a few minutes."

It was the day of the baby party for Mrs Prezzioso. It was also about three days before Mrs P's birthday, so a friend had invited her to lunch in a posh restaurant to celebrate. The lunch was just a ruse, though. The friend was getting Mrs P out of the house so that Stacey, Claudia, Mr P and I could prepare for the party and surprise Mrs P when her friend brought her home.

Mr P had thought of everything. He'd told Mrs P's friend to bring her back at around one-thirty, no earlier. He'd invited the guests for one o'clock and told them to park their cars down the street so Mrs P wouldn't get suspicious. And anything he'd had to buy for the party he'd hidden in the attic.

I reached the Prezziosos' before Stacey and Claud did, since I live close by. But they showed up about ten minutes later – just in time for chaos. When I'd arrived, things had been relatively calm. I mean, relative to the way they became ten minutes later.

Jenny had answered the door, still in her pyjamas. Mr P was just behind her. "Come in, come in!" he said, smiling. I stepped inside, took off my coat, and hung it in the coat cupboard. Mr P continued, "I think everything is in order. The cake is being delivered, I've got the stuff out of the attic, and the caterers are on their way with the food."

"Terrific," I said. I grinned at Jenny. "Are you excited? There's going to be a party here today."

"And Mary Anne is going to get you all dressed up," added her father.

"I don't want to get dressed up," said Jenny flatly.

"Well, I'm afraid you have to," Mr P said, not sounding quite so calm. "Mummy will want you to look pretty."

Just when Jenny looked as if she was going to throw a fit, the bell rang. I was sure it was Claudia and Stacey, so I opened the door. Standing on the front step was a man from the bakery, carrying a large white box tied up with string.

"Mr Prezzioso, it's the cake," I said.

"Oh, good." Mr P edged past me and held open the door for the delivery man. "The stork cake, right?" Mr P said. "With 'Congratulations' on it?"

The man shook his head. "Nope. What I've got here is a pink flowery cake. Says 'Happy Birthday, Ginnie' on it."

He looked unconcerned, but I could see Mr P growing edgy.

"That's not our cake," said Jenny's father. "Ours is for a baby party."

"Hm," said the man.

"Could you check your van?" asked Mr P. "I specifically ordered a stork cake for midday today."

"All right-y." The man returned to his van.

While he did so, the phone rang. All I could hear of Mr P's end of the conversation was groaning. When he got off the phone he said to me, "That was the catering service. They're going to be late with the food. But they promised to be here between one and one-fifteen. That's cutting it close. . . Oh, I *knew* things were going too well this morning."

And that's when Claud and Stacey arrived – with Jenny whining and complaining, the delivery man searching through his truck, and Mr P going mad over the caterers.

But things began to change. The delivery man found the right cake. Stacey and Claudia took over the decorating and set up the food table. And I managed to get Jenny upstairs.

"Look," I said. "Your father has laid out some clothes for you to wear."

"It's one of my grown-up outfits," replied Jenny. (It was the pink pinafore dress and hat ensemble she'd shown Mallory.)

"Well, it's lovely. Okay. Out of your pyjamas."

"No."

"Yes. Out of your pyjamas and into those clothes."

Jenny didn't reply, but she made a face. And then she refused to take off her pyjamas or put on the new outfit, so I had to do everything for her.

"I don't see why I have to get dressed up," she said. "The party is for the baby, not me. People are going to bring presents and they'll all be for that stupid old baby."

"That stupid old baby is going to be your brother or sister, remember?"

"Yes . . . OW!"

I was brushing Jenny's hair, but I hadn't hit so much as a tiny tangle.

"Do you want to wear some of your jewellery?" I asked, when her hair had been thoroughly brushed and was shining.

"No."

And that was that.

Jewellery or not, Mr P thought Jenny looked fine – when I finally got her back down the stairs. She balked, complained and thought of excuses for staying in her room, every step of the way.

"Hey, Jenny!" I said. "Look at the living room. Look what Claud and Stacey have done to it."

They had transformed it. I think Jenny was impressed, but she didn't want to let on. *I* let on, however. "This is beautiful, you two!" I exclaimed. The room was like a pastel cloud. Pale pink, blue and yellow streamers lazily criss-crossed the ceiling. Bunches of balloons had been fastened here and there. On the food table was an airy yellow tablecloth, bouquets of flowers and a huge fold-out stork carrying a bundle in its beak. Out of the bundle peeped a doll's face.

Jenny looked at the stork intently. "What is that bird doing?" she asked.

I tried to explain.

"You mean storks bring babies?"

"Well, no—" Stacey began to say.

But Jenny wasn't paying attention. "'Cause if *that's* true," she went on, "I'll just make a big sign for our roof, and it will say, 'DO NOT LEAVE ANY BABIES HERE. EVER'."

Stacey and Claudia and I looked at each other helplessly. Finally Claudia said, "I don't think that will work. You know how fat your mummy's tummy has become? Well, that's because the baby is—"

"I think Jenny should discuss this with her parents," I interrupted. Then, to distract Jenny, I said, "Hey, look how Claudia has decorated that cradle. That's where all the presents will go." I indicated the crepe paper and flowers that adorned the cradle.

Jenny narrowed her eyes. "The presents are going in *there*? That used to be *my* cradle. When I was a baby."

"I give up," I whispered to Stacey and Claudia.

Luckily, things started to happen then. The first guests arrived, along with the catered food. Mr P talked to the guests, while my friends and I arranged the food on the table. Almost before I knew it, Mr P was looking around and announcing, "Everyone's here. And our guest of honour should be back in about five minutes."

The guests hid themselves in the dining room and kitchen. I pulled Jenny behind an armchair and said, "Shh."

"Why are we hiding and whispering?" she asked me.

"Because any second now your mummy is going to walk through the front door, and everyone is going to jump out and say 'Surprise!'."

Jenny looked interested, at least. And when the door did open and her mother did step into the living room, Jenny was the first to jump out.

Mrs P was properly surprised. I mean, *really* surprised. For a second, her mouth just formed an O. Then she buried her face in her hands and laughed, cried and blushed, all at the same time, as her friends surrounded her. When she composed herself, Mr P led her to a chair next to the cradle. And then the fun began.

Mrs P reached into the cradle and pulled out a gift. "From Margery," she read. "Thank you!"

The woman named Margery dug around in her handbag and unearthed a smaller package. "I didn't forget the new big sister!" she exclaimed, and handed the present to Jenny.

"For *me*?" Jenny beamed. She opened her small present while her mother opened a much larger one. The larger one turned out to be an acute stuffed teddy bear. Jenny's gift was a pair of plastic hairslides. She couldn't hide her disappointment. And didn't even try to, as guest after guest handed her some small item while her mother opened much more elaborate gifts for the baby.

"Jenny, you could at least say thank you," I whispered to her.

Jenny did not answer me. I decided that teaching her manners was not part of my babysitting job. So I sat back and enjoyed the rest of the party. (Later, Stacey and Claudia and I agreed that the party had been fun, but that if we ever heard another person say, "Oh, isn't that *cute*?" we'd strangle them.)

At last the guests began to leave. When everyone had gone, my friends and I walked around with rubbish bags, stuffing them with crumpled, lipstick-stained paper napkins; empty cups; bits of crepe paper; scraps of food; and a mountain of wrapping paper.

"So, Jenny," I said. "What did you think of the party?"

Jenny looked at her little pile of gifts. "Yucky," she said.

"But all those people brought you presents," Claudia pointed out.

"The baby got better ones."

I glanced at Mrs P, still sitting in her chair, but she was engrossed in a baby book she'd been given.

"Jenny—" I started to say.

Jenny interrupted me. "You know what? I HATE THAT BABY!"

12th CHAPTER

The following Friday was Valentine's Day. At breakfast, Dad, Sharon, Dawn and I exchanged silly cards. We laughed, but I had to force myself to stop thinking about Logan. Here it was, the most romantic day of the year, and we probably wouldn't even speak to each other. A few days earlier I'd been in a stationery shop and had seen the perfect card for Logan. It was huge, and cost a lot of money for a card. I didn't buy it. Not because it was too expensive, but because there was no point. I cried a little, right there in the shop. By Valentine's Day I felt better. It was impossible not to, what with the funny cards, and Sharon putting red food colouring in the butter so we could have a pink spread on our toast.

And after school, the BSC held a small party before the Friday meeting.

"Lovehearts!" Claud announced. "I've got Lovehearts and heart-shaped sweets and even . . . chocolate covered cherries!"

It was a sugar-fest (although Claud had thoughtfully provided pretzels for Stacey and Dawn, our non-chocolate eaters).

We lolled around and talked about school and friends. We giggled. Stacey was in the process of painting everyone's fingernails red when Kristy suddenly announced, "Okay! Come to order! It's time to start the meeting."

Automatically, I checked Claud's digital clock. It read 5:30 on the dot. I couldn't believe it. Throughout the entire party, Kristy had been clock-watching.

Oh, well. That's Kristy for you.

The meeting went by quickly. At six o'clock, as we were getting ready to leave, I said to Dawn, "Remind Dad and your mum that I won't be home until about ten tonight, okay?"

"Oh, that's right," Dawn replied. "You'll be at Logan's sitting for Kerry and Hunter." She paused, then added, "How do you feel about that?"

"I don't know," I said honestly. "I mean, I like Kerry and Hunter, and I'm flattered that they specifically asked for *me* to be their sitter. But I don't know if I can face seeing Logan and Olivia leave the house on their date."

"Who's Olivia?" asked Dawn, Jessi, Kristy, Stacey, Mal and Claud.

I realized two things then: that everyone had been listening to my conversation with Dawn, and that the non-existent Olivia had become real to me. Did that mean I was cracking up?

My friends were waiting for an answer, so I mumbled something and then dashed out of Claud's room. Behind me I could hear Stacey saying, "What? His cousin?" and Mallory saying, "I think she said, 'No one'."

Anyway, I walked quickly to Logan's house. The evening was cold, so I stuffed my hands in my pockets. I was glad I was wearing jeans and an old ski sweater under my parka. I didn't look glamorous, but I was warm.

A few minutes later, I reached the Brunos'. (I could have found my way there blind-folded.) I stood on the front step, reached up to press the doorbell – and froze. My finger wouldn't move. I was too afraid of what I'd find in there. Logan and his girlfriend ready for their date? Mrs Bruno taking pictures of them?

Oh, well. I had to be an adult about this. I forced myself to ring the bell.

Instead of running footsteps, I heard nothing. Silence. I noticed that the Brunos' house looked pretty dark. Had I got my dates mixed up? No, Logan had definitely said Valentine's Day, and this was Valentine's Day. Wrong house? No way.

Just as I was wondering what could possibly be wrong – and just as I was getting a tiny bit scared – the front door creaked open. Shadowed against a dim light from the kitchen down the hall stood Logan. He was wearing a tuxedo and holding a box containing a flower.

Oh, this was just too much. A flower (an orchid) for Olivia? I half expected Logan to say, "Oh, it's just you," and to look over my shoulder to see if Olivia was arriving yet.

Instead, Logan smiled slowly and shyly at me. "Hi, Mary Anne," he said. Then he added, "Happy Valentine's Day."

"Hi, Logan," I replied.

"Come on in."

Logan held the door open for me, and I slipped past him, into the hall. "Where are Hunter and Kerry?" I asked as I took off my jacket. "I've never heard your house this quiet."

"Oh, they're here," Logan told me. "They're down in the TV room with Mum and Dad. I made them promise to stay there all evening."

"I thought your parents were going out tonight," I said, puzzled and somewhat apprehensive. "That's why I—"

Logan interrupted me by putting his finger to my lips. "Shh," he said. "Come and see." He took my hand and led me to the dining room. There I saw the table set for a romantic dinner for two. Candles burned in silver holders. A white cloth covered the table. The Brunos' best china gleamed next to crystal glasses and sparkling silverware.

Torture.

Logan was making me see how he and Olivia were going to spend Valentine's Day evening. How low could a person get?

I was about so say something when Logan spoke up first. "Surprise," he said softly. He opened the box and presented me with the orchid.

"Huh?" I said, stupidly.

"This is for us, Mary Anne. You're not here to babysit. That was . . . well, it was a trick. It was the only way I could give you this present, this evening. Anyway, like I said, everyone's in the TV room. They won't bother us. Tonight is our night."

My jaw dropped open. "I thought we were going to cool off our—"

"We did," said Logan. "And now I'm ready to try warming it up again. Here, have a seat. My family helped me make this special dinner just for us."

I was completely overwhelmed. So I sat down. I think that if Logan had said (as gently and as sweetly as he had spoken just now), "Here. Shave your head, get each of your ears pierced four times and your nose once, and go and be a shepherd in the mountains," I would have done it.

“Are you hungry?” Logan asked. He was standing at my elbow, like a waiter.

“Yes,” I admitted.

“Good. We’ll be eating soon. But first I have some things for you. Just a minute. Stay right here.”

Logan disappeared into the kitchen, swinging the door shut behind him. When he returned, his arms were loaded. Grinning, he put a small gift-wrapped package by my plate, and then a red heart-shaped box. After that, he handed me a single red rose. “For you,” he said.

“But you’ve already given me a flower,” I replied, looking at the orchid. I was completely bewildered.

“Red roses are traditional on Valentine’s Day.”

I wasn’t sure what to do with the rose (its stem was *very* long; also thorny), so I just laid it next to my plate on the white tablecloth.

Logan was nudging the present and the heart-shaped box closer to me. (He still hadn’t sat down.) “Go on. Open them,” he said.

“Only if you’ll sit down, too,” I said with a nervous smile. I just couldn’t believe what was going on. It had happened too fast. I was supposed to be babysitting, but here I was in a candlelit room, a world of romance. And Logan, all dressed up, was presenting me with gift after gift, while I sat dumbfounded, feeling guilty because I hadn't even bought Logan that card I'd seen.

Logan sat. I looked at the boxes in front of me. "Which one first?" I asked.

"Mmm . . . that one." Logan pointed to the heart-shaped box.

In all honesty, I must say that the box was pretty gaudy. It was adorned with a gigantic pink plastic rose and tied with red voile. (Or toile. Whatever that stuff is that wedding veils are made of.)

I slipped off the voile or toile. Inside the box were five kilos of chocolates. "Yum," I said. "Thanks, Logan."

"Any time. Let's save them for dessert. Open the other present."

I reached for the small silver-wrapped box and unwrapped it. When I lifted the lid I saw . . . a bracelet made of tiny gold hearts linked together.

I gasped. And Logan leaned over and kissed my cheek.

At that moment I still felt overwhelmed. But I felt something new, too. It was a gnawing sense of dread.

I was in over my head with Logan. This was not at all the way things were supposed to be working out. And I didn't know what to do, how to make things right.

"Logan, this is beautiful," I ventured.

"I knew you'd like it," was Logan's answer. He fastened it around my wrist.

It really was beautiful – but now I had to say sheepishly, "Logan, I didn't get anything for you. I saw a card, but. . ." My voice trailed off.

"That's okay," he said. "Eating dinner with you is enough of a gift."

I wanted to cry.

Logan went back into the kitchen then, and returned carrying two plates of food – lasagne, broccoli with some sort of sauce on it, and a serving of salad.

"Wow!" I couldn't help being impressed.

"Just remember," said Logan, as he put one of the plates in front of me, "I had a little help with this."

"And now you're forcing your family to spend the evening in the TV room?"

"Under penalty of death," replied Logan.

We began to eat. For a while, we ate in silence. When the silence became excruciating, I said, "Logan, I feel *really* bad that I don't have anything for you. You've given me flowers, chocolates, a bracelet and dinner."

"Don't worry about it. I've been planning this as a surprise. How could you have known about it?"

I just shook my head.

We made it through dinner. We made it through dessert (chocolate cake and chocolates – Claudia would have been in heaven). As soon as dessert was over, I looked at my watch.

"Logan, I'd better go," I said.

"Okay, I'll ask Mum or Dad to drive us to your house."

"Wait! Before we leave I have to say something." My heart was pounding but I was determined to speak up. "Logan – Logan, when I said we should cool off our relationship, I meant it."

"I know. And we did cool it off. But as I said, I'm ready to start it up again."

I'm not, I thought. Logan hadn't understood at all.

The bracelet on my wrist felt as heavy as an iron chain.

13th CHAPTER

Saturday

Big news! What an exciting day. Mr Prezzioso called this morning. He sounded frantic. And he had a right to sound that way. Mrs P was ready to go to the hospital to have the baby! Since it was an emergency sitting job, Mr P just started calling each of us BSC members, trying to find someone who could come stay with Jenny for the day. I was the first one he reached. And, oh, I just love babies!...

As you can tell, Jessi was ecstatic over her unexpected sitting job. Jenny is not one of her favourite sitting charges, but new babies *are* exciting, and besides, Mr P really did need someone to come over quickly.

So Jessi's Aunt Cecelia drove her to the Prezziosos'. Jessi knew that accepting this job without consulting Kristy or the other club members was okay. It was an emergency. Besides, Mr P had said over the phone, "Your friends are either out already, or their lines are busy."

"Well, I'm free," Jessi had told him. Two minutes later, she was sitting beside Cecelia in the front seat of her aunt's car.

Before she knew it, her aunt had pulled to a stop in front of the Prezziosos'.

"Bye, Aunt Cecelia!" Jessi called as she scrambled out of the door. "I'll phone when I hear any news. If I don't phone, I'll be home by six. Mr Prezzioso said that either he would come home then or, if he needed to stay at the hospital, Mrs Frank from down the street will come and spend the night with Jenny."

Aunt Cecelia smiled. "That's fine," she said. "I can't wait to hear the news." Jessi closed the door then, and her aunt drove slowly and carefully down the street, pausing once to let a squirrel cross the road.

Jessi, however, literally *sprinted* to Jenny's front door. She didn't even have to ring the bell. The door was flung open by Mr P

Sitting nearby, on a chair in the hall, was Mrs P, a suitcase next to her. Both Mr and Mrs P looked pretty tired. I suppose you don't sleep very well when you're expecting a baby.

"Where's Jenny?" was the first thing Jessi asked after she and the Prezziosos had hastily greeted one another.

"Still asleep," said Mrs P, with a smile. "Jenny could sleep until midday every day, but we don't usually let her. However, we thought it would be okay today."

"So Jenny doesn't know you're leaving for the hospital?" asked Jessi, astounded. This did not seem like a very good situation to her.

"No," replied Mr P, "but when she gets up, tell her I'll try to phone her several times today. With any luck, one of the calls will be to say that the baby has arrived. But I'll phone no matter what. We don't want Jenny to think we've abandoned her."

"Dear?" spoke up Mrs P. "I really think we should leave now." She grimaced.

"Oh! Oh, right," exclaimed her husband, sounding nervous again. He turned once more to Jessi. "You know where the emergency numbers are, you know where we'll be, and if you have any problems, Mrs Frank will be at home all day."

"Dear?" said Mrs P again.

With that Mr P appeared to forget about Jessi. He helped his wife to her feet, picked up the suitcase, and walked her out of the door, which Jessi held open for them. As they made their way slowly down the front path, Mrs P leaned heavily on Mr P and Jessi had a sense of déjà vu. She remembered her old house in Oakley, New Jersey, she and Becca standing at *their* front door, their grandmother behind them, as all three watched Mr Ramsey escort Mrs Ramsey to the family car. Later that night, Squirt had been born.

Gosh, thought Jessi. That was about a year and a half ago. It could have been yesterday. And now Squirt was walking, climbing stairs. . .

Jessi shook her head. The Prezziosos' car backed hurriedly down the drive and into the street. Jessi watched until it was out of sight. Then she closed the front door and tiptoed up the stairs to Jenny's room. Her door was ajar, so Jessi peered in. Jenny lay sprawled on her back, the covers kicked off, one arm slung over the side of the bed.

Jessi smiled, then tiptoed back downstairs. I'll make Jenny a nice breakfast, she thought. Maybe that will take the sting out of waking up to find her parents gone – and her position as an only child about to come to an end.

Jessi had laid the table, poured orange juice for Jenny, and was putting out bread and cereal, when Jenny shuffled into the kitchen.

"Morning, sleepy-head," teased Jessi. Then she added, "Do you remember who I am?" (She doesn't sit for Jenny very often.)

"Jessi?" said Jenny questioningly.

"That's right! You've got a good memory."

"You're a babysitter," was Jenny's reply. She sounded as if she was accusing Jessi of committing a crime.

"That's right," said Jessi again.

"Then where are my mummy and daddy?"

"Why don't you sit down and have some breakfast," suggested Jessi. "I'll tell you everything while you're eating."

"Okay." Reluctantly, Jenny climbed on to her chair.

Jessi handed her a piece of toast and a bowl of cereal. Then she sat down opposite Jenny. "Something wonderful happened this morning while you were asleep," she began, choosing her words carefully.

"What?" asked Jenny suspiciously.

"Your mummy decided she was ready to have the baby. So she and your daddy went to the hospital. Pretty soon you'll have a new brother or sister. Oh, and your daddy promised to phone you today whenever he can. So you'll get to talk to him on the phone."

Jenny stopped eating her cereal, her spoon halfway to her mouth. She looked bewildered, then puzzled. Finally she said, "What about the stork?"

"The stork?" repeated Jessi. And then she remembered. She had read the BSC notebook and knew about Jenny's conversation with Stacey and Claud and me before Mrs P's baby party.

Uh-oh, thought Jessi. But she composed herself and said, "Jenny, storks don't bring babies. That's just a silly story. Babies grow inside mummies."

Jenny looked quite thoughtful for several moments. She returned her spoon to her bowl. Then she opened her mouth (Jessi braced herself for the worst) and said, "I *thought* that stork thing sounded funny!"

And that was the end of the conversation. Jessi breathed a sigh of relief.

When breakfast was over, Jessi took Jenny upstairs to help her brush her teeth and get dressed. She let Jenny choose her own outfit (something she was pretty sure fussy Mrs P never did). She decided it wouldn't matter. Mrs P wouldn't see Jenny that day anyway.

Jenny had just finished putting on her clothes – a pink denim skirt, a red shirt, yellow knee socks and blue sandals – when the phone rang.

"Maybe it's Daddy!" Jenny shrieked. "Maybe my baby is here." (*Her* baby? wondered Jessi.) "Can I answer the phone? Please?"

"Do you know how to?" asked Jessi.

"Yes! Mummy taught me. It is a very grown-up thing to do. You can listen if you want." Jenny was already heading for the phone in her parents' bedroom.

"Okay," said Jessi. "Go for it."

Jenny snatched up the receiver. "Hello, Prezziosos'. Who's calling, please?" She listened for a moment. Then she said, "What? . . . What?" and then, "I have to ask." She took the phone away from her ear. "Jessi," she said, "the man wouldn't tell me his name. But he wants to know if we want to buy some . . . cyclopediments?"

Jessi, suppressing a smile, said, "Tell him no, then say thank you and goodbye and hang up the phone."

Jenny did as she was told. Almost immediately the phone rang again. And Jenny snatched it up again. "Daddy!" she cried a moment later. "The stork story isn't true after all. Do I have a new baby yet?" She paused, then said, "Oh. Okay. Do you *promise* you'll phone later? . . . Okay. Bye." Jenny sounded disappointed.

"Don't worry," said Jessi, confused because she thought Jenny didn't *want* the baby. "You'll have a new brother or sister by tonight. Or maybe tomorrow."

"Stupid old baby," muttered Jenny, kicking at a chest of drawers. "I didn't know Mummy and Daddy would have to go away to get the baby. It'll never be just me and Mummy and Daddy again. The baby's got them all to itself right now. And I'll never have them to myself again."

Oh, thought Jessi. So *that* was why Jenny wanted the baby to come home soon. She didn't want it to have too much time alone with her parents. And she probably thought that if she took care of the baby as "hers", then Mr and Mrs P would have more time to spend with Jenny.

It was very complicated.

Jessi managed to entertain Jenny for the rest of the morning. She made a few phone calls to let some of the other BSC members know what was going on. She gave Jenny lunch.

Jenny was just finishing her peanut butter sandwich when the phone rang again. Jenny made a leap for it. "I hope it's my daddy!" she cried.

It was, but he didn't have any news. No baby yet.

Jenny was becoming edgy. And cranky.

"How about a nap?" asked Jessi tiredly.

"NO!"

"Okay, okay."

At 4:15, the phone rang again. "You get it this time," said Jenny, who was slumped in a chair, the picture of depression.

So Jessi did. And it was Mr P. "The baby's here!" he said excitedly. "It's a girl, she weighs seven and a half pounds, and she's twenty-one inches long. Her name is Andrea."

"Congratulations!" shouted Jessi. "Wait, let me put Jenny on the phone."

Jenny listened to her father with absolutely no expression on her face. Then she said goodbye and slumped back into her chair.

Jessi hardly noticed. She phoned her family and every single club member, including Logan and Shannon, to spread the news. When she finally got off the phone, she said excitedly to Jenny, "So what do you think? You have a baby sister now."

Jenny narrowed her eyes. "I wanted a brother," she said, and marched up to her room.

Jessi watched her helplessly.

14th CHAPTER

Mrs Prezzioso and Andrea stayed in the hospital for three days. On Tuesday afternoon Mr P was allowed to bring them home. The day before, he had phoned during the BSC meeting to arrange for a sitter for Jenny for the afternoon. I had got the job.

When I rang the Prezziosos' bell on Tuesday, I was greeted by Mrs Frank, who had been staying with Jenny since the night before. I had a feeling that Jenny's life since Saturday had consisted of a string of babysitters. I also had a feeling that Jenny was not going to be in a good mood. I was right about both things.

I said goodbye to Mrs Frank and let her out of the front door. Then I walked into the living room, where Jenny and Mrs Frank had obviously been reading books.

"Hey, Jen," I greeted her. "Andrea comes *home* today!" I sounded as perky and as excited as I was able.

"So?" countered Jenny.

"Well, today is pretty important. You're a big sister and your baby sister is coming home."

Jenny didn't answer me.

"Your dad's going to drive everyone home in an hour or so."

"Yup." Jenny finally looked up from her copy of *The Little Engine That Could*. "And I will never have Mummy and Daddy all to myself again."

"Oh, Jen." I sat on the floor beside her. "That's not true. Mummies and daddies have time for more than one child. Think about Mal's family."

"I know." (Jenny heaved a sigh that was probably heard in China.) "But it won't be the same."

"No. You're right. It won't be the same. I bet your mum and dad will make special time just for you, though."

"Maybe."

"You know what?" I said. "My mum died when I was little, so I grew up without brothers or sisters. It was just my dad and me. And sometimes I was really lonely. I wished and wished for a brother or sister. Especially a *baby* brother or sister. I wanted to have someone to take care of."

"You did?"

"Yup. Anyway, then my dad married Dawn's mum, so now Dawn is my sister. She's not a baby sister to take care of, and every now and then we fight, but mostly we're glad to have each other. Sometimes at night when we're supposed to be in bed, one of us will sneak into the other's room and we'll stay up late, talking and talking in the dark."

"That sounds like fun," said Jenny . . . uncertainly.

"What's the matter?" I asked her.

"Babies seem like a lot of work. And Mummy wants me to do grown-up, big-girl things."

"But you'll still be your mummy's little girl. Nothing will change that."

"Yes it will!" Jenny shouted suddenly, startling me. "Andrea will change everything. I'll have to give her bottles the way I practised on that stupid old doll, and I'll have to—"

"Whoa, Jenny. Calm down," I told her. "You won't know how things will be with Andrea until you actually see her." Jenny got up and stomped around the living room. "Okay, kiddo," I said. "Outdoors."

"Why?"

"Because you've got a lot of energy to get rid of, and I'm going to teach you a new game. It's really good fun."

"What is it?" asked Jenny suspiciously.

"It's called Flamingo Fight."

Jenny giggled. "Okay," she said.

So we put on our jackets and mittens and went outside. Luckily the snow that had fallen had long since melted, and the grass was dry. (You need a soft, dry outdoor place that's not too near the street to play Flamingo Fight, because you fall over a lot.)

"Oh, wait," I said to Jenny as soon as we were outdoors. "I've got to get us blindfolds. You sit right here on the front steps and don't move. I'll be back in just a second."

I dashed inside, grabbed two woollen scarves from the Prezziosos' coat cupboard, and dashed back out. Jenny was sitting where I'd left her.

"Okay. First thing," I began. "Do you know what a flamingo is?"

Smiling, Jenny got up. Then she tried to balance on one leg.

"That's right!" I said. "A flamingo is a bird that stands on only one of its legs. It tucks the other one up under its body. You can pretend to be a flamingo by bending your leg up behind you and holding your foot with your hand. Then you can hop around on your other leg."

"Okay," said Jenny, trying it. "But what about the fight?"

"Well, what you do in a flamingo fight is try to make the other person fall over. If you can do that, you win. But there are some rules. You have to tie a scarf around your face so that you can't see. Then, we call out to each other so that I know where you are, and you know where I am. We try to bump into each other. If I make you fall down, I'm the winner. If you make me fall down, you're the winner. One important thing, though. We can't use our hands. We just hop and bump around in the darkness."

Jenny was laughing by then. "Let's play!" she cried.

So I tied a scarf around Jenny's eyes (I was careful not to cover her nose) and made sure she couldn't see. Then I tied a scarf around my eyes. "Jen?" I said.

"Yeah. I'm here."

"Are you holding one foot up?"

"Yup."

"Okay. Then get ready to . . . flamingo fight!"

I hopped in the direction in which I'd heard Jenny say, "Yup." But I didn't run into anything. "Jen?" I called. I heard giggling from the opposite direction, turned round, and hopped towards the sound. Suddenly I bumped into Jenny. "Flamingo fight!" I cried.

Laughing, Jenny and I kept bumping into each other, until I finally lost my balance and fell over.

"You win!" I said. "The score is one nil, in favour of you."

"Yea!" shouted Jenny.

Twenty minutes later, the game was tied five to five, and Jenny and I were desperately trying to knock each other over, when we heard the honking of a car.

"I think that's Mummy and Daddy . . . and Andrea!" exclaimed Jenny. In her excitement, she rushed towards the drive, ran into me, and knocked me to the ground.

"Hey, you win!" I told Jenny, slipping the scarf from over my eyes.

Then, "Jen, wait!" I called, realizing that Jenny was tearing towards the drive blindfolded. I caught up with her and removed *her* scarf. The two of us stood at the edge of the drive and watched Mr P park the car.

He pulled gently to a stop by the front path, got out of the car, and hurried round to Mrs P's door. Then he took the baby from her, and Mrs P climbed slowly out of the car herself. She knelt down and held her arms open wide. "Jenny!" she said. "I missed you."

Jenny flew towards her mother, and I thought, Oh, what a nice reunion.

But at the last moment, Jenny veered to the side, stood on tiptoe in front of her father, and said, "Let me see Andrea."

I couldn't tell whether Mrs P looked hurt or relieved or proud or all three things at once. At any rate, she and I both watched as Mr P bent down, cradling the baby, and Jenny got her first look at her sister.

Andrea was wrapped up in blankets. Only her face and her tiny hands showed.

She was wide awake and she looked as if she were staring solemnly at her sister, who stared back at her.

For a few moments, Jenny and Andrea continued to stare at each other. Then Andrea's hands moved slightly and Jenny held out a tentative finger. She touched one hand. She leaned over for a closer look.

"She has fingernails!" said Jenny softly. "She has real fingernails, but they're so *little*." She paused and said, "Ooh, Andrea is *much* better than my doll. Can I hold her, Daddy?"

"When we're inside," replied Mr P. "And before we go in, why don't you give your mum a big hug? She missed you."

"I missed you, too, Mummy," said Jenny, as everyone stood up. "I'm glad you came back." She hugged Mrs P around the legs.

Jenny took her mother's hand and they followed Mr P and Andrea inside. *I* followed Jenny and her mother.

The first thing Jenny said when we were indoors was, "Can I hold the baby now?"

"Let's take off our coats first," replied her mother.

So we did. A few minutes later, Jenny was sitting in an armchair, her feet sticking out in front of her, and Mr P and I were watching as Jenny's mother placed Andrea in her sister's waiting arms.

I hope that the Prezziosos saw what I saw then: as Jenny looked down at her new sister, and gently stroked a hand, an arm, a cheek, her whole face changed.

I could tell it was love at first sight.

Jenny loved Andrea, her new sister.

Oh, of course, there would be tough times ahead for them. They would quarrel, fight, slam doors, not speak to each other, go on car trips and divide the back seat in half so that neither sister touched the other's belongings. Just like Dawn and me. We fight sometimes. But mostly we're good friends. We stick up for each other and we have fun together.

I could tell that that was the way things would be for Jenny and Andrea, too.

Jenny bent over. She and Andrea were nose to nose. "Hello, Andrea," said Jenny. "I'm your big sister. I know you can't do many things yet, so I will help you. Maybe when you're three or four I'll teach you how to play Flamingo Fight. I'll be seven or eight by then. I'll be going to school and you won't, so I'll tell you all about school."

Jenny stopped talking. She stroked the black downy hair on Andrea's head. "Don't worry, Mummy," said Jenny, looking up. "I remember about the soft spot. I won't hurt the baby."

By that time, the Prezziosos were filming this scene on their camcorder. But Mrs P stopped watching her daughters long enough to pay me. Then I went home.

15th CHAPTER

Wow.

I did some heavy thinking as I walked from Jenny's house to mine.

I was thinking about relationships. I thought about Dawn and me, and what good friends we are. Even when we fight, we learn something from our fights. We learn how to listen to each other and respect each other.

I was thinking about Jenny and Andrea. In my wildest dreams I had never imagined that Andrea's homecoming would have worked out the way it had. Not with the conversations the BSC members had been having with Jenny. Not with Jenny throwing her doll around her room. Not with Jenny's fears about no longer being her parents' "one and only".

I suppose that sometimes some family members *never* get on together, but I don't think that happens often. Usually when people are angry some sort of love is underlying the feelings that show, the feelings on the outside. When people love each other – whether they're brothers and sisters, parents and children, best friends, husbands and wives, or girlfriends and boyfriends – that love leads to an understanding. That's why I can (usually) ignore my father when he gets into one of his orderliness frenzies. It's why my stepmother doesn't force me to eat the foods (such as tofu) that she and Dawn adore. And it's why Dawn and I can argue and make up again.

Then I thought about Logan and me. What did this say about us? I had tried to be understanding of Logan, but was he understanding of me? He used to be, that's for sure. I remembered my thirteenth birthday. There had been a surprise party. Since I'm shy, you can imagine how I felt about being surprised with a cake and presents. I *hated* being the centre of attention. Being the centre of attention is as awful as performing and public speaking. I'm terrified of those things. And when I ran out on my own party that evening, Logan understood. He gave me a chance to get myself together. Then we talked about things, and Logan never made me the centre of attention again, if he could possibly help it. He didn't mind when I'd agree to go to a school dance – and then not dance. He let me make up my mind about going to Hallowe'en parties in costumes or in ordinary clothes. . . He *used* to be that way.

Now he wasn't.

I felt that he didn't listen to me any more. He thought only about what *he* wanted, while I tried to understand him and what he wanted, and to make allowances for him. Not that he would have forced me to dance at a school disco – or would he have? I wasn't sure. What I *was* sure about, though, was that he expected me to be available for him at all times. He seemed to have forgotten that I had a family and another life, and that they did not include Logan.

Logan wanted me to be "Logan's girl", and I didn't want to be anybody's girl. Ever. I may not be as independent as my sister, but I have rights and feelings like anyone else.

I didn't want to be owned.

By the time I reached our house, I had made a decision.

First, I went to my room. I opened my jewellery box, removed something from it, and slipped it into my pocket.

Then I telephoned Logan.

"Hi," I said when he picked up the phone. "It's me."

"Hi, you!"

"Logan, I've got to talk to you. Now. Can we meet in the park?"

"It's late, Mary Anne. It's getting dark outside. Why do you have to meet me somewhere? Can't we just talk? Or can't we see each other at school tomorrow? I'm not—"

"No," I interrupted.

"Mary *Anne*."

"Logan, when *you* call *me* on the spur of the moment and want me to go out, I usually do it. Now I'm asking you to do the same thing for me." I paused. Then I went on, "We'll meet at the bench by the skating pond."

"Oh, okay! Remember that snowy afternoon in the park? That was great, wasn't it?"

"Yeah. But Logan, you don't need to bring your skates. I can't stay out very long."

"Me, neither," replied Logan agreeably. "See you in a few minutes."

We hung up the phone.

"Dawn!" I called. (She was in her room, studying.) "I'm going to meet Logan in the park now."

"*Now?*"

"Yeah. I know it's late, but I only have to see him for a few minutes. I'll be back before six o'clock."

"You shouldn't let Logan push you around like this," was Dawn's reply.

I almost told her that I was doing the pushing this time, but I didn't have time.

Besides, by this evening I'd probably have a lot more to tell her, so I just yelled, "Later!" Then I put on my parka and mittens and ran out of the door and all the way to the park.

The park looked very different than it had a few weeks earlier. The snow was gone. Scrubby brown grass showed in its place. The tree branches were bare, dark against the late afternoon sky. No snow outlined them, turning them into fairy trees. Only a few people were still enjoying the park; the children had left.

And yet just *seeing* the park brought back all sorts of memories. It brought back good times that Logan and I had shared there. And those memories led to other memories.

I pictured Logan and me wearing cat costumes to the Hallowe'en Hop.

I pictured us on a joint babysitting job for Jackie Rodowsky. That was before Logan and I were boyfriend and girlfriend.

I remembered the first time I had spotted Logan at school, when he was the new boy – and I couldn't take my eyes off him.

I could not *believe* what I was going to do.

When I reached the bench it was empty.

I sat down and waited.

Logan was not likely to be late.

And he wasn't. I'd been sitting alone for less than a minute when I heard him call, "Hi, Mary Anne!"

He was loping towards me, jogging through the park. Smiling.

Oh, I thought. What am I doing? What am I going to do to Logan? What am I going to do to us?

But my mind was made up.

Logan sank down next to me. He tilted my chin towards him so we could kiss, but I pulled away.

"What's wrong?" asked Logan. "Here we are in the park. Don't—"

I put my hand over Logan's mouth to make him stop talking. It was Logan's turn to pull away. But then he leaned towards me and tried to kiss me again. Why wasn't he getting the message?

Oh.

Because I wasn't talking. I thought my actions were enough, but maybe not. After all, Logan couldn't read my thoughts.

"Logan . . . Logan?" I began.

"Yes? Yes?" Logan laughed at his joke.

"Logan, this is serious," I said. (Logan's smile vanished.) "Remember how I said we needed to cool off our relationship?"

"Of course," answered Logan. "And we did."

"No. *I* did. You never took it seriously."

"I did!" exclaimed Logan indignantly.

"But then you decided to start things up again, without asking me."

"I don't have to ask your permission for everything."

"No, but you need to listen to me. And understand me. I don't feel as if you do either of those things any more. You haven't for a long time." I could feel my hands growing clammy in my mittens, but I was determined to say what I'd planned to say. "I was the one who asked to cool off our relationship for a while, and you agreed. Don't you think it would have been courteous to consult me when you felt we were ready to start seeing more of each other?"

"Courteous?" repeated Logan. "Who are you? Miss Manners?"

"No, I'm Mary Anne Spier and I am a person. An independent person who likes to think for herself and have some freedom." (I was shaking; wondering just how independent I was – or wanted to be.)

"What exactly are you saying, Mary Anne?"

"I want to break up with you," I replied. I didn't even hesitate before I said it.

"You *what*?"

"I want to break up with you. It's time to do that. This relationship isn't going anywhere. I don't know about you, but I'm not happy."

"Mary Anne—"

Logan stopped talking when I stood up, took off one mitten, and reached into my pocket. From it, I pulled the heart bracelet that Logan had given me on Valentine's Day. Then I reached for Logan's hand, dropped the bracelet into it, and closed his fingers around the linked hearts.

"I can't keep this," I told him.

"You're serious, aren't you?" said Logan.

"Yes," I replied softly.

Logan opened his hand. He looked at the bracelet coiled in it. Then he looked back at me. "I suppose this means we're – we're not—" Logan had to stop speaking because his voice had choked up. (I was choked up, too.)

"Goodbye, Logan," I said.

"Goodbye, Mary Anne."

The Babysitters Club

JESSI AND THE DANCE SCHOOL PHANTOM

The author gratefully acknowledges
Ellen Miles
for her help in
preparing this manuscript.

1st CHAPTER

"And now mesdemoiselles, if you please: a *pas de bourrée couru*, *en cinquième* with *port de bras*, ending in an *arabesque*. One at a time, please . . . and begin!" Mme Noelle banged her stick on the floor to emphasize her words.

A stranger might have thought they'd wandered into some other world – and in a way, they'd be right. A ballet studio is another world – a world where movement is everything, and where words are shorthand for what our bodies should be doing.

Pah deh boure-ay koo-roo? On sankeeyem? With por deh brah? And an arabesk? Sounds crazy, but what Mme Noelle, our teacher, wanted us to do was to move on our toes across the floor, holding our arms in graceful patterns, and end by standing on one toe with our arms held out to the sides. That's what all those words meant. They're French.

I don't speak French, but I know those words, and a lot of others, because French is the language of ballet, and I've been studying ballet since I was four. I'm eleven now, so that's a long time!

"Jessica Romsey, please take your turn!" said Mme Noelle.

Jessica Romsey, that's me. Except most people call me Jessi, and my last name's Ramsey, not Romsey. It's just that in the elegant accent of Mme Noelle's, everything comes out sounding kind of – well, kind of glamorous.

I closed my eyes for a second, picturing what I was about to do. I wanted to do the best *pàs de bourrée* I'd ever done. Why? Because this was the final stage in the final auditions for a big production that was going to be put on by my ballet school. We were going to be putting on *The Sleeping Beauty*. And I was trying out for the lead!

I took a deep breath, let it out slowly, and rose on to my toes. Then I began. I was so focused that I was hardly aware of Mme Noëlle's attention, but I knew she was watching every single muscle in my body, checking to make sure that I was in complete control.

Normally, as I *bourrée*'d past her, Madame would be making comments like, "Long neck, Mademoiselle Romsey!" or, "Use zee onkles!" (That's 'ankles', just in case you were wondering.) But this wasn't a class. This was an audition. And I was on my own.

I finished the *bourrée* and went into an *arabesque*, stretching my arms gracefully (I hoped). Then I clomped off the stage area, my toe shoes clacking with every step.

I watched the other girls do what I'd done, one at a time. There were a lot of good dancers in my class, which makes sense – it is, after all, an advanced class. Take Mary Bramstedt, for example. Just then she was *bourrée*-ing across the floor, in perfect form. She always seems to be in perfect form. But I think (and this is just my personal opinion – I'd never say it out loud) that there's something missing when she dances. Something like – I know this might sound really silly but – passion. She's a bit like a robot, you know?

I don't think anyone could mistake me for a robot – and not just because I'm not always in perfect form. As far as I know, there aren't too many black robots running around – in fact, there are probably even fewer black robots than there are black ballerinas.

Luckily, there are a few black ballerinas now. Twenty years ago, there weren't any. And someone like me, with skin the colour of cocoa and eyes like coal, could never have dreamed of joining a ballet company. But now I can dream. And it makes me glad, because I absolutely, positively *love* to dance.

So does Carrie Steinfeld, and it was showing as she did her *bourrée.* She's a great dancer – one of the best in the class. She's also one of the oldest students in the class, and she'll be graduating soon. This might be her last chance to get a starring role in a production – a role that would really give her an edge if she could add it to her résumé.

Without having had a role like Princess Aurora, the leading part in *The Sleeping Beauty*, Carrie might have a hard time getting into another dance school for older students. And she'd have hardly any chance at all of joining a ballet company. The ballet world is very competitive.

"Very nice, Mademoiselle Steinfeld," said Mme Noelle. I bit my lip. She hadn't said anything when I'd finished *my bourrée.* I tried not to worry about it. It might not mean a thing, after all.

I found Mme Noelle very intimidating when I first joined this school, back when my family moved to Stoneybrook, Connecticut. That was not too long ago, when my dad was transferred to the Stamford office of his firm. The move was hard on the whole family.

It was tough for the usual reasons – leaving friends and family, coming to a strange new place – but there were other reasons that made it even worse. The neighbourhood we used to live in, in New Jersey, was completely integrated. So were the schools. But in Stoneybrook, it's different. Here there are very few black families. People just weren't used to seeing black faces – and they didn't make us feel very welcome. In fact, it was the opposite.

But in time, we've all made friends in Stoneybrook, and our lives have settled down. I'd have to say that my family is pretty happy here now. And for me, one of the best parts of the move was getting into this dance school. The school isn't actually in Stoneybrook – it's in Stamford, where my dad's office is. It's one of the best on the East Coast – if you don't count the really big ones in New York City. And Mme Noelle is known throughout the ballet community as an excellent teacher. I don't find her *quite* so intimidating any more.

I looked up to see that Katie Beth Parsons had just finished her routine. She looked pretty happy with herself, but then she usually does. She's one of Madame's pets – she has been since she was the youngest member of the class when she joined it. Now that I've joined, she isn't the youngest any more (she's twelve), but she's still a favourite of Madame's.

"Nice work, Katie Beth," I said as she came off the stage.

She looked at me suspiciously. "Thanks," she said, as if she weren't sure whether or not I meant the compliment. Katie Beth and I have not always been the best of friends – in fact, there have been times when we were downright enemies – but we've been getting on pretty well lately. Still, the atmosphere at most auditions isn't the friendliest.

Katie Beth pulled at the elastic of her leotard as she stood next to me, watching the rest of the students complete the routine. "I hate this stupid thing," she said. "I wish we could wear whatever we wanted instead of these."

We were all wearing exactly the same outfits: a black leotard with pink tights. It's a bit like the uniform for my class. I could just imagine the scene if we were allowed to wear anything: there'd be so much neon in the place that it would look like Times Square. I myself don't really mind having to wear the same thing to each class – in fact, it's good to have one less thing to decide on as I pack my dance bag.

And it's not as if we can't express our individuality. There's room for that in how we each decide to do our hair. The only requirement is that it be "off zee face", as Mme Noelle puts it. I like to wrap mine into a tight bun or to plait it. Carrie usually has some kind of ponytail on the side of her head. And Hilary – well, Hilary's a totally different story.

Hilary Morgan always has the best of everything. A brand-new leotard every few weeks. New toe shoes as often as she needs them. (The rest of us have to make them last – toe shoes are awfully expensive.) And she doesn't do her own hair – she gets it "done" in a very posh French plait a few times a week.

It's not that Hilary's family is all that rich (although they're certainly not poor). It's just that Hilary's career as a dancer is top priority with her mum. Mrs Morgan used to be a ballet dancer herself, but she gave up her career to have a family. As I understand it (from what I've overheard in the dressing room) she's one of the worst "stage mothers" in the history of the school. She really *pushes* Hilary all the time; I know because I've seen her do it. She actually sits and watches our entire two-hour class sometimes!

Luckily, she wasn't watching that day – we didn't need any distractions, I don't think Mme Noelle would have tolerated a visitor during auditions anyway.

All of a sudden, I noticed that the last dancers had finished. Auditions were over. Mme Noelle called us all out on to the stage. She looked us up and down without saying a word. Then she smiled.

"All of my demoiselles have done very, very well today," she said. "But only one can be zee Princess Aurora." Suddenly she clapped her hands three times. "Go now!"

she said. "Change zee clothes. When you are ready, come back. I will give my decision zen."

We all scurried into the dressing room and raced to be the first out of our leotards. Everybody was talking at once, asking the others how they'd looked as they performed.

"Did you notice when I shook on the *arabesque*?" asked Lisa Jones, as she pulled on an oversized sweat shirt. I like Lisa, but sometimes she worries too much about her performance in class.

I shook my head. "Sorry, but I wasn't paying that much attention," I said. "I think I was on Mars for a while there." That's what it had felt like – I'd been concentrating so hard that I felt as if I'd been on a different planet.

"I thought I'd die by the time I *bourrée*'d across that huge stage," said Hilary. "It's not fair that the stage is so much bigger than our usual studio."

"Of course it's fair," said Carrie. "We all have to do the same thing on the same stage, don't we?"

"I suppose so," said Hilary. But she didn't sound convinced.

I stuffed my leotard and tights into my dance bag, and then carefully wrapped the ribbons around my toe shoes and laid them on top. You have to take very good care of them, otherwise they won't last.

"I just hope Madame noticed how much I've been working on my arm movements," said Carrie. She stuffed her toe shoes into her bag, got up, and left the dressing room.

"Actually, she'd better hope that Madame *didn't* notice she's completely over the hill," said Hilary, giggling.

Over the hill! It was true that Carrie was one of the oldest students in class, but really! She's only a few years older than me! Ballet may *look* like a graceful, dainty world – but it's not. It's as tough and competitive as any sport. I could have spoken up in Carrie's defence, but I held my tongue. I don't like to get involved in any of the gossip and back-biting that often goes on in the changing room.

Hilary looked in the mirror and patted her still perfectly plaited hair. "I'm dying to dance Princess Aurora," she said. "What a great part." Then she spun on her heel and headed out of the room.

"The rest of us had better pray that she doesn't get that part," said Katie Beth. "If she does, we'll have to put up with Mrs Morgan practically sitting in our laps during every rehearsal!"

"I know," said Lisa. "I think Hilary's mum would dance the part *for* her, if she could."

I shook my head and kept quiet. Everybody was being pretty catty that day. I suppose the auditions brought it out.

Finally we had all finished changing. We sat in a semicircle on the floor of the dance studio, facing Mme Noelle. She was seated on a chair, and she looked very serious.

"Zee *Sleeping Beauty* is one of zee most beautiful ballets in zee world," she began. "To perform in it is a privilege, no matter how small zee role."

Right. But none of us wanted "zee small roles". We all wanted the lead.

"To begin," said Mme Noelle, "zee part of zee Lilac Fairy will be donced by Lisa Jones."

Lisa smiled. I don't think she had really expected to get the lead. The Lilac Fairy is a pretty good role, and she looked happy to get it.

"Next," said Mme Noelle, "zee part of zee Bluebird of Happiness." That part is usually played by a man, but it sounded like someone from our class would be playing it instead. There aren't too many boys in the school – and there are none in our class. "Zis will be donced by Carrie Steinfeld."

Carrie let out a breath, then pressed her lips together and tried to smile at Mme Noelle. "Thank you," she said. "I know that the Bluebird's *pas de deux* is famous. I will try to do it justice."

I had to hand it to her – she handled the disappointment well.

"And now," said Mme Noelle, "I will tell zee news you are all waiting for." She paused. "Zere is only one student in zis class who has zee talent and zee *je ne sais quoi* to bring zee role of Princess Aurora to life."

Zhuh-nuh-seh-kwah? What on earth did *that* mean? I'd never heard the expression before.

"Zat student is Mademoiselle Romsey," finished Mme Noelle.

I was still trying to figure out what she meant, and I didn't really hear my name. The next thing I knew, Lisa was giving me a quick hug. "All right, Jessi," she said. "You did it again!" She seemed genuinely happy for me.

"Congratulations," said Katie Beth sort of half-heartedly. I smiled vaguely. It still hadn't sunk in that I had won the role. That meant that I had got yet *another* lead in a production! I'd loved dancing in *Swan Lake*. And playing Swanilda in *Coppélia* had been pretty incredible. But the Princess Aurora! It was the role of a lifetime.

When I finally came to my senses, I was alone in the room. Except for Mme Noelle. She was smiling gently at me. "Congratulations, Jessica," she said. "You earned zee part."

"Thank you, Madame," I said, blushing. "But there's one thing I want to know. What does 'zhuh-nuh-seh-kwah' *mean*?"

"It simply means 'zat certain something' – zat indescribable feeling," she answered. "And you, mademoiselle, possess it."

I blushed again. Then I thanked her once more, said goodbye, and ran out to wait for my lift home.

Hilary Morgan's mother pulled up just as I reached the outside stairs, where we all wait for our parents. Hilary started to walk towards the car, looking as if she was going to a funeral.

"Did you get the lead?" called Mrs Morgan loudly.

Hilary shook her head. I saw Mrs Morgan frown and heard her start to lecture as Hilary got into the car. "Didn't I *tell* you. . ." she began.

I turned away – I just couldn't listen to any more. Part of me almost wished that Hilary had got the part. Poor Hilary. But – I have to admit it – a bigger part of me was so happy I could hardly stand it. "Princess Aurora," I said to myself softly. "Princess Aurora."

2nd CHAPTER

After Hilary had left, I sat down to wait for my dad. I was still in a state of shock about getting the lead, but I thought that – just for fun – I'd play it cool with him.

Pretty soon, Daddy pulled up in front of the steps. I opened the car door and slid in, throwing my dance bag on to the back seat.

"Hi, darling!" he said, giving me a kiss. He started the car, and I saw him looking at me out of the corner of his eye as he pulled into the traffic. He was being careful not to be pushy – but I could tell he was dying to know how the auditions had gone. "How did it go?" he asked casually.

"Pretty well," I answered, just as casually. "I mean, okay, I suppose." I was bursting with my news, but I suppose I also felt like holding it in for a little while.

We'd only gone about three blocks before I couldn't stand it any more. "Daddy!" I said. "I did it! I'm Aurora!"

He turned to grin at me. "All right!" he said, punching the air with his fist. "I knew you could do it." A horn honked, and Daddy straightened out the car.

"I want to hear all about it," he said, "but let's wait till we're home, so you can tell everybody all at once." Then he pulled the car over to the kerb and turned off the engine. "Wait here," he said. "I'm going to run into the shop for some ice cream. We've got something to celebrate tonight!"

The minute we pulled into our drive, Becca came running out of the front door. "Did you get the part?" she asked excitedly. Mama was right behind her, carrying Squirt. Aunt Cecelia stood in the doorway, holding a tea-towel.

Becca is my little sister. She's eight and a half, and she's a really great kid, even if she does drive me up the wall sometimes. She's really bright, and she has a great imagination. Becca loves to come and see me in my productions. In fact, she'd probably like to be in one herself – except for one thing. Becca has the worst case of stage fright I've ever seen.

Squirt, who was now looking at me and saying, "Buh!" with a big smile on his face, is just a toddler. Squirt's not his real name, of course. His real name is John Philip Ramsey, Jr – but Squirt suits him much better. He was nicknamed that by the nurses at the hospital where he was born, because he was the smallest baby there. He only weighed five pounds, eight ounces back then! Now he's like a big ape – a big, squirmy ape, who was doing his best to get out of Mama's arms.

"I'll take him," I said. "C'mere, Squirtman." I took him from Mama and balanced him on my hip. I smiled at him. "How does it feel to be carried by a princess?" I asked.

Mama gasped. "You got the part?" she asked.

"Yup," I answered. "Princess Aurora, at your service."

Becca was all over me, shrieking and smacking my arm.

"Okay, Becca," said Aunt Cecelia. "Let's let the princess come in and have her dinner." Aunt Cecelia likes to try to keep things calm. She's Daddy's older sister, and she came to live with us not long ago, when Mama decided to go back to work and realized she'd need help with Squirt in order to do that.

At first, having Aunt Cecelia living with us seemed like a big mistake. Becca and I thought she was too strict and too unfair. She treated us like babies. But she learned to give us some credit for being able to take care of ourselves – and we learned to like her better. Now we're glad she's here.

At dinner, I filled my family in on the details of the audition. And over ice cream (I had a tiny bit, even though I really have to watch what I eat, especially when we're preparing for a performance). I told them all about *The Sleeping Beauty*.

"You all know the story," I said. "It's just like the fairy tale. It starts with the christening of the baby Princess Aurora. All the fairies do beautiful dances as they present their gifts."

"Then the bad fairy comes, right?" asked Becca.

"That's right. The funny thing is that the bad fairy is usually played by a man in a wig," I said. "Anyway, the bad fairy puts a curse on the baby, telling her that she will prick her finger and die on her sixteenth birthday. A good fairy, called the Lilac Fairy, can't get rid of the curse. But she at least makes it so that Aurora will sleep for a hundred years instead of die."

"Then what happens?" asked Daddy. I suppose he doesn't remember fairy tales as well as the rest of us.

"Well, I come on stage in the next act, which is my sixteenth birthday party. Four princes present me with roses, and I do this gorgeous slow dance called the 'Rose Adagio'. It's really hard. Then the bad witch, in disguise, sneaks into the party and hands me a spindle for making yarn and I prick my finger on it and fall into a deep sleep.

"A hundred years later," I went on, "this prince is looking for me. He sees a vision of me – which is really me, of course – and we dance together. Then the prince tries to find me, and when he finally does, he kisses me—"

"Ugh!" interrupted Becca. "Do you really have to kiss a boy? I'd rather kiss Misty any day!" Misty is our pet hamster.

I ignored her. "– and I wake up, and then there's the wedding, where I dance with all these different fairy-tale characters, like the Bluebird of Happiness. I don't really know what that has to do with the plot, but it's a great dance. And then I dance with the prince again at the very end." I was exhausted just thinking about it.

"It sounds like a beautiful ballet," said Mama.

"It is," I said. "And you should hear the music. It's by Tchaikovsky, the same composer who wrote the music for *Swan Lake*."

After dinner, I ran upstairs (Mama said I could be excused from table clearing and dish washing, since it was a special night) to phone Mallory. I couldn't wait to tell her my news, and I knew she'd spread it around to our friends.

Who is Mallory? Maybe I should tell you about her – and about my other friends, too.

Mallory Pike is my best friend, and the first friend I made when my family moved to Stoneybrook. She's terrific. She's clever and funny, and we have great times together. We both love reading – especially horse stories, like *Misty of Chincoteague* – but Mal also likes writing. One day she hopes to be a writer and illustrator of children's books, which I think is a great idea.

Part of what makes Mallory fun is that she's easy-going and doesn't get fazed by much. I think that's because she comes from a huge – and I mean huge – family. Mallory is eleven like me, and she has seven little brothers and sisters! Three of them are triplets, believe it or not. Their names are Adam, Jordan and Byron, and they're ten. Then comes Vanessa – she's nine – and Nicky, who's eight, followed by Margo, who's seven. The baby of the family is Claire. She's five. The Pike household is never boring. Actually, I think that Mal sometimes envies my (relatively) quiet family. She doesn't get much private time.

Even though she's the oldest, Mallory feels that her parents still treat her like a kid. (I can relate to that!) She had to work really hard on her parents – just like I did – to convince them to let her get her ears pierced. Her next project is to get contact lenses, but I think that's a long way off. With her red hair and freckles, and her glasses and her brace, Mal has a hard time feeling glamorous – even with pierced ears. But you know what? I bet she's going to be a real beauty one day. She just has to be patient. (I should talk. I'm as impatient as she is.)

When I first moved to Stoneybrook, I felt so lonely. I'd just left my best friend, Keisha (who also happens to be my cousin) behind, and I wondered if I'd ever find another best friend. But as it turned out, I not only found Mallory, which was great, but a whole group of other friends. These friends are all very different from each other, but they have one thing in common. They love babysitting, just like I do. And that's why they formed the Babysitters Club. I'm lucky to be a member and to have them all as friends. Mallory and I are the youngest in the club, by the way. Everyone else is thirteen.

Kristy Thomas is the chairman of the BSC. She's great. When I first met Kristy, I was a little intimidated – she's very straightforward (sometimes she's even got a big mouth) and energetic. But now I like her, and admire her, a lot. She's always having these great ideas – and she acts on them, too. She's not just a dreamer.

Kristy's family is pretty complicated to describe, but here goes. First of all, her parents got divorced years ago, after her dad walked out, leaving Kristy's mum to take care of Kristy, and her brothers. (She's got two older brothers, Charlie and Sam, and a younger one called David Michael.) Mrs Thomas did a good job of being a single parent. But then she met Watson Brewer, who's a real millionaire. They fell in love and got married, and Kristy and her family moved across town to live in Watson's mansion.

But it's not just the six of them in that gigantic house. Watson had also been married before, and he's got two kids – Karen (she's seven) and Andrew (he's four). They stay with the Brewers and Thomases every other weekend and for two weeks in the summer. Karen and Andrew love Kristy, and she loves them, too. No wicked step-families here!

You'd think that a family that size would be enough. But you'd be wrong. Kristy's mum and Watson recently decided to adopt Emily Michelle, this two-and-a-half-year-old Vietnamese girl. (She's really sweet!) And then Nannie, Kristy's grandmother, moved in to help take care of Emily. Wow! Now that's a big family. And I haven't even told you about Shannon and Boo-Boo. (Don't worry, they're not more kids. Shannon's a dog and Boo-Boo's a cat.) And, there are some goldfish.

So that's Kristy. Oh! I forgot to tell you what she looks like. Kristy is on the short side, and she's got brown hair and brown eyes. And she's a bit of a tomboy – that is, she doesn't care much about clothes or make-up – she likes playing baseball, and she's not all that interested in boys.

Kristy's best friend (I think they've been best friends all their lives) is Mary Anne Spier. She and Kristy look alike, with their brown hair and brown eyes (although Mary Anne cares a bit more about clothes), but other than that they're very different. You've heard the saying "opposites attract"? That describes Mary Anne and Kristy. While Kristy is assertive and loud-mouthed, Mary Anne is very quiet and shy, and incredibly sensitive.

I'm not sure why she's like that, but sometimes I think it may have to do with the way she grew up. Mary Anne's mother died when Mary Anne was tiny, and so her dad was the one who brought her up. I've heard that he used to be very strict with her – but he seems to be pretty laid-back now. He even dealt well with the fact that Mary Anne had a steady boyfriend for a while (she's the only one of us club members who did). I suppose it helped that he likes Logan. (That's Logan Bruno, Mary Anne's ex-boyfriend. He's in the club, too, actually – but I'll tell you about that later.)

Maybe part of what changed Mr Spier was falling in love and getting married again. Now that's a romantic story. He met up with an old girlfriend from high school, started going out with her again, and then he married her. And the best part of the story is that the old girlfriend happens to be Dawn Schafer's mother! Who is Dawn Schafer?

Dawn is another member of the club, and she's not only Mary Anne's stepsister; she's her best friend, too. (That's right, Mary Anne has two best friends.) Dawn's mum grew up in Stoneybrook but then moved to California, got married, and had two kids – Dawn and her younger brother, Jeff. But then she got divorced and moved back to Stoneybrook – a fact for which we're all thankful, since that move brought us Dawn. The only bad part about the move was that Jeff missed California and his dad so much that he ended up moving back there to live. So her family's split up, but Dawn handles it well.

Dawn is truly gorgeous. She's got incredibly long, white-blonde hair and she dresses in a style all her own. She wears all these great, casual clothes in bright colours. Nobody else in Stoneybrook dresses like that – you could pick Dawn out as a California girl in a minute. She's different in other ways, too: she loves the sun and the sea, and she adores health food. Bean sprouts are to Dawn what Hula Hoops are to Claudia.

Claudia – that's Claudia Kishi, the vice-chairman of the BSC – is the Junk Food Queen. I've never seen anyone eat the way she does and still have such a great figure and perfect skin. I don't know how she does it, but Claudia always looks great. She has an incredible sense of style. She's also a great artist, which might have something to do with it.

Claudia is Japanese-American and very exotic-looking. She's got this long, silky black hair that she wears in a million different ways, and gorgeous almond-shaped eyes. Her family is pretty small – there's just her and her sister, Janine (who's a real – I swear it – genius), and their parents. Claudia's grandmother Mimi used to live with them, but she died not long ago. I get the feeling that Claud still misses Mimi all the time; they were very, very close.

Unlike her genius sister, Claudia is not a great pupil. It's not that she's stupid, but there are other things she'd rather do with her time than study – like sculpt or paint or make collages. She'd also like to spend her time munching on junk food while reading Nancy Drew books, but there's a limit to how much of that she can do, especially since her parents disapprove of both activities. Which is why you never know when you're in Claudia's room where you might find a Twix or Maltesers or a Snickers bar. She hides them. Everywhere. Just like she hides her Nancy Drew books.

But even though Claudia's parents are strict about some things, they're pretty easy-going about others. Like clothes.

Mallory and I are always arguing with our parents for the right to wear certain things – like mini-skirts or big T-shirts over leggings. But Claudia's parents seem to let her wear whatever she wants. I think they see her outfits as part of her artistic expression. (I'm so jealous!)

Stacey McGill is a really cool dresser, too. In fact, I think that's why she and Claudia became best friends at first. And one of the reasons Stacey's a sophisticated dresser is that she grew up in New York City. That's right, New York City – home of some of the best ballet companies in the world, not to mention the greatest restaurants, dance clubs, department stores. . .

But Stacey likes Stoneybrook. She first came here when her dad was transferred to Stamford, but then she actually moved back to New York when he was transferred again. The rest of the club members thought they'd lost Stacey for ever. But then they heard bad news and good news. The bad news was that Stacey's parents were getting a divorce. The good news was that she and her mum were moving to Stoneybrook again!

Unfortunately, they couldn't move into their old house. Why? Because my family had moved into it in the meantime! They did find another nice house, though, and of course, Stacey was back in the club straight away.

Stacey's very cool, as you might expect her to be. She gets her blonde hair permed every now and then, and as I said before, she rivals Claudia for "Trendiest Dresser in Stoneybrook".

There's one thing about Stacey – she's a diabetic. That means she has to take really good care of herself, watch her diet like a hawk, and (I could never do this!) give herself daily injections of insulin. Stacey doesn't seem to let it get to her, though – she's usually in a great mood.

Speaking of great moods, that night I was in about the best mood possible. The time right after you learn that you've won a great part is always the best – before the hard work of rehearsal begins. As I passed the hall mirror on my way to phone Mallory, I gave myself a big smile. "Hey, Aurora!" I said. "What's new?"

3rd CHAPTER

"*Love* your leg warmers, Lisa," said Carrie. "Are they new?"

We were all in the dressing room, getting ready for our first day of rehearsals for *The Sleeping Beauty.* I was still pretty excited about being chosen to play Princess Aurora, but I knew enough to keep my mouth shut. Most of my classmates were probably happy for me, but nobody likes a gloating prima ballerina.

"They really are great, Lisa," I said. "Where'd you get them?"

"My mum got them in town," she answered. "At Capezio's. She gave them to me last night. They're lilac, because I'm playing the Lilac Fairy."

Lisa seemed happy with her role, and I was glad. I have this weird thing sometimes, where even though I'm thrilled to get the lead, I feel pretty bad about it, too. Because if I got it, that means that somebody else didn't. Does that make any sense?

I threw my dance bag down next to my locker and started to change. It seems like I'm always in a hurry in the dressing room, but so is everybody else. There's the feeling that Mme Noelle is waiting for us in the studio, getting more and more impatient by the minute. And having Mme Noelle in a bad mood is bad news.

I threw off my school clothes (jeans, a new red sweater and my red high-tops) and stuffed them into my locker. It's never a good idea to put things on the benches in the dressing room, even for a minute. They'd get all mixed up with everybody else's stuff and there would be mass confusion.

Then I groped around in my dance bag and pulled out my leotard and tights. I shimmied into them in about three seconds (after years of practice) and then reached for my toe shoes. I could put them on in the studio while I was listening to Mme Noelle give us the rehearsal schedule.

My toe shoes weren't in the bag.

I checked again. No toe shoes. My red high-tops were in there, but no toe shoes. Now, you have to understand that I have been dancing for seven years. For at least the last four I have packed my own dance bag. And I have never, *ever* once forgotten anything. Other girls would have to dance with bare legs when they forgot their tights, or in old swimsuits when they'd left their leotards at home. Not me. Never. I am always prepared. It's just the way I am.

"Mesdemoiselles!" called Mme Noelle from outside the dressing room. "Are we plonning to donce today?" She clapped her hands loudly, just once. That meant, in Madame's special shorthand, "Get into the studio, NOW!"

I panicked. I bent over my dance bag and practically turned it inside out. They *had* to be in there! I clearly remembered putting them in the bag the night before, after they'd aired out enough so that they'd be ready to wear again.

I looked around the dressing room. There were heaps of clothing everywhere – tangled leg warmers on the benches, leotards hanging by one sleeve from a locker door – but not a toe shoe in sight. What was I going to do?

Everybody else was hurrying out of the dressing room. Mary stopped for a moment as she passed my locker.

"What's the matter, Jessi?" she asked.

I told her that my toe shoes were missing. Her eyes grew round. She knew how serious this was.

"I wish I could lend you a pair, but my spare ones are at home," she said.

"That's okay," I said. "I really couldn't dance in anyone else's shoes anyway." My toe shoes are unique – everybody's are.

And every dancer has a different way of taking care of them. There's a whole routine with toe shoes – you have to break them in (I do it by banging them against the banister on the staircase at home), and sew ribbons on to them, and stuff the toes with lambswool. So even though they don't last very long (I usually need a new pair every week or so), each pair has a lot of time invested in it. And each pair ends up fitting your feet, and your feet alone.

I do, of course, have a spare pair of toe shoes. But guess where *they* were? Right – they were at home.

"This is terrible," I said. By then I was alone in the dressing room. I could hear Mme Noelle's voice, just faintly. She was taking the register in the studio. In about three seconds she'd realize that I wasn't there.

I was going to have to go into the studio barefoot.

I took a deep breath and started to walk. I stopped at the dressing room door and took one last look around the room. There was not a single toe shoe anywhere. I looked down at my feet. This was going to be humiliating. And Mme Noelle wasn't going to like it all.

At least my entrance was quiet. Bare feet make a lot less noise than toe shoes, which tend to make clunking noises when you try to walk normally.

But, as quiet as I was, everybody, including Mme Noelle, looked at me as I walked into the studio.

"Ah," said Madame. "Zee Princess Aurora hos decided to join us." She gestured to a spot on the floor. "Please, your highness, take a seat."

Then she saw my feet.

"But where are your shoes, Mademoiselle Romsey?" she asked, her eyebrows raised high.

I felt so ashamed. "I – I don't know," I said. "I packed them last night, but now they're not in my bag," I felt hot, then suddenly cold, all over.

"But you cannot rehearse wizout zem!" she said. "And we cannot rehearse wizout you." She stood up. "You must look for zem again. Perhops zey are benease some ozair girl's clothes. Come!" She clapped her hands and gestured to the class to follow her.

I felt like such a jerk, walking back into the dressing room with the whole class marching behind me. When we got there, we started to tear the place apart. Mme Noelle stood at the door of the room as we searched. She had a funny look on her face, as if she smelled a dead fish or something. Usually, she made a point of staying out of the dressing room – and it was obvious that she wasn't enjoying this little visit.

"What is *zot*?" she asked, pointing at

Carrie's neon green, pink and yellow jacket, which was tossed over a basin.

"That's my jacket," said Carrie.

"I see," sniffed Mme Noelle.

"I think it's wicked cool," said Katie Beth. "I wish I had one."

"Perhops if you young ladies were more careful with your sings, zis would not hoppen," said Mme Noelle, looking at me.

I felt tears stinging my eyes. It wasn't fair! True, everybody's stuff was strewn all over the room. But I'm actually a pretty neat person. *My* stuff is usually put away in my locker. And I'm always prepared for class. At least I always *have* been.

I looked around at my classmates. They'd finished poking through the piles of stuff and were looking back at me. I picked up my dance bag one more time and checked it. No luck. It was empty, except for my high-tops. Too bad I couldn't dance in those.

I looked at Mme Noelle and shrugged my shoulders. "I'm sorry," I said. "They're not here."

She gave me a glance that said, as clearly as words would have, "Jessica Romsey, I am most disappointed in you." Then, out loud, she simply said, "Come."

We trooped back into the studio and got ready to warm up at the *barre*. I was just going to have to do the exercises barefoot. Mme Noelle put on some music and led us through a few minutes of *pliés* (plee-ay –

that's when you sink down, keeping your bottom tucked in and only bending at the knee) and *relevés* (reh-leh-vays – that's when you go up on your toes.)

I saw her look at me as I *relevé*d. Everybody else was *en pointe* – that is, *really* up on their toes. I was kind of just pretending. Madame shook her head, her lips in a tight line.

"Zis will not do," she said suddenly. "If Mademoiselle Romsey cannot practise *en pointe*, zere is no reason to rehearse today. After all, she is zee Princess Aurora, and we cannot do very much wizout her." She turned her back on us and lifted the needle from the record. "Zis rehearsal is concelled."

I was shocked. This was worse than I ever could have imagined! Everybody groaned. I knew how they felt. There's nothing worse than missing a day of dancing – it throws off your whole routine. And we needed every rehearsal that was scheduled. The performance wasn't all that far off.

"Isn't there any way we can still rehearse?" asked Lisa.

"What if we just look for the shoes one more time?" asked Hilary. "If Jessi says she brought them, they *must* be in that room somewhere."

Mme Noelle didn't look happy about the idea, but she agreed. "One more time, she said. "But zen, rehearsal is off."

I *hated* having her angry with me.

We all paraded back into the dressing room. I brought up the rear – I wasn't too enthusiastic about another pointless search. Just as I entered the room, I heard Katie Beth squeal.

"Hey, *here* they are," she said, holding up a pair of toe shoes. They were mine. I could tell from across the room. "They were in your bag the whole time, Jessi."

I ran over to her and grabbed them without even saying thanks. My shoes! I'd never been so happy to see them. But I knew Katie Beth was wrong. Those shoes had not been in my bag the whole time. I knew it as surely as I knew my own name.

"Very good, Katie Beth," said Madame. "Zee mystery is solved. Now let us get on wiz zee rehearsal!"

She led us back into the studio and the rehearsal began for real. I put on my toe shoes as Madame told us about the first part of the dance we would be practising.

"And zen," she said, "zee Princess Aurora enters wiz a *glissade*. . ." She made a movement that suggested what I was supposed to do. ". . .and zen a *relevé en arabesque*." Again, she illustrated what she meant.

I love to watch Mme Noelle move. She doesn't dress in leotards for class – she just wears a poloneck and a long black skirt. And when she demonstrates steps, she doesn't do them full out. But every move she makes is just so – so full of grace is the only way I can describe it. You can see all those years of dance training in the slightest motion of her arm. I don't think she knows *how* to move like an ordinary person any more. I wonder if I'll ever have that kind of poise.

For me, for now, ballet is more like hard work. The stuff I do without having to think about is stuff I've been doing nearly every day for seven years. And everything new I learn is based on those foundations. It takes a long, long time to learn to dance.

I tried to concentrate on learning my steps. I was doing the best I could to forget about the whole miserable scene before rehearsal. But I couldn't get it out of my head.

Mme Noelle couldn't either – that was obvious. She was very impatient with me, and since I was feeling distracted, she kept having to repeat directions. That didn't help.

"Long neck, Mademoiselle Romsey!" she said. "You are not doncing zee part of a hunchback. You are a princess – please act like one."

I stretched my neck and proceeded to stumble in the middle of my *glissade*. I heard somebody giggle behind me. Wonderful! I just knew that everybody in the class was now convinced that I was a complete air-head. Once again I tried to concentrate.

"STEP!" said Mme Noelle suddenly, clapping her hands. I was out of rhythm. This just wasn't my day. She went to the record player and started the music from the beginning. "And . . . again," she said, nodding at me. "I want nossing but grace from all of you," she said. "I want absolutely magnificent, glorious grace."

Right.

I worked harder and harder, forgetting the time, forgetting my lost shoes, forgetting everything except the music and how I was moving to it.

Before I knew it, Mme Noelle was clapping her hands. "Okay, mesdemoiselles," she said. "Next time we will do better, am I right?"

I met her eyes and nodded. She gave me a tight smile – I suppose she had forgiven me.

I walked to the dressing room, relieved that rehearsal was finally over. I changed back into my school clothes and reached into my dance bag for my high-tops. I was thinking that the next rehearsal would just *have* to go better than this one – it certainly couldn't be any worse. Then I pulled my left trainer out of the bag and saw something stuck between the laces.

It was a note. And this is what it said: BEWARE. Nothing more, nothing less. Just . . . BEWARE.

I couldn't work out what it was supposed to mean. Beware of what? Beware of whom?

I thought it was pretty strange. But I was too tired from rehearsal to wonder about it for long. I shoved it into my bag and headed out of the door.

4th CHAPTER

I was still feeling a little shaky by the time I got to Claudia's for that day's Babysitters Club meeting, but I tried not to let it show as I slipped into my usual spot next to Mallory on the floor. As usual, I had arrived about two and a half seconds before Kristy called the meeting to order. (I nearly always get there just before 5:30 pm because of dance class, but nobody gives me a hard time about it, which I'm thankful for.)

I think I forgot to mention that our club always meets at Claudia's house, in her room. This is why: Claudia, the vice-chairman of the club, has her own phone and her own personal phone number. That means that we're not tying up any adult's phone while we take calls during meetings.

Let me go back and explain a little bit about how the club began and how it works. The whole thing was Kristy's idea originally. Remember how I told you that she's always having good ideas? Well, this was the ultimate good idea, and here's how it happened. One afternoon, way back before Kristy's mum married Watson Brewer, David Michael needed a babysitter. Usually Kristy or her brothers would have looked after him, but this time none of them could. Mrs Thomas made about three zillion phone calls looking for a sitter, but she wasn't having any luck.

That's when Kristy had her brainstorm. What if parents could reach a whole group of sitters, just by making one phone call? It seemed like a great idea. Kristy talked to her two friends Mary Anne and Claudia (who were interested) and they started a club – The Babysitters Club (or the BSC). Three people didn't seem like enough for a club, though, so Claudia asked Stacey, whom she was becoming friends with, to join. It was just the four of them until Dawn moved to town and became friends with Mary Anne. Dawn had done some babysitting out in California, so they asked her to be a member, too.

Mallory and I joined the BSC during the time that Stacey was back in New York, before her parents got divorced. The rest of the club members were feeling kind of overwhelmed with jobs, and we were available, so it worked out for everyone. Even though (we think) we're lowly sixth-graders and can only sit during the day (except for our own families), I think we fit in pretty well.

So, all together there are seven of us now, and it seems as if the club is just the right size. In fact, I don't think Claudia's room could hold many more people without bursting at the seams.

The way the club works is pretty simple. We meet on Mondays, Wednesdays and Fridays from 5:30 to 6:00. Parents can call during those times to arrange for a sitter. (Most of the parents have been using us for ever; new clients find out about us through the leaflets we distribute from time to time, or by word of mouth.)

Kristy is the club chairman, and she takes her job pretty seriously: she's all business at meetings. She always sits in Claudia's director's chair, with a visor on her head and a pencil behind her ear. She calls each meeting to order just as the digital clock flips to 5:30. Sometimes she asks us if we've read the club notebook. (We always say yes, because we always have.)

The club notebook, in case you're wondering, is where we record every job we go on. We write down what happened, who it happened to, why it happened, and anything else we can think of. Seriously, it's a good thing that we have it. Reading it keeps us up to date on our clients and what's going on with them. The only thing is, it's a bit time consuming to write all that stuff down – and then to read what everybody else has written. But it's worth it. By the way, the notebook was Kristy's idea (of course).

Anyway, let's get back to answering the phone. When a call comes in, someone takes it (we all dive for it) and finds out when and where the job will be. Then we tell the parent that we'll call them straight back. Next, Mary Anne, the club secretary, checks the record book. (It's different from the notebook.)

The record book is quite an amazing thing. In it, Mary Anne keeps track of all our schedules: Claudia's art classes, my dance classes and rehearsals, Mal's dental appointments . . . you get the idea. Then, when a call comes in, she only needs to take a quick peep to see which of us is free. In the record book is a lot of other stuff besides our schedules. It has records about all our clients: names, addresses, phone numbers – and also information about the kids we sit for, like who's allergic to what.

Anyway, once Mary Anne finds out who's free, it's usually a simple matter to decide which of those sitters gets the job. We rarely squabble over jobs, since there's always enough work to go around. Then we phone back the parent and confirm the job. And that's it!

Well, not quite. I forgot to tell you about the treasury. Stacey, the maths genius, is in charge of that. As treasurer, she can tell you in about three seconds exactly how much money we have available.

Where does the money come from? Well, it's like this. We keep all the money we earn on jobs – that's ours. But every Monday, we pay club subs. (Not without a lot of complaining, I might add – we hate to part with our hard-earned money.) The subs are used for club things, like paying Kristy's brother Charlie to drive her to and from meetings since she lives too far away to walk now.

We also use the money for the occasional pizza bash or for sleepover munchies. (We're not all business, all the time!) And we use some of it for supplies for our Kid-Kits. Kid-Kits are yet another of Kristy's great ideas. They're really just cardboard boxes, but we've each decorated our own with all kinds of stickers and sequins and stuff. The boxes are stocked with things that kids love – crayons and books and puzzles and paper dolls . . . stuff like that. We bring them on any job where they might come in handy.

Okay, so Kristy is the chairman, Claudia is vice-chairman, Mary Anne is secretary, and Stacey is treasurer. You might be wondering where that leaves Dawn, Mallory and me. Well, Dawn is what we call an alternate officer. That means that any time one of the others can't make it to the meetings, Dawn fills in for them. She has to know how to do everyone else's job.

Mallory and I are junior officers, which really doesn't mean much at all, except that we're younger and that we can only sit during the afternoons. This is fine with me – I don't know if I'm really ready to sit in some strange house alone at night! (I do sit for my own brother and sister at night, and Mal sits at her house – but that's different.)

There are also two other members whom I haven't told you about. They're associate members, and they don't come to meetings. But they do take jobs, when the rest of us are all booked up – and that's been a big help more than once. Logan Bruno, Mary Anne's ex-boyfriend, is one of the associate members. (He's really nice – and you should hear his great Southern accent. He moved to Stoneybrook from Louisville, Kentucky, and he sounds like someone out of *Gone With the Wind*. He and Mary Anne are still good friends, by the way.) The other associate member is Shannon Kilbourne, a girl who lives in Kristy's new neighbourhood. I don't know her very well, but she seems nice.

So there I was, sitting by Mallory on the floor of Claudia's room, ready for the meeting to start. Claudia, Mary Anne and Dawn were all sitting cross-legged on the bed. Kristy was in the director's chair, and

Stacey was sitting in Claudia's desk chair, leaning right back in it. She looked as if she was about to topple over at any minute.

"Did you see that outfit Jennifer Cooke had on today? I mean, she looked like a cross between Princess Di and Minnie Mouse!" said Claud all of a sudden.

That was all it took to make Stacey – and the chair – fall over. Stacey was fine. She just lay there on the floor, laughing until she was almost crying. "Who does she think she is, anyway – just because she's won some beauty contests. All that make-up – it's too much!"

I was giggling, trying to imagine the outfit Claudia had described, when Kristy spoke up, "Order!" she said. It was 5:30. And our meetings *always* start on time.

Stacey got up from the floor and brushed off her jeans. She was wiping the tears from her eyes and trying to stifle her laughter. Kristy gave her a Look, which meant settle down, but Stacey was too far gone. You know how it is when you're not *supposed* to be laughing – like in the library, or during a science lesson – but you can't stop? That's how Stacey was.

She just kept shaking her head and saying "Minnie Mouse" and then breaking into giggles all over again. Kristy looked a little annoyed.

Luckily for Stacey, the phone rang then. Kristy dived for it. "Babysitters Club," she said, answering it. Then, "Okay, Mrs Perkins. No problem. I'll call you right back." Kristy hung up and looked around the room. The phone call had given Stacey the chance to get serious. "Mrs Perkins needs a sitter for Laura," said Kristy.

Laura is a baby. We usually sit for her *and* her two big sisters. "What about Myriah and Gabbie?" asked Mallory.

"The Perkinses are taking them to that big show in Stamford," said Kristy. "You know," she continued, "the one with Minnie Mouse on ice skates."

That did it. We *all* cracked up, including Kristy, and laughed until we were rolling on the floor. We didn't stop until the phone rang again.

We were busy handling calls and setting up jobs for a while, so I had to wait for a chance to tell everybody about the disastrous rehearsal I'd had that afternoon. But finally there was a lull in the action, and I told the awful tale.

"Oh, Jessi!" said Mallory. "Did you just *die* of embarrassment when you had to come out barefoot? I would have."

I admitted that it had been pretty bad. "But the worst thing was that Madame Noelle was angry with me," I said.

Mary Anne smiled sympathetically. "You really care a lot about what she thinks of you, don't you?" she asked.

"I know how that is," said Claudia. "It's like if I don't finish a project in time for art class. I hate it when I let my teacher down."

"But it all worked out okay, right?" asked Dawn. "I mean, you found your toe shoes and everything. But I wonder about that note."

I nodded even though the note didn't have me all that worried. "It's just that I hate starting out a new production with a rehearsal like that," I said. Everybody was being so nice. There's nothing like supportive friends when you're feeling like a total loser. I noticed, though, that Kristy hadn't said anything. Maybe she just wasn't that interested in my stories.

"Well, it's all over now," I said, getting ready to change the subject. I didn't want to make Kristy annoyed with me for taking up so much meeting time.

"Right, Jessi. Next time will be better," said Kristy quickly. "Now listen, everyone. I've got a great idea."

Everybody groaned, just to tease Kristy. How can anyone get so many great ideas all the time? No wonder she wasn't interested in my story – she'd been waiting impatiently the whole time, dying to tell us about her latest brainstorm.

"It seems to me that we haven't done anything really special with the kids we sit for lately," said Kristy. "You know, there hasn't been a big party, or a carnival, or anything – not for a long time."

"That's true," said Dawn. "But what can we do that would be new and exciting?"

"Are you ready for this?" asked Kristy, grinning. "We're going to have – a pet show!" She looked around the room. "I was remembering that Louie was in a pet show once," she continued. (Louie was a great collie that Kristy used to have. I never met him, though: he died before I moved here.) "It was at the library, and it was really good fun. Louie won second prize! I was so proud of him."

Everybody loved Kristy's idea.

"The kids are going to think this is brilliant," said Mallory. "It'll be a chance to get together and show off their pets. But where should we have it? We need lots of room."

"I was thinking it could be in Dawn and Mary Anne's garden," said Kristy. "It's one of the biggest gardens, and their house is pretty close to a lot of the kids' houses."

"Sounds great!" said Dawn. "I'm sure my mum won't mind."

"How are we going to let everyone know about this?" asked Stacey. "It's going to take a lot of planning.

"I'll make invitations," said Claudia. "We'll send them out to all our clients to let them know the time and place. We'd better pick a date a few weeks away, though –

everybody's going to need time to get ready for this."

"We're also going to need prize rosettes, refreshments and all kinds of other things," said Mary Anne. You could practically see the gears turning as she considered the details. She's a great organizer.

We worked on plans for the pet show for the rest of the meeting (between phone calls, that is). And I got so caught up in the whole thing that I almost forgot about my horrible rehearsal.

Almost.

5th CHAPTER

When the time came for the second rehearsal of *The Sleeping Beauty*, Princess Aurora was Princess Prepared. As I unpacked my dance bag in the dressing room, I almost had to laugh. I'd brought not just my spare toe shoes, but a spare dance outfit. The whole thing.

Two pairs of pink tights. Two black leotards. Two hairbands (it wouldn't do to have my hairband disappear and have to dance with my hair in my face – Mme Noelle would be furious). Two pairs of leg warmers (one white, one purple) and two baggy old grey sweat shirts, for warm-ups. I wasn't taking any chances.

As I changed, I watched my things like a hawk. When I walked across the room to check my hair in the mirror, I kept looking over my shoulder to make sure nobody went near my bag. I must have looked pretty paranoid. But I didn't care. Knowing that I had everything I needed for the class made me feel safe. I was sure that everything would go smoothly that day.

"Coming, Jessi?" asked Katie Beth. "I see you've brought your toe shoes this time."

I gritted my teeth. Sometimes Katie Beth can be really irritating. "For your information," I answered, "I brought them *last* time, too."

"Of course, Jessi," said Katie Beth. "Anything you say." She ran on ahead, into the studio. I walked behind her, giving her dirty looks.

"Why zee cloudy face, Mademoiselle Romsey?" asked Madame as I walked into the room.

I changed my frown to a smile, in a flash. "Good afternoon, Madame Noelle," I said, trying to sound happy. By then she was busy choosing the records for the day's practice, and she just nodded at me.

"All right, mesdemoiselles," she said. "Let us begin zee warm-up."

We took our places at the *barre* and began to work through the familiar exercises that I could probably do in my sleep. Sometimes I wonder just how many *pliés* I've done over the years, rising and falling to the sound of tinkly piano music.

When I was younger, taking beginner's classes, we used to play fun little games. For example, the teacher used to let us guess what the music was after each exercise. The records were always classical arrangements of simple songs like "Three Blind Mice", and we were very competitive about seeing who could guess right most often.

But games like that are out of the question now. Mme Noelle's class is serious. We don't giggle, we don't whisper and we don't ask questions like, "What's fifth position, again?" But you know what? Even though the early days were fun, I like this ultra-serious kind of class even better.

I like working hard. I like concentrating. And I love the fact that all the painstaking, repetitive work I do is worth it. You know why? Because it lets me fly. That's how I feel sometimes; when I'm in the middle of a *tour jeté* (toor jet-tay – that's just a big jump), I feel like I'm flying. And then it doesn't seem like work at all – it feels effortless, and graceful and . . . just wonderful.

When we'd finished our warm-up, we left the *barre* and stood in the middle of the room, while Mme Noelle changed the record. Soon, Tchaikovsky's music filled the air. It was beautiful.

Madame stood in front of the room, working out the steps she was about to teach us. She made motions with her hands, and whispered words like *glissade* and *piqué* to herself. While I waited for her to be ready, I looked into the big mirror that covered one wall of the studio.

I checked my posture. Good, but not good enough. I pulled up my head ("As if there is a string from the ceiling, holding you up," as Mme Noelle always says) and pulled in my stomach. I held out my right arm and arranged my hand as gracefully as I could. There! That looked good.

You might think that the other girls in class would think I was weird for looking at myself that way, but no. They were all doing it, too. Ballet pupils are always checking their form, because their form is important. You've got to be "just so" all the time.

"Mademoiselle Romsey," said Mme Noelle. "And Mademoiselle Steinfeld and Mademoiselle Jones. Attention, please."

She was ready to show us our steps. I paid close attention – you don't want to have to ask Mme Noelle to go over the steps more than once.

She gave us the whole routine in a flurry of French words. We followed along, practising without doing the steps full out. Just as she was getting to the last *arabesque*, Carrie lost her balance, knocked into me, and fell down.

"Jessi, you klutz!" she said loudly.

Me? I couldn't believe it. I hadn't had anything to do with it! Carrie was the klutz, not me. I looked up at Mme Noelle and opened my mouth to defend myself. But when I saw the look she was giving me, I decided to forget it. She clearly hadn't forgotten the episode of the toe shoes, and I was better off just keeping quiet.

So instead of sticking up for myself, I helped Carrie to her feet. Did she thank me? Three guesses.

"Again, mesdemoiselles," said Madame, barely pausing for Carrie to catch her breath. "And *one*, two, three. . ."

We went back into the routine. I was fighting to regain the concentration I had lost when Carrie knocked into me. We worked through the steps, counting carefully as we leaped and spun. It was beginning to feel good – but I knew we had a long way to go before it would *look* good.

But then, once again, on the final *arabesque*, Carrie knocked into me – hard. This time she didn't quite fall, but our collision definitely drew Mme Noelle's attention. She frowned at me.

"But I didn't—" I began, and then I just stopped. I sounded like a baby, back in the beginner's ballet class. That kind of excuse didn't belong here. If Carrie – and Mme Noelle – wanted to blame me for what was happening, there was no point in trying to turn that blame around. It would only make me look worse.

This time, instead of speaking out, I put all my energy into the steps we were learning. I became more and more focused on what we were doing and just tried to steer clear of Carrie Steinfeld. It wasn't easy at first, but after a while I forgot about everything except how it felt to dance.

There were no other major catastrophes for the rest of the rehearsal. And when it ended, Mme Noelle nodded at me approvingly. I think she must have sensed how hard I was working.

After rehearsal, I collapsed on to the bench in the dressing room as I pulled out my dance bag. I felt tired, but in a good way – and I felt satisfied with my dancing that day. I took my hair out of its ponytail and shook it out. Then I reached into my dance bag and I knew straight away that something was wrong.

My jeans and my shirt were still in there, and so were my sneakers. But my whole spare outfit had gone. No black leotard, no pink tights. No leg warmers (I'd worn the white ones, so it was the purple ones that were missing) and no sweat shirt. No spare toe shoes, either.

"Oh, my lord," I said, under my breath. (That's one of Claudia's favourite expressions, and we've all picked it up.) I looked around to see if anyone was noticing me noticing my empty bag. They were all busy with their own stuff.

I shrugged. What was I going to do about it? There was a thief in our midst (as they would say in a Nancy Drew book) but I wasn't going to catch her that night. I was too exhausted even to think about it.

I pulled on my school clothes and bent over to tie my shoes. Then I saw it. Once again, a note was tucked into the laces of my left trainer. Only this time, the note was written in blood!

I gasped. Oh, how creepy. Hiding my toe shoes was no big deal. Stealing my extra dance clothes was worse, but it still wasn't a capital offence. But a note written in blood! Ugh! For a minute I thought I was going to pass out.

Then I looked closer and saw that it wasn't blood at all. It was just red ink. But this time, it didn't say BEWARE. It said: WATCH YOUR STEP. As I read it, I shivered. Then I crumpled it up and stuck it into my bag. This was getting scary. Somebody was really out to get me. But why?

I left the dressing room as quickly and quietly as I could. I didn't want to draw attention to myself. My dad picked me up, and I barely spoke to him during the ride home. He didn't try to get me to talk, even though I could tell he'd noticed that something was wrong. He's pretty sensitive that way.

As we pulled into the drive, I made a real effort to forget all about the disturbing events of the day. I just didn't want to think about the note, or what it might mean, for a while.

Fortunately, Becca had something besides *The Sleeping Beauty* on her mind that evening. The minute I came into the house, she came flying down the stairs, waving a piece of paper in the air.

"Why didn't you *tell* me?" she yelled happily. "I can't believe you kept this a secret."

"Tell you what?" I asked. I really didn't know what she was talking about. "What secret?"

"The pet show!" she shrieked. "It's going to be great!"

I'd forgotten all about it. "Let's see the invitation," I said. Becca handed it to me, and I unfolded it.

CALLING ALL KIDS! it said, in big capital letters. Each of the letters had little animals climbing all over it – puppies and kittens and monkeys and all kinds of other beasts. Claudia is *so* talented.

The reason it said "all kids" instead of "pet owners" was that we'd decided to invite all of our regular customers – whether they had pets or not. That way, a kid like Jamie Newton, who doesn't have a pet, could still come to the show and have fun.

Underneath the headline were more pictures of animals, and then the information about the pet show: where it was going to be held, and when, and what kinds of pets could be entered. ("Bring your goldfish! Bring your pony! Bring any pet you have!")

Becca was nearly beside herself. "It came in the post today, Jessi!" she cried. "It had my name on it! I'm invited!"

I didn't want to spoil things by telling her that *everyone* was invited. "That's great, Becca," I said. "A pet show will be fun, won't it?"

She nodded. Then her smile faded.

"But we haven't got a pony. We haven't even got a dog! All we have is Misty." She looked worried.

"Misty's a great pet," I said. "She's friendly, and clean, and she knows her name—"

"But she's just a hamster," said Becca. "There's no way she can win a prize at a big pet show like this."

I thought about all the other pets that would probably be entered in the show. Nobody had a pony, at least as far as I knew. But there were a lot of dogs in the neighbourhood – dogs that knew how to do all kinds of tricks. There were a lot of beautiful cats, too. Would a boring little hamster be able to compete? Becca might have a point, there, I thought. But I didn't want her to worry about it.

"Winning a prize isn't everything, Becca," I said. "Just being in the show will be fun." I thought I sounded very grown-up and reasonable.

A tear ran down Becca's cheek. "I wish we had a dog," she said. "Then I could give it a bath, and put a ribbon around its neck, and teach it some really great tricks. Then it would win first prize!" She sniffed. Obviously, she wasn't convinced by my reasonable little speech. "Silly old Misty is just going to sit there, wiggling her nose."

"C'mon, Becca," I said. "You love 'silly old Misty'. Remember when we got her, how excited you were?"

Misty was born during one of my craziest sitting jobs. I'd been pet sitting for this couple, the Mancusis. They haven't got any kids, but they certainly have a lot of pets. They have three dogs, five cats, some birds, two guinea pigs, lots of fish, a snake (ugh!) called Barney, a lot of rabbits and an aquarium full of turtles.

The Mancusis also have hamsters, and when I was sitting, one of the hamsters got ill. It was awful! I didn't know what was wrong with him, and I had to miss an important meeting of the club to take him to the vet.

Well, you've probably guessed the rest of the story. "He" was really a "she" – and she was pregnant. She was going to give birth very, very soon. And not long after the babies were born (there were a lot of them!), the Mancusis came home. They were very happy with the way I'd handled the whole thing, and they offered me a baby hamster of my own.

Of course, we didn't take Misty home until she was old enough to leave her mother. The Pikes got a hamster, too, and so did one of the kids we sit for, Jackie Rodowsky. Becca was thrilled to pieces when we got Misty – but now the thrill seemed to be wearing off. There was nothing I could say to convince her that winning a prize didn't matter. Maybe this pet show wasn't such a great idea after all.

6th CHAPTER

Saturday

Total pet-mania. I can't believe how excited the kids are about the pet show. I hate to admit this (I really, *really* hate to admit this), but maybe, just maybe, this pet show was not the best idea in the world. I mean, it seems to be getting just a little out of hand already—and there's still a lot of time before the show.

Kristy must have been feeling really overwhelmed, for her to admit that one of her ideas might not have been totally and completely perfect. Well, let's just say that I've never heard her come close to admitting anything like that before.

That Saturday afternoon, Kristy was sitting for her brother David Michael; her adopted sister, Emily Michelle and her stepsister and stepbrother Karen and Andrew. Kristy had her hands full.

It was a beautiful, sunny day, and they were all sitting on the back-porch steps. Well, actually, they weren't just 'sitting'. David Michael was hanging over the railing, making burping noises, while Karen shrieked at him to stop. Emily was zooming her Tonka truck around Kristy's feet, screaming with glee every time she made a sharp turn. And Andrew was off in his own little world, examining an ant that he'd found crawling on the porch.

In between burps and shrieks and screams, they were all talking about – guess what – the pet show. All except Emily Michelle, that is. She doesn't talk much yet.

"I wonder who'll get second prize," David Michael said. "Maybe one of the cats."

"What do you mean, second prize?" asked Karen. "What about *first* prize?"

"Well, I don't need to wonder about that," David Michael answered. "I know which pet will get first prize. Shannon will. And I'm going to enter her, so I'll get to keep the blue ribbon." He paused to think for a moment. "I wonder where I should hang it in my room," he said.

"What makes you so sure that Shannon will win?" asked Kristy.

"Well, she'll be the biggest pet in the show," said David Michael. (Shannon *is* pretty big – she's a Bernese mountain dog, and she'll be the size of a Saint Bernard when she's fully grown.) "*And* she's got the best personality, right?"

Kristy had to admit that Shannon *was* pretty sweet – not to mention clever and loyal.

"And she's the best-looking!" finished David Michael triumphantly. "Mega-Dog!"

Kristy raised her eyebrows. "Well, we'll see," she said vaguely. She was thinking that it might not look too good if a dog from her own family won first prize in a pet show that had been her idea to begin with.

"I don't think Shannon's so great," Andrew said. He'd got bored with the ant and had started to listen to David Michael's boasting. "Midgie's cuter than her any day. Midgie's going to win. I just know it."

Midgie is this little mongrel (he's cute and intelligent, but he is definitely a mongrel) belonging to Andrew's stepfather, Seth.

"Did Seth say you could enter Midgie?" asked Kristy.

"Yup!" said Andrew proudly. "And I'm going to give him a bath, and put ribbons in his hair. He'll look great!"

"If you put ribbons in his hair, he's going to look like even more of a wimp than he already is!" said Karen.

"Wimp?" asked Andrew.

"Yeah," said Karen. "Midgie's a wimp. He's afraid of his own shadow. He'll never win a prize – not unless you train him to do some tricks or something. And you haven't got time for that."

Andrew looked downcast, but Kristy put her hand on his shoulder and gave him a squeeze. "Don't worry, Andrew," she said. "Midgie's a lovely little dog, and you'll have a good time entering him in the pet show. And that's all that matters, right? Having a good time?"

(Does that sound familiar? Kristy and I had come up with the same reasonable, grown-up-sounding line. I only wished that some of the kids would start to agree with it.)

"Well, I'm going to have a good time," said Karen.

"Great!" said Kristy.

"Because *my* pet is definitely going to win first prize," Karen finished.

Kristy rolled her eyes. "Which pet are you entering?" she asked.

"Well, that's the only problem," said Karen. "I can't decide between Rocky and Emily Junior."

Rocky is Seth's cat. And Emily Junior is (ugh) a rat! Emily Junior lives with Karen's mother and stepfather, instead of at Watson's house.

"Rocky's a bit funny-looking," mused Karen. "I'd probably have to dress her up or something."

Kristy pictured Rocky in Karen's dressing-up clothes – her "lovely lady" clothes, as she calls them. High heels, a big hat . . . or maybe a wedding veil. Kristy tried not to laugh out loud.

"But if I entered Emily Junior, she'd probably be the only rat there. Maybe she'd win a prize just for that," Karen continued. "The only thing is that I'd probably have to give her a bath, and I don't know how much she'd like that," she added. "I just can't decide."

"What about Boo-Boo?" asked David Michael. "Doesn't anybody want to enter Boo-Boo?"

Everybody laughed. Why? Because Boo-Boo is not just any cat. Boo-Boo is the oldest, fattest and *meanest* cat you've ever seen.

"He's too nasty," said Karen. "He'd probably hiss at the judges."

"Yeah," said Andrew. "And how could we even pick him up to carry him to the show? He's too fat."

Obviously, Boo-Boo was out of the question as a pet-show contestant.

"But what about Emily Michelle?" asked David Michael. "She hasn't got a pet to enter."

"Pet!" said Emily Michelle, smiling and clapping her hands.

David Michael started to laugh all of a sudden.

"What's so funny?" asked Karen.

"What if *Emily* enters Boo-Boo?" he said.

Kristy thought of Emily trying to lug Boo-Boo to the pet show. "That cat is almost bigger than *she* is!" she said, laughing.

Karen and Andrew cracked up, too. Then Karen got serious. "But Emily's too young to enter a pet, right?" she asked Kristy.

"I think so," said Kristy. "She doesn't really understand what we're talking about." It was true. Emily Michelle was playing happily with her Tonka truck, totally absorbed in shifting a little pile of pebbles from one area to another

"Rrrr. . ." said Emily, making a pretty good truck noise.

As the afternoon wore on, some of the other kids in Kristy's neighbourhood came over to play. Hannie and Linny Papadakis were the first to arrive. They'd brought their little sister, Sari, to play with Emily. They're just about the same age, even though Sari's more advanced in some ways than Emily. Emily is having a difficult time learning certain games – maybe because she had a very hard time for the first year or so of her life in Vietnam.

Hannie (she's seven, and in the same class at school as Karen) and Linny (he's eight, and he's David Michael's best friend) were just as excited about the pet show as everybody else. It was all they could talk about.

It was the same with Scott and Timmy Hsu, who live down the street, and Max and Amanda Delaney. They all gathered on Kristy's front lawn, and nobody wanted to talk about anything but the pet show.

Karen and Amanda are friends, even though Amanda can be kind of stuck-up. (Which is why Hannie can't stand her.) Max, who's six, is always trying to be friends with the other kids, but it seems that David Michael and Linny would rather avoid him.

Scott and Timmy Hsu are good kids, and everybody likes them. In fact, Hannie and Scott are married! (Well, they're pretend married. Karen's just got married, too, to a boy in her class.)

Anyway, with all these kids, some of whom like each other and some of whom might be looking for a fight, Kristy thought it would be a good idea to forget the pet show for a while and organize a game.

"How about freeze tag?" she yelled over the commotion.

"Yeah!" cried David Michael. "I'm It!"

Everybody scattered, and David Michael started trying to tag them. Emily was the only one who didn't quite "get" the rules of the game. Whenever David Michael tagged her, she collapsed in a heap on the ground, giggling and shrieking as if he were tickling her to death.

"She won't stop wriggling!" complained David Michael to Kristy. "She's supposed to freeze."

Kristy told David Michael that Emily was just too young. "C'mon, Emily-bird," she said, scooping her up. "You and I will watch from the porch."

The game went on for some time, until the older kids, at least, had had a chance to be It. Then everybody flopped down on the grass, panting. Kristy brought out paper cups and a jug of lemonade and passed out some to all the kids.

Then they began talking about the pet show again. Karen was the one who brought it up. "Which one of you is going to enter Priscilla?" she asked Amanda and Max. (Priscilla is the Delaneys' cat.) Karen's always got her nose in everyone's business. She's a bit like a young Kristy. She's full of energy and good ideas, and sometimes she gets herself into trouble by saying things before she's really thought them out.

Like this time.

For a moment, neither Max nor Amanda answered her question. Then they both spoke up at once.

"Me!" said Max.

"I am!" said Amanda.

"She's *my* cat!" they both said, in perfect unison.

Uh-oh, said Kristy to herself. Trouble.

"Priscilla will be the most beautiful cat in the show," said Amanda. "Nobody else around here owns a pedigree white Persian that cost four hundred dollars." Amanda has a habit of pointing out how much everything costs. I suppose she *is* kind of stuck-up sometimes – but she's basically a good kid. "And I intend to get first prize with her," she finished.

Before Max could argue with his sister, Hannie jumped into the battle. "What do you mean, Priscilla is the most beautiful cat around? Pat the cat is prettier than that old dust mop any day! And cleverer, too."

Pat the cat is Hannie's kitten. All the Papadakises' pets have funny rhyming names. There's Pat the cat, Noodle the poodle and Myrtle the turtle.

"Dust mop!" repeated Amanda, outraged. "How dare you—"

"And she's a stupid dust mop, too," said Hannie. "She can't even do any tricks."

"So what?" asked Amanda. "She's a cat, not a dog. Cats aren't supposed to do tricks."

"Pat the cat can do tricks," said Hannie. "She can dance around on her hind legs." She smiled meanly at Amanda. "The judges are going to love her," she said.

Kristy thought it was time to change the subject – or at least to get the focus of the conversation off cats.

"Who are you going to enter, Linny?" she asked.

He smiled at her. Linny can be a little shy, but he's great if you draw him out. "I'm going to enter Myrtle," he said. "I'm going to paint her shell so she looks really cool."

"Great!" said Kristy. Then she looked over at Scott and Timmy. They looked a little downcast. "What about you two?" she asked.

"We haven't got any pets," said Timmy. "So I suppose we can't enter the show."

Before Kristy could begin to comfort them, Karen spoke up. "You can borrow Boo-Boo!" she said. "He might not win, but at least you'd have a pet to enter." Timmy's eyes lit up.

"And you can borrow Noodle, Scott!" said Hannie. "After all, you are my husband. Noodle's sort of your pet, too, right?"

Kristy looked seriously at Hannie and Karen. "Are you two sure about that?" she asked. "Lending your pet to somebody is quite a big deal." She didn't want to see any more fights spring up.

"Hmmmm. . ." said Karen. "Maybe you're right. Forget it, Timmy. What if Boo-Boo did win a prize? Then I'd be furious."

"I didn't think of that," said Hannie. "I take it back, Scott. You can't have Noodle after all."

Scott looked stunned. "I thought you said that he was my pet, too!" he said. "Does this mean we're getting a divorce?"

"I don't know," said Hannie. "Maybe. But anyway, you'll have to find your own pet."

Kristy groaned. It looked as if the honeymoon was over for those two. And it looked as if her latest idea might end up being more trouble than it was worth. The pet show was supposed to be fun – but the kids seemed to be taking it a little too seriously.

7th CHAPTER

"Hey, Princess," said Lisa. "How's it going?"

I smiled. "Fine," I said. "I'm raring to go today, aren't you?"

Lisa nodded.

"You'd better be," said Hilary, overhearing me. "You haven't been doing too well so far. Sleeping Beauty's sleeping on the job."

I ignored her. I knew that none of the things that had happened at the first and second rehearsal had been my fault. But today would be different. Today, things would go smoothly.

It was the day of the third rehearsal, and it was time to change out of my school clothes. I pulled on my new pink tights and my new black leotard. Over the tights I pulled on my new (blue) leg warmers. I put on my new baggy sweat shirt.

"Woo, new outfit!" said Lisa. "Nice!"

"Thanks!" I said.

How did I get all those brand-new things? I used my hard-earned babysitting money, that's how. And I hated having to do it. Of course it's nice to have new things – I retired my older things to serve as spares right away. Still, it doesn't really seem fair. I'm trying to save that money for other things. But there was no way I could get by with just one of everything – I'd learned that lesson well enough. So I bit the bullet and paid out the money.

I'd even stretched my cash to buy one other thing – something that I hoped would prevent anyone from taking my stuff ever again. It was a new dance bag. The old one had been big enough, and it was still in pretty good shape. But the new one has something that the old one didn't have. The new one has a zip at either end, and the zip tabs meet in the middle. Guess what? There's a tiny padlock that I can use to lock the zips together.

Can you believe I actually have to lock up a grimy old leotard and a ratty pair of leg warmers? As my parents would say, "What is the world coming to?"

By the time I'd finished putting up my hair, everybody else was in the studio. Good. For some reason, I didn't want them to see me locking up my bag. I closed the bag, took out the tiny key, and made sure the little padlock was locked tight.

Then I put the key on the thin gold chain I was wearing around my neck.

Mme Noelle doesn't really approve of wearing jewellery in class, so I usually don't. But she says it's okay as long as it doesn't get in the way. I tucked the necklace under my leotard and checked in the mirror. It hardly showed, so Madame probably wouldn't even notice it.

Once rehearsal started, I forgot about the key. For a change, nothing bad was happening to me, and I was free to concentrate on practising my steps. Mme Noelle was giving me approving looks.

"Beautiful!" she said, as I *bourée*'d across the floor. "But *smile*, Mademoiselle Romsey. Relax and enjoy it!"

Oh, sure. Have you ever tiptoed across a whole floor, moving nothing but your legs in the tiniest, controlled movements? I tried to smile, but my feet were killing me. A ballet dancer's feet are almost *always* killing her.

We changed to another step, and I had a chance to relax for a moment as I waited my turn to show Mme Noelle my technique. Lisa Jones did a lovely *arabesque* at the back of the room. She was just practising while she waited her turn. Carrie was on the floor, showing Mme Noelle her stuff.

After I took my turn, I stood again in the little knot of dancers, waiting for Madame to tell us what was next. I heard Hilary whispering behind me, and turned quickly to warn her to be quiet. (Madame *hates* it when we whisper.) Just as I turned, I heard a tiny *clink*. I looked down. Uh-oh. My necklace had dropped to the ground. The catch must have come unfastened.

I knelt quickly and grabbed it before anyone saw. Then, still kneeling, I scrambled to fasten it around my neck. When I stood up, I realized that I'd missed Mme Noelle's directions. I had no idea what we were supposed to do next – and I was out in front of the group, which meant I might have to go first.

I looked around desperately. Mme Noelle's back was turned – she was just about to put the needle down onto the record. Carrie was standing next to me.

"Quick!" I said. "What did she say?"

"*Tour jetés*," replied Carrie. "One of us at a time, across the room."

I tried to catch my breath. *Tour jetés.* No problem.

"Lead off, Mademoiselle Romsey!" said Mme Noelle.

Oh, boy. I gathered myself together and took a deep breath. Then I took off, running diagonally across the room and executing a perfect *tour jeté*. (Which is a big, running leap, in case you've forgotten.) Well, almost perfect. The only problem with it was the landing.

I landed like a sack of potatoes, sprawled out all over the floor. For just a second, I had no idea where I was. I shook my head and blinked. How could I have fallen so hard? Then I felt a sharp pain. My ankle was killing me. Everybody rushed over to where I was lying.

"Jessi, are you okay?" asked Katie Beth. "What happened?"

I sat up, rubbing my ankle. "I don't know. It seemed as if I'd slipped on something when I landed." I looked around me, checking the floor. "Look!" I said, pointing to a nearby spot. "It's all wet."

Hilary knelt to look at it. "Boy, that's slippery," she said. "No wonder you fell."

"Where'd that mess come from, anyway?" asked another girl.

Then Mme Noelle worked her way into the circle of girls standing around me. "You are all right, Mademoiselle Romsey?" she asked. I nodded. "Good," she said. "All of you, back to your places," she added, waving the girls away from me. She helped me up, and then she examined the wet spot on the floor.

She clapped her hands. "Lisa Jones!" she said. "Please to run and fetch zee man who cleans zee floors!" Lisa ran out of the door and headed for the caretaker's room.

Madame turned back to me. I was standing there with all my weight on my right leg. My left one didn't seem to want to hold me up. "How does zee onkle feel?"

she asked me, looking intently into my eyes.

I couldn't lie. "It – it hurts," I said. All I wanted to do was to keep on dancing. I could hardly stand the fact that I'd interrupted rehearsal for the third time in a row. But my ankle did hurt. A lot.

"Come," said Mme Noelle. She walked with me over to the side of the room (or rather, she walked; I limped), sat me down on a chair, and knelt in front of me. "Let's have a look," she said.

She picked up my foot and examined my ankle. Mme Noelle has seen a lot of injuries in her years of dancing – ballerinas are always hurting themselves. So she knew what she was doing. Anyway, even I could see that my ankle was swelling up and beginning to look bruised.

"Not so bad," said Mme Noelle. "It is not sprained, I sink. Just a strain. But you must see zee doctor." She looked into my face. "Tell me," she said. "Why were you performing zee *tour jeté*?"

"What do you mean?" I asked. "That's what we were supposed to be doing, wasn't it?"

She shook her head. "You were not listening well, mademoiselle. I said nossing about zee *tour jeté*. You were all to show me your best *glissade changée*."

I felt such a fool. I must have misunderstood Carrie. "I'm so sorry, Madame

Noelle," I said. "You're right. I wasn't listening well." I hung my head, ashamed. I just hate to disappoint her.

"It is all right, Jessica," said Mme Noelle gently. "Zee important sing for now is for your onkle to have zee chonce to heal." She smiled at me.

Then she dropped the bomb. "You must not donce for several days."

Not dance! But what about the production? How were they going to rehearse *The Sleeping Beauty* without me?

Mme Noelle answered my question before I even had a chance to ask it. She stood up and faced the class. "Mademoiselle Parsons," she said in a louder voice, gesturing to Katie Beth. "You will take over zee role of Princess Aurora—"

I couldn't believe my ears. Had I lost the lead role just because I'd slipped on some stupid wet spot?

"– for zee next rehearsal, and perhops some uthers, until Jessica is able to donce again," she finished.

Phew. I was relieved. At least I hadn't completely lost my chance to perform as Princess Aurora. But still, I felt like crying. There haven't been too many times in my life when I've been unable to dance – but there's nothing that can make me quite as miserable. Mme Noelle says that injuries are a part of a "doncer's" life, and that we'd better get used to them. I don't know if I'll *ever* be able to take things like this gracefully.

Mme Noelle clapped her hands. "Shall we continue?" she said. Then she turned back to me. "I would like to allow you to stay and watch zee rehearsal, but I sink you need to get off zat foot. Perhops you should have your father take you to zee doctor, and then you can go home and lie down."

I nodded miserably and limped out of the studio. I couldn't help noticing, as I crossed the floor, that Katie Beth was absolutely beaming. I'm not saying that she was happy to see me get hurt – but she certainly didn't look all that heartbroken about it.

I smiled broadly at her. I wasn't about to give her the satisfaction of seeing me miserable.

I headed for the pay phone and phoned my father's office. "Mr Ramsey, please," I said when somebody answered. Then my dad picked up his extension. Just hearing his voice say "Hello?" made all the tears I'd been holding inside well up and overflow.

"Daddy!" I wailed, feeling like a two-year-old.

"Jessi!" he said. "What is it? Are you all right?" He sounded frantic.

I hadn't meant to scare him. I took a deep breath and started again. "I'm okay," I said, sniffling a little. "It's just that I hurt my ankle during rehearsal. Madame Noelle says I should see a doctor." I drew a ragged breath. "Oh, Daddy, she says I can't dance for a while!"

"It'll be okay, sweetie," he said. "Now you sit tight. I'm on my way."

I hung up the phone and went into the dressing room to change. This had been the worst of three bad rehearsals, and in a way I was just grateful that it was over.

I looked up at the framed picture of Mikhail Baryshnikov that hangs above one of the basins. He looked back at me, smiling his cocky smile. "Oh, Misha," I said. (I feel as if I know him – he's my favourite dancer of all time – so it seems okay to use his nickname.) "I just want to crawl under a rock."

He kept on smiling, and I could swear I heard him say, "Oh, Jessi, relax. So you can't dance for a few days. If that's the worst that happens, that's not so bad."

I knew Misha was right. And if my mother were there she'd agree with him. "Get over it, Jessi!" she'd say. I decided to take their advice – even if it *was* all in my mind.

It was time to put all this bad luck behind me. So I had to take a break from dancing. Big deal. When I came back, I'd be rested and better than ever.

I pulled my new dance bag out from under the bench, and my heart sank. A piece of paper was jammed over the padlock. Another note. I picked it up carefully and unfolded it. I read it and gasped. Here's what it said: I TOLD YOU SO. FROM NOW ON, WATCH OUT.

I felt a chill run down my spine. I thought of the wet spot on the floor, and how I'd slipped and fallen. Had somebody *planned* my fall? And if so, who? And why? How could anybody do such a mean thing? My head was full of questions. And my ankle was throbbing. I changed and got out of that place as quickly as I could.

8th CHAPTER

"I'm sorry, Jessi, but I have to agree with your teacher," said Dr Dellenkamp. My dad had driven me straight to her surgery. She held my ankle gently as she examined it. "This looks like a pretty bad strain. Still, it could have been worse."

I nodded glumly. "I know. I could have sprained it, or even broken it, right?"

"According to what you told me, I'd have to say that you got off lightly," she agreed. "But it's important that you give even a minor injury like this plenty of time to heal."

"How long do I have to stay off my foot?" I asked. I held my breath as I waited for her answer. Was that one fall – which happened so quickly – going to ruin my chance to dance the part of Princess Aurora?

"About three days, I'd say," she answered. "Longer if it's still sore by then."

Three days. That wasn't so bad. I ran over the rehearsal schedule in my mind. I would only have to miss one rehearsal. I gave a sigh of relief.

"Now let's wrap it well," said Dr Dellenkamp, pulling a bandage out of a drawer. "And I'm going to give you some crutches to use, too. You really need to keep your weight off that ankle." She smiled at me. "Sound okay?"

I nodded. "Whatever you say. I just want to be dancing again as soon as possible."

My ankle hurt pretty badly that night, especially when I was trying to get to sleep. It throbbed painfully and kept me awake. Maybe it was lucky that I didn't have to dance at rehearsal the next day – I was wiped out.

It felt funny to sit on a chair against the wall in the studio and watch everybody else rehearse. Katie Beth was in her element, dancing my part. Carrie kept shooting glances my way – and maybe it was all in my mind, but she looked a bit guilty to me. I started to wonder . . . had one of them been writing those notes? Was it only coincidence that water had spilled on the floor? And had I really misunderstood Carrie – or had she told me to do the wrong step on purpose?

I didn't like being so suspicious – but I was really beginning to feel scared. It seemed that *somebody* was out to get me –

and the stakes were pretty high. Somebody wanted me out of the way so that she could dance the lead role – that seemed obvious. And she didn't care if I got hurt in the process.

After rehearsal, some of the girls gathered around the chair where I sat.

"How are you feeling, Jessi?" That was Hilary, sounding syrupy sweet. She'd never cared about my welfare before. . .

"I'm okay," I said. "It doesn't hurt very badly. I think I'll be able to dance again by the next rehearsal."

"That's great!" said Lisa.

I looked at her closely. Was she really being sincere? Suddenly, it seemed as if any one of the girls in my class could be suspected of trying to get rid of me. What a terrible feeling!

I waited until everybody else had cleared out. Then I hopped into the dressing room on my crutches. It was embarrassing to limp around like a cripple – I didn't want anyone laughing at me. I checked my locker, just to make sure there wasn't a mouldy old leotard in there that I should take home and put in the wash.

There wasn't. But there *was* another note. "What's going on here?" I said out loud, as I unfolded it. Once again I saw that blood-red ink. IT COULD HAVE BEEN WORSE, it said, echoing Dr

Dellenkamp's words. But then it went on. TOO BAD IT WASN'T.

At the next BSC meeting, I poured out the story to my friends. I hadn't talked about it very much yet – mainly because I was embarrassed. It had seemed silly. Until now.

"This person, whoever she is, sounds really mean, Jessi," said Mary Anne. "This is serious."

"I know," I said. "I'm starting to get scared. What if I *really* get hurt?"

"That's what worries me," said Mallory. "But what are you going to do? Maybe you should talk to Madame Noelle."

"I can't do that," I said. "She'd never believe that such things were going on in her school. She'd think I was making it all up." I paused for a moment, while Kristy answered the phone. Should I tell them what I'd been thinking of doing?

"Actually," I said, when the job at the Papadakises' had been arranged, "I've been thinking that maybe I should just pull out of the production. I love that role, but it's not worth risking my life for it."

Mallory gasped. "Give up the production!" she said. "You're mad, Jessi. That may be the best part you've ever got. You can't let them scare you out of it."

"Mal's right," said Claud. "You can't give up. I've already bought a new outfit to wear to your opening night." She laughed. "I'm only kidding. But really, we'll help you work out what to do."

Dawn leaned forward. "Hey, Jessi, have you still got the notes?"

I nodded. "They're right here," I said, digging into my new high-security dance bag.

"Let's see them," she said. I handed them over, and she started to examine each one closely. "Hmm, I can see why you're feeling scared," she said, after she'd read each one. She passed them round to the others. There was a pause while everybody read them – and while Stacey answered a couple of job calls.

"Still, Jessi," said Kristy after a few minutes. "The *idea* was to scare you. You can't give this person the satisfaction."

"I've got an idea," said Mallory suddenly. "What if we came to watch one of your rehearsals? We could be – what d'you call it? Objective observers? And maybe we could pinpoint the suspect."

I thought about it for a minute. "Our next rehearsal is on the stage where the performance is going to be held," I said slowly, working it out. "If you sat at the back of the theatre, maybe no one would notice you."

"It sounds like fun," said Stacey. "But that's in Stamford, right? How are we going to get there?"

"No problem," said Kristy. "I bet Charlie would drive us."

Just then the phone rang, and Kristy jumped to answer it. By the time the job had been assigned, I had decided that the plan sounded good. I agreed not to drop out of the production, at least not until my friends could observe a rehearsal.

"Now that that's settled," said Kristy, "what about the pet show? I know I sounded a bit down on it in my notebook entry, but don't you think it'll still be fun?"

She sounded as if she needed to be convinced.

"I do!" said Mary Anne. "And I know the kids do, even if it is stirring up some competition. They're having fun already."

"I know," said Mallory. "I babysat for the Perkins girls yesterday afternoon, and you should have seen them trying to give Chewy a bath. What a mess!"

Chewy is Chewbacca, the Perkinses' dog. He's a black Labrador retriever, and boy, is he crazy! He's the most energetic dog I've ever seen – and since he's also big and strong, sometimes he creates total chaos in that house.

"First of all," said Mallory, "every time they finally wrestled him into the bath, he'd jump out again and shake water off all over the bathroom."

"Oh, no!" said Dawn, groaning. "I hope Mrs Perkins was prepared for that."

"She said that whatever the girls wanted to do was okay," said Mallory. "I suppose she realizes that it's only water. Anyway, then they'd get him into the bath, and one of them would have to get in *with* him to try to hold him. The other one would pick up the bar of soap and start scrubbing. Then the soap would slip out of her hands and on to the floor, and Chewy—"

"Would jump out to retrieve it, I bet!" finished Dawn. "That dog can never let anything drop to the ground without running to pick it up."

"No joke!" said Mallory. "He looked pretty surprised the first time he picked up the soap. It must have tasted so gross! But he kept doing it again and again."

"So did he finally get clean?" asked Stacey.

"He was getting there," said Mallory. "But then Gabbie left the room for a minute and came back carrying RC."

That's RC for Rat Catcher, the Perkinses' brown tiger cat.

"She must have thought RC needed a bath, too – because the next thing I knew, she'd dumped her in the bath with Chewy!"

Oh, my lord.

"RC jumped right out and streaked out of the door, looking like a drowned rat. And Chewy chased after her. Water was flying all over the place!" said Mallory.

By now we were hysterical, imagining the scene.

"Of course, RC ran under the porch, and Chewy followed her. Both of them got covered with dirt. So the whole thing was a waste!"

"I'm sure Chewy would have got dirty again by the time of the pet show, anyway," said Mary Anne.

"That's what I tried to tell Gabbie and Myriah," said Mallory. "But they were too upset to listen. What a day! It took us the rest of the afternoon to clean up the bathroom."

"I had a similar experience with Linny Papadakis and his turtle," said Kristy.

"He gave his *turtle* a bath?" asked Claudia.

"No, he didn't exactly give Myrtle a bath," said Kristy. "What happened was—" But she was interrupted by a job call. Mrs Barrett needed a sitter for Buddy, Suzi and Marnie. Mallory got the job. Then Kristy went on with her story.

"Linny spent all afternoon painting Myrtle's shell," she said. "He used these water-based poster paints, since I'd told him that his model paints might not be very good for Myrtle. You know what? He did a great job. Myrtle looked really cool when he was finished."

"What did he paint?" asked Claudia.

"There were these red lightning bolts running down the sides of the shell, and yellow stars," said Kristy. "And all kinds of other things. We took Myrtle outside with us afterwards, so that Linny could admire her once in a while as he played."

"Sounds as if a disaster is coming up!" said Mary Anne.

"You're right," said Kristy. "Linny got involved in a game of Statues with some other kids, and Myrtle crawled over to this plastic pool at the back of the garden. By the time we got to her, all the paint had washed off."

"Oh, poor Linny!" I said.

"I know," said Kristy. "He was really crushed. But at least he learned that he's got to keep Myrtle away from water if he wants the paint job to last."

We talked about the pet show for the rest of our meeting that day – it was clearly the "main event" for a lot of kids in Stoneybrook. I only hoped we'd all live through it.

9th CHAPTER

Thursday

Why, oh why did we ever think that a pet show would be fun? So far it seems to be causing nothing but messes, and tears, and trouble of every kind. I should have known that the pet show had something to do with the way Buddy and Suzi were acting... Oh, well, I suppose it worked out in the end. And so will the pet show. Right, everyone? Right?

Poor Mallory. She realized the minute she entered the Barrett's house that she was in for a bad afternoon. As usual, Mrs Barrett was running late (she's sort of disorganized), and she left without giving Mallory any instructions about the job. (We always get to jobs on time – or even early – so that parents can let us know if they have any special instructions for us. But in Mrs Barrett's case, arriving early hardly ever does any good.)

Mrs Barrett was divorced not too long ago, and I suppose looking after three kids on her own isn't easy. I'll say one thing, though – it hasn't taken a toll on her appearance. Mrs Barrett is totally gorgeous. She looks like a model, with her beautiful chestnut-coloured hair. Anyway, Mrs Barrett rushed out as Mallory came in, leaving a cloud of perfumed air behind her.

She also left three grumpy kids. Buddy, who's eight, is usually in a pretty good mood – he's always got a lot of energy. But that afternoon he seemed sulky and withdrawn. And five-year-old Suzi's round face looked crabby. She can pout with the best of them. Mallory said that Suzi's lower lip was stuck out about as far as it could go.

Marnie, the baby (she's two), was wailing like a fire engine. Mallory scooped her up. "What is it, Marnie?" she asked. But the answer was obvious. Marnie's nappy was soaking wet.

"C'mon, you two," said Mallory to Buddy and Suzi. "Keep me company while I change your sister. Then we'll have a snack, okay?"

Buddy shot Suzi a Look. "Do I have to?" he asked. "I don't even want to be in the same room as her." He pointed at Suzi, who pouted even harder.

"Guess what, Buddy Barrett," said Suzi.

"What?" said Buddy, flatly.

"You're a nut!" Ordinarily, this joke gets a big laugh out of both of them. But this time, Buddy just shook his head.

"Guess what," he said back to Suzi.

"What?" she asked.

"Your whole family's a nut," Buddy sneered.

"Ha, ha!" said Suzi triumphantly. "You're *in* my family. That means you're a nut, just like I said."

Mallory could see that this was going nowhere. "Okay, okay," she said. "C'mon, let's get this nappy changing over with. Suzi, where has your mum been keeping the nappies lately?" The Barretts' house is pretty messy. "A pigsty", Stacey called it, the first time she sat there.

Sometimes we try to tidy up while we're there, but Mallory didn't think that was a good idea, with Buddy and Suzi in such bad moods. So she asked Suzi to lead her to the nappies (Suzi and Marnie share a room), and asked Buddy to help her distract

Marnie while she changed the wet nappy.

"Moonie, Meanie, Mownie!" said Buddy, dancing around the changing table and making faces while Mallory wiped Marnie's bottom. His technique wasn't brilliant, but Mal had to admit that it worked. Marnie was smiling and waving at him, instead of crying and kicking. She's usually not too keen on having her nappy changed, so the distraction helped a lot.

"Thanks, Buddy," said Mallory. "Thanks, Suzi. You two were a big help." She lifted up the newly dry Marnie, who was making what Buddy and Suzi call her "ham face", which she only does when she's happy. Then she led them back downstairs. "Now let's have a snack and you can tell me why you're both feeling so grumpy today."

"I'm not grumpy!" whined Suzi.

"Yes, you are!" said Buddy. "But I'm not. I'm *happy*!" He gave Mallory a big – and very false – smile.

Mallory shrugged and turned to get some crisps out of the cupboard.

"Ow!" she heard, behind her. She turned around. Suzi was rubbing her shin. "He kicked me," she said, pointing at Buddy. Mallory gave Buddy a Look.

"Buddy, don't kick your sister," she said, turning back to the cupboard.

"Hey!" This time it was Buddy's voice.

"What is it?" asked Mallory. She'd had just about enough of their squabbling.

"She poked me!" said Buddy.

"Did not!" yelled Suzi.

"Gobbydoo," said Marnie, waving her hands in the air.

Mallory put her hands on her hips. "Okay, that's it. I want to know what's going on between you two. You usually get on okay together. So what's the problem today?"

Suzi looked at Buddy.

Buddy glared at Suzi.

"It's Pow," they both said at once.

"I want to enter him in the pet show," said Buddy. "He's my dog. I got him for my second birthday, when he was just a puppy. Suzi wasn't even born yet then."

"But Mummy said he belongs to all of us now!" said Suzi. "And I help you feed him sometimes. *I* want to put him in the pet show!"

Pow is the Barretts' basset hound. Buddy sometimes likes to tell sitters that Pow is the meanest dog in the world. But he's not. He's sleepy and slow and puts up very well with the kids' teasing.

Mallory sighed. She'd left her own house hearing a similar fight between her brothers and sisters. Ever since the Pikes had got their invitation to the pet show, they'd been squabbling over which one of them should be able to enter Frodo.

Frodo is the Pikes' hamster. They got him when my family got Misty, which means that he and Misty are brother and sister. I'm not great at long division, but I do know one thing: one hamster doesn't go evenly into seven kids. Mallory told me later she'd given up on helping her brothers and sisters decide which of them should enter Frodo in the show. It seemed impossible.

"I know you two can sort this out," said Mallory to Buddy and Suzi. Actually, she had her doubts about that, but she knew she had to say something. "It's really nothing to fight about. Let's finish our snack and go outside to play." Being outside just *had* to be better than being cooped up inside with these sour-pusses, she thought.

After the kids had eaten, Mallory tidied up the kitchen (including washing a sink full of breakfast plates that Mrs Barrett had left behind). Then she herded her charges out of the door. Marnie climbed into her buggy, and Mallory pushed her down the front path. Suzi ran to show Mal all the flowers that she and her mum had planted. Buddy tagged along behind them, making faces behind Suzi's back.

Then Mal saw him smile and wave. She looked up to see Haley and Matt Braddock waving back. Mallory smiled with relief. Great! Now Buddy and Suzi would have something to do besides pick on each other.

She called hello, and also made the "hello" sign to Matt. Matt's deaf, so we've all learned at least a little bit of sign language. Haley makes a great interpreter (she's fluent in sign) but it's nice to be able to "speak" to Matt directly, too.

Matt signed back. Then he and Buddy signed quickly to each other.

"What are they saying?" Mallory asked Haley.

"Matt asked if Buddy wanted to play with a ball, and Buddy said yes," she answered. "Hey, can me and Suzi play, too?" she asked the boys, signing as she spoke.

The game was organized within minutes, and Mal and Marnie settled down to watch.

"And it's a high pop fly to centre field!" yelled Buddy, after he'd hit a blooper over Matt's (the pitcher's) head. "A triple!" He ran around the garden, pretending to tag the bases.

Then it was Haley's turn to bat. "Watch out," she said, swinging the bat. "I'm going to hit it out of the park!" She put down the bat to sign the same thing to Matt. He signed something back, laughing.

"What do you mean, girls can't hit?" yelled Haley. She gave a mighty swing and missed completely. "Drat," she said. She shook back her hair and dug her feet into the grass. "Pitch me another one," she said, signing along. This time, she connected. Buddy (still standing on "third base") and Matt watched the ball fly over their heads.

Haley forgot to run – she just stood there and watched the ball disappear.

And disappear it did – right on to the porch roof. "Great hit, Haley!" said Mallory.

"Yeah, just great!" said Buddy. "Now we've lost the ball. Why couldn't you have just hit it into the back garden?" he asked Haley. "Then Pow would have found it, no matter where it went."

"Oh, Pow Pow Pow," said Haley. "All I ever hear about these days is what a great dog Pow is and how he's going to win the pet show." She frowned at Buddy. "I don't think Pow is *that* great a dog," she added.

"Well, he's a lot better than no dog at all," said Buddy.

Haley bit her lip. Just then, Matt came over and looked at her questioningly. She signed to him, letting him know what Buddy had said. Matt gave Buddy a dirty look. Then he signed back to Haley.

"He says, "So what if we don't have a pet?" Haley explained. "We're still invited to the pet show, you know."

"But you can't win a prize," said Suzi.

"Well, what makes you so sure *you'll* win any prizes with that fat old mongrel?" asked Haley.

Suzi burst into tears. "Pow is *not* a mongrel," she wailed. "He's a pedigree basset hound."

Mallory decided it was time to step in. "Okay, everyone. Let's not fight about it—" she began. But Buddy was shouting at Suzi, drowning Mallory out.

"You're right, he's a basset hound. But you're not going to win any prizes with him, anyway. *I* am!"

Oh, no, thought Mallory. Not *that* one again. She stepped towards Buddy, ready to separate him from the others before he got any angrier.

Just then, Haley shrieked. "You don't have to *pinch* me!" she said angrily to Suzi. Then she took Matt's hand and started to drag him out of the garden. "C'mon," she said, forgetting to sign as she spoke. "Let's get out of here."

Matt seemed to know what she'd said even without the signs. He gave one last angry glance back at Buddy and Suzi, and stalked out of the garden at his sister's side.

"Oh, great," said Mallory. "Look, it's time to stop this fighting." She sat Buddy and Suzi down on the porch steps. Marnie, still in her buggy, had fallen asleep – and the fight hadn't even woken her up.

"Look, you two. There's no rule that says that only one person can enter each pet in the pet show," said Mallory. She'd been thinking the problem over, and had come to realize that this was the only solution. "Why don't you enter Pow – together!"

Buddy and Suzi looked at each other hopefully. Mal could see that they both thought it was a good idea, but neither one wanted to be the first to give in.

"You could be in charge of his looks, Suzi," said Mal, trying to push the idea. "And Buddy, you could teach him some new tricks. How about it?"

Buddy and Suzi smiled at each other. "Yeah!" said Buddy. "Maybe I can teach him how to roll over, just like Aunt Jo's dog does!"

"And I can give him a bath, and paint his toenails pink, and put ribbons on him," said Suzi. "He'll look so, so beautiful!"

They ran off to find Pow, leaving Mal alone on the porch. She shook her head and spoke to the still-sleeping Marnie. "Sweetie, that was a close one," she said. "I thought they were going to really fall out this time." Marnie shifted in the buggy and smiled in her sleep.

Later that afternoon, her job over, Mal walked back to her house. She was hoping desperately that her brothers and sisters would have settled the Frodo issue while she was away. She couldn't take any more arguments that day.

Luckily for her, they had. For some reason – nobody knew why – the triplets had suddenly given up their claim to Frodo. They'd said that Nicky could enter him in the show, and Nicky had generously agreed to share him with Vanessa, Claire and Margo.

Mallory was too grateful for the peaceful atmosphere at home – and too tired – to wonder about the triplets' motives for very long. She knew they must be up to something. But she'd wait for the pet show to find out what they had up their sleeves.

10th CHAPTER

"Claudia, do you *mind*?"

"What, Stacey?"

"Your elbow. It's in my ear!"

"I can't help it, Stace! There's nowhere else to put it."

"Can't you move over a little?"

"Not with Mallory on my lap, I can't. Anyway, I don't think I'll ever be able to move my legs again – there's no feeling left in them."

Mallory squealed. "Stop it, Claudia! I'm not really that heavy, am I?" she asked, trying to shift her weight.

Six of us were packed into Charlie's car, the Junk Bucket (Mary Anne couldn't come; she had a sitting job), and believe me, it was a tight squeeze. It was a rainy Saturday afternoon. We were on our way to Stamford. I had a rehearsal, and everybody else was coming to watch it.

Kristy and I were in the front seat with Charlie; I got to sit in the front so that I could give him directions to the civic centre. Dawn, Stacey, Claudia and Mallory were all jammed into the back seat, and they'd been complaining about how squashed they were ever since we'd pulled out of Claudia's drive. (We'd all met there to wait for Charlie and Kristy.)

"Hey, who pinched me?" asked Dawn. Then there was a whole lot of squealing and giggling from the back seat, while everybody pinched everybody else.

"Hey, calm down back there," said Charlie, looking in the rear-view mirror. "How am I supposed to drive with all that racket?"

They were quiet for a moment. Then, as Charlie stopped at a red light, Dawn saw a cute boy walking across the street, holding a newspaper over his head to keep off the rain. "Wooo!" she said loudly. "Follow that man!"

"Dawn!" said Kristy, blushing. "Stop it! What if he hears you?"

"He can't hear her," said Claudia. "The windows are rolled up. Watch – I'll prove it. Hey, gorgeous!"

The guy turned around and stared at the Junk Bucket. All of us ducked down in our seats, giggling. "Can you believe it?" asked Claud. "Do you think he heard me? Oh, I'm going to die!"

"Well, please don't die in my car," said Charlie. "What would I tell your parents? Now, come on, quieten down."

"Okay, Charlie," said Claud. "I'm sorry." For a few minutes, there was silence from the back seat. Then the giggling started up again, as Stacey and Claudia discussed Jennifer Cooke's latest outfit.

I was hoping that Charlie wouldn't get too annoyed and dump us all on the street to walk the rest of the way. I was nervous enough about this rehearsal, and I at least wanted to be on time for it. But Charlie kept his cool. And actually, I was glad of the distraction that the rest of my friends were providing. It kept me from thinking too much about the rehearsal.

Why was I so nervous? Well, for one thing, I was worried about my dancing lately. All the little "accidents" during class and the notes were really throwing me off, and I knew I wasn't dancing as well as I usually do. I was worried that Mme Noelle would lose patience with me if I didn't shape up soon.

Also, I knew that I really shouldn't be letting my friends come to this rehearsal. I hadn't asked Madame's permission – mainly because I'd been pretty sure she'd say no – and I was worried that they'd be caught. Then we'd *all* be in trouble.

I was also a little nervous about having to dance in front of an audience – even if they were my friends – so early into a production. Usually there was absolutely no audience until the dress rehearsal. Would having them there affect my performance? What would they think of my dancing?

I tried to shove all my worries to the back of my mind. "Hey, Mal," I said, "let's get our hair done there, sometime!" I pointed out the window to this funny little beauty shop I've always noticed on my way into Stamford. Carmelita's Casa de Beauty, it was called. There were pictures in the window of ladies with towering hairdos, their hair teased and curled into fluffy mounds.

"Great," said Mallory. "We'll look like poodles." She giggled. "Maybe we'd win first prize at the pet show!"

"The pet show," groaned Kristy. "Please, let's forget about the pet show for one day. I've heard enough about it to last a lifetime!"

Just then, Charlie pulled into the civic centre's car park. "Okay, everybody out!" he said. "Jessi, how are they supposed to get inside?" he asked me.

"They can use that side door," I said, pointing. "Can you help everyone sneak in? It's going to be dark in the back of the theatre."

By then, the BSC members had piled out of the back seat. "Good luck, Jessi," said Mallory. "We'll be watching!"

"And taking notes," said Dawn. She held up a little notebook and a tiny torch shaped like a pen.

"Wow!" I said. "You lot are serious about this detective stuff. Please be careful – and don't get caught."

"We won't," said Claudia. "Don't worry – just forget we're even here. Have a good rehearsal, Jessi!"

I waved at them as they headed for the side entrance, led by Charlie. I knew he'd help get them settled before he took off to do the errands he'd been planning to do for his mother and Watson.

Then I turned and went into the backstage entrance. I shivered a little as I opened the door, remembering the excitement of the other performances I'd danced in. I only hoped that *The Sleeping Beauty* would come off as well as they had.

I changed quickly in the crowded dressing room, and then headed for the stage. Mme Noelle was waiting. I peered past her, into the darkened theatre. Where were my friends? I couldn't see – or hear them – anywhere. Good. If I couldn't see them, nobody else could, either.

"Are we ready to donce today?" asked Mme Noelle, looking at me curiously. She must have been wondering what I was looking for.

"Ready, Madame," I answered. And I was. So far, the rehearsal looked as if it was going to go smoothly. None of my clothes had disappeared, no notes had been shoved into my bag. Today I was going to concentrate on my dancing.

At first, it was hard to forget that my friends were sitting out there in the dark, watching my every move. But before long, I did forget. I got caught up in the beautiful – and difficult – movements of the ballet, and I forgot everything. My ankle was completely healed. It felt as strong as ever.

It was a great rehearsal. I danced well, and so did everyone else. We went through pretty much the whole ballet, with plenty of stops and starts and corrections from Mme Noelle.

"Watch zee shoulder, Mademoiselle Romsey," she called as I danced. "It is still dropping during your *glissade*."

I concentrated even harder, paying attention to nothing but my muscles and my form. I didn't come close to stumbling or falling, and neither did anyone else.

"Very good!" said Mme Noelle when we were finished. "All of you are doncing wiz incredible grace today. Zee performance will be a success!"

She clapped her hands and sent us to the dressing room. While I was changing into my street clothes I thought about the rehearsal. I hoped it hadn't been a total waste of time for my friends. After all, nothing had happened. I have to admit that I had secretly been hoping that something *would* happen – just so they could see it for themselves.

But that day's rehearsal had been completely normal. And there was nothing suspicious in the dressing room, either. No notes, no stolen belongings. Dawn sneaked into the dressing room after a load of people had gone. She wanted to "investigate" – but there was nothing new for me to show her. Had the mystery been in my mind all along? Maybe I was just imagining things. Maybe I was going crazy.

"No way!" said Claudia, when I said this in the car on the way home. "I'm sure there's foul play going on. And I can guess who might be responsible, too!"

"You *can*?" I asked. "How?"

"Just by watching everybody closely," she said. "And by trying to decide what Nancy Drew would think if she were in this situation."

"She's right," said Dawn. "I know *I* saw a few things going on. For example, why did Katie Beth make a face when Mme Noelle told you that your bore-ay – whatever *that* is – was 'close to perfect'?"

Luckily, my friends had been to enough of my performances to identify most of the dancers in my class.

"I suppose she might have been a little jealous," I said thoughtfully. "After all, she got to dance my role while my ankle was healing, and Mme Noelle never said anything like that about her *bourrée*."

"So . . . would she get your part if you couldn't dance it?" asked Stacey. "I mean, that would explain everything, wouldn't it? She's trying to get rid of you so she can have the lead role."

I shifted in my seat until I was looking at Stacey. "I don't know. . ." I said slowly. "I don't think that's necessarily the answer. Because if I couldn't dance, Mme Noelle would probably reaudition the whole class for the part. She's always fair that way. I don't think Katie Beth would automatically get the part – and Katie Beth must know that, too."

"What about Hilary?" asked Claudia.

"What about her?" I asked.

"Why does she look so worried all the time?" asked Claudia. "It's as if she's terrified that she might do something wrong."

I explained about Hilary's mother – how pushy she is, and how she always expects Hilary to be perfect. "I know she's under a lot of pressure," I said. "I feel a bit sorry for her."

"Well, don't lose any sleep over it," said Claudia. "She's not too crazy about you."

"What do you mean?" I asked.

"Oh, just a feeling I got from watching her," said Claudia. "You know how they say 'If looks could kill'? Well – she was giving *you* some looks that could stop an elephant in its tracks, if you know what I mean."

I thought that over for a minute. "So who else do you all suspect?" I asked.

"What about Lisa Jones?" asked Mallory. "She just seems so sweet and good all the time. Nobody's *that* nice."

"You know something?" I said. "She really *is* that nice. She was worried about me when I hurt my ankle. She was the only one who phoned me at home that night to see how I was."

"Maybe she just wanted to find out early if you were going to be dropping out," said Kristy.

"No," I said. "I'm positive she isn't a suspect. We'll have to rule her out. I like Lisa too much to be suspicious of her."

"Okay, forget Lisa," said Claudia. "What about that old Carrie Steinfeld? What's her story?"

"Well," I said, giggling, "you hit the nail on the head by calling her 'old'. Carrie's the oldest one in our class, and this is the last performance she'll be in." I told them a little about why she needed good roles on her résumé. "I know that getting the lead would have meant a lot to her," I went on. "But she did get a pretty big part. I think the Lilac Fairy will help her out. Anyway, she's a good dancer. I'm sure she won't have any trouble getting into another school."

"*You* might be sure, but maybe she's not," said Claud. "Personally, I think she's a suspect."

"I agree," said Mallory. "And I think Hilary Morgan is one, too – just based on those dirty looks she was giving you."

"Hmmmm. . ." I said. "Just the two of them?"

"No," said Kristy. "I've got to vote for Katie Beth, too. Remember, you two were enemies way back when—"

"But we made up!" I said, interrupting.

"I know," said Kristy. "But I think she's still got it in for you. And she wants that role so badly she can almost taste it."

"I don't agree," said Dawn. "I mean, if she was going to get it automatically, fine. But she'll have to audition just like everybody else, and even *I* can tell that there are plenty of better dancers in the class.

We argued back and forth for a while, but by the time we had reached Stoneybrook we'd narrowed it down to three suspects: Katie Beth, Carrie and Hilary. Now all I had to do was to keep a close eye on all of them. My friends were sure it'd be easy to catch the guilty party.

Charlie dropped me off at my house, and as I waved goodbye, I felt grateful to my friends. I also felt relieved. I wasn't positive that we were any nearer to identifying the 'phantom of the dance school', as Claudia had begun to call her. But I felt a little more in control of the situation. At least we'd begun to work on the mystery. And I knew that with everyone's help, I could solve it eventually.

11th CHAPTER

I watched the three suspects as closely as I could during the next few rehearsals, but things went pretty smoothly. Our practice was starting to pay off. The performance was coming together, and I was feeling more and more confident as I danced the part of Princess Aurora.

I began to think that maybe the phantom really *had* been just in my mind. Then, mysterious things began to happen again.

First, I reached into my dance bag after one rehearsal, and I found my old leotard – the one that had been stolen. But there was no way I could wear it again. It had been cut to shreds. Somebody had gone after that leotard with a sharp pair of scissors. That was creepy.

Then, during another rehearsal, I got shoved – by someone I didn't see – into some scenery that was being painted. My leotard was covered with red paint, and Mme Noelle wasn't pleased. Neither was I. I had spent all my savings to replace my dance outfit when it was stolen, so I had to borrow money from my parents to replace it again.

This role was becoming expensive.

Sometimes I wondered if it was worthwhile – if I should just give up playing Princess Aurora. But then I would spend two hours working with Mme Noelle on a segment of the ballet, and I would realize that there was no way I could give up that kind of experience.

My favourite part of the ballet was the dance I had to do when I first came on stage – the Rose Adagio. Some dancers have said that it's this dance that makes the role of Princess Aurora such a challenge, because you have to do it "cold" – without warming up with some easier dancing first.

But I loved that dance. It was full of slow, graceful movements. According to the fairy tale, this dance shows the princess being presented to the court on her sixteenth birthday. She is meeting four princes. They all want to marry her, even though she's so young.

Each prince gives her a beautiful rose, and she dances with them. But after dancing, she gives the flowers to her mother. She's having too much fun to think about serious things like marriage.

The dance that she does (or rather, that I did) with the princes is very difficult. Mme Noelle worked with us for a long time before we could do it well. The way it went was this: as I finished dancing with each prince, he helped me to balance on the point of one toe – and then he took away his hand and left me balancing there until the next prince came to dance with me.

"Do not wobble, Mademoiselle Romsey!" cried Mme Noelle as I did my best to balance on one toe. "Smile!"

I tried to smile.

"Remember, you are a joyous young princess. You must show us zee excitement and hoppiness of youth!"

I tried to act "hoppy". It wasn't easy, especially with Hilary Morgan glaring at me from the sidelines. Sometimes I felt bad about how much time Mme Noelle was spending with me, but the fact was that my role was very demanding. Still, I could tell that the other girls were jealous, and I really couldn't blame them. I would have been jealous, too.

But my phantom took jealousy a little too far. When I went into the dressing room on the day I'd been working on the Rose Adagio, I saw it straight away. A note – in that same red ink – with a red rose attached. WATCH OUT FOR THE THORNS, it said.

I stood looking at it for a moment. It gave me a creepy feeling in the pit of my stomach. Then I folded the note and tucked it into my bag. I looked at the rose, thinking that I'd take it home to my mum – at least it was pretty, and it probably smelled good. But when I picked it up, a thorn pricked my finger. "Ouch!" I said out loud. I squeezed my finger and a drop of blood oozed out.

I looked around the dressing room to see who was there. Sure enough, all three suspects were among the dancers who were busy changing. Hilary was at the mirror, checking her hair. Katie Beth was by her locker – she was packing her dance clothes into her bag. And Carrie was just about to leave, but when she heard my little cry of pain, she turned around.

"Are you okay, Jessi?" she asked, coming over to me. Then she saw the rose. "Hey, that's pretty. Who's sending you flowers?"

I shrugged.

"A secret admirer, huh? Hey, everybody, Jessi's got a boyfriend!" she yelled.

I was really embarrassed. I tossed the rose into the wastepaper bin and got out of the dressing room as soon as I could, trying not to listen to the teasing that was going on. Dancing the Rose Adagio was never quite as much fun after that day. I was always thinking of that thorn pricking my finger, like a bee sting – and of that drop of red blood appearing afterwards.

But unlike Princess Aurora, I didn't fall asleep for a hundred years after I pricked my finger. Instead, I became more alert. I was dying to catch the phantom in the act.

I thought of hiding in the dressing room so that I could be there when she stuck a note into my bag. But that wouldn't work. Mme Noelle would notice my absence from rehearsal straight away, since I was in almost every act. All I could do was wait – and watch.

I watched very closely. I tried to pay attention to where each of the three suspects were at all times. But it wasn't easy. Mme Noelle kept me busy throughout almost every rehearsal.

One day, Carrie bumped into me about three times during rehearsal. That day, I was sure that she was the phantom.

At another rehearsal, I overheard Hilary whispering mean things about me to Lisa Jones. I was convinced that Hilary was the one who was out to get me.

Then Katie Beth started to give me funny looks. I'd catch her watching me as I put on my toe shoes, or staring at me during exercises at the *barre*. I certainly couldn't rule her out, either.

I was getting more and more confused, and to make matters worse, the notes kept on coming.

GIVE UP THE ROLE BEFORE IT'S TOO LATE, said one. I shook my head and tucked it into my bag with the rest.

After the next rehearsal, there was another. YOU HAVE BEEN WARNED, it said.

But you know what? Instead of scaring me, those notes started to make me angrier and angrier. I became more determined to solve this mystery and find out who the phantom was. Then I'd tell everything to Mme Noelle, and the performance – with me as Princess Aurora – would go off without a hitch.

One day, Carrie was absent from rehearsals. She was at home with flu, according to Madame. That day we worked extra hard on one of the most difficult parts of the dance.

When we're learning a dance, Mme Noelle makes us do the movements over and over again, until it finally looks right. Even once we've learned the basic steps, we keep repeating them. If we do even one little thing wrong, she makes us do it over again. If we do it right, we *still have* to do it again – for luck.

Rehearsals can be so exhausting.

That day, I was ready to drop as I headed for the dressing room. The last thing I needed was to find another note. But there it was, in that creepy red ink. TAKE A REST, SLEEPING BEAUTY!

I rolled my eyes as I put the note away. When was this going to end?

Then I realized something. Carrie was absent. And I'd still received a note. Finally, I was getting somewhere with this mystery. I could rule out Carrie, which would leave me with only two suspects.

Unless . . . had Carrie only been *pretending* to be ill – and got someone to leave the note *for* her? I shook my head. That was pretty unlikely. She wouldn't miss a rehearsal unless she really had to.

So it was down to Katie Beth and Hilary. How was I going to work out which one of them it was? I decided just to wait and see what would happen. If I could rule one of them out, I'd have my phantom.

Carrie was still ill at the next rehearsal. I felt sorry for her, missing all that practice time. Now that I knew she wasn't the phantom, I sort of missed having her around.

But it was a relief to have to watch only two suspects instead of three. I found that I could concentrate better – and it showed in my dancing. Mme Noelle told me that I was *magnifique* that day. That's "magnificent" in French.

It always feels great when Mme Noelle compliments you. She doesn't say nice things unless she really means them. So that afternoon I was feeling terrific. I danced the Rose Adagio without missing a step. My *pas de deux* with the Bluebird of Happiness was nearly perfect. And I got through the scene where the prince kisses me without giggling once. It was a great rehearsal.

It was great, that is, until I almost got flattened by some scenery.

In that theatre, most of the scenery is painted on huge flats that can be raised and lowered on ropes. When they're in the raised position, the ropes are securely tied so they can't fall. And when it's time for the scene to change, the flat is slowly let down to the floor. Each flat must weigh about a ton – they're so big!

There were a lot of different flats for the *Sleeping Beauty* scenery. There was the grand ballroom, the magic forest, and the sleeping castle, where Princess Aurora lies awaiting her prince. I'd got used to the flats moving up and down during rehearsals, while the stage managers practised their cues just as we practised ours.

Anyway, that day I had just finished my final dance with the prince, and I was walking to the back of the stage so that I could collapse quietly while Mme Noelle went over her notes on who – and what – needed improvement.

I didn't even see the flat falling. Before I knew what was happening, someone had pushed me out of the way. The flat hit the stage with a loud crash, right where I had been standing only seconds before.

I felt dizzy. Was this another "accident"? I looked around, trying to get my bearings. Someone was standing next to me, asking if I was all right. It was Katie Beth. She was the one who'd pushed me out of the way.

"Thanks, Katie Beth!" I said, as soon as I could speak. "I hate to imagine what would have happened if that thing had hit me!"

"I'm glad it didn't," she said, smiling at me. "Are you sure you're okay?"

She was being so nice. I felt terrible for ever being suspicious of her. "I'm fine," I said. "Thanks again."

Rehearsal ended a few minutes later. I walked off the stage and into the dressing room, thinking hard. So Carrie wasn't sending me those notes, and obviously Katie Beth wasn't either. Was Hilary really the phantom? And if she was, how could I prove it?

That's what I asked my friends later that day at a club meeting. I'd filled them in on my detective work so far, and they were excited to hear that the list of suspects had been narrowed down to one.

"You're almost there!" said Stacey.

"But I still have to prove that Hilary is the phantom," I said. "Any ideas?"

Everybody thought for a few minutes. Finally Kristy said, "You have to set up some kind of trap for her. Let her prove her own guilt."

"But how?" asked Claudia. Then a light seemed to turn on in her eyes. "Let me see those notes again, Jessi!"

I handed them to her. Luckily I'd saved every one. Dawn leaned over to examine them again with Claudia.

"You don't see writing like this every day," said Dawn. "I noticed that before, when I looked at the first few."

"You're right," said Claudia slowly. "And I know why the writing looks so different. It's because the writer is using a special pen – the kind you do calligraphy with."

"Calligraphy? What's that?" asked Mary Anne.

"It's the special writing on wedding invitations and stuff like that," said Claudia. "It's pretty and slanted – and some parts of the letters are thick and other parts are thin. A girl in my art class has a calligraphy pen. It has a sharp, flat point and you can write thick *or* thin, depending on how you hold the pen."

"So what are you getting at?" asked Kristy.

"Well, all Jessi has to do is to trap Hilary into writing something, so she can see if the samples match," said Claud, smiling.

"Whoa!" said Stacey. "Claud, you're the Nancy Drew of Stoneybrook."

Claudia blushed. "Oh, yeah?" she said. "Well, if I'm Nancy Drew, who's Bess?"

We all laughed. Bess is Nancy Drew's

plump sidekick, the one who's always eating.

"How come detectives always have a chubby friend?" asked Mallory. "There's one in the Hardy Boys, too – and in the Three Investigators. Have you ever noticed that?"

Claudia laughed. "I know. I suppose it's all just part of being a super crime solver. So, Stace, you're just going to have to gain some weight!" She stuck an elbow into Stacey's side, and we all cracked up.

I thought Claudia's idea was great. Now all I had to do was work out how to get Hilary to write something – in front of me.

12th CHAPTER

For the next few days, I spent most of my free time just thinking. I had to work out a foolproof way to trap Hilary. But for a long time I couldn't think of a single good idea.

During rehearsals, I watched Hilary out of the corner of my eye. She was no fool, I knew that. It wasn't going to be easy to trick her into confessing. But that's what I had to do.

For a while I considered looking through her locker, checking to see if she owned a pen like the one Claud had described. But that seemed risky – and it didn't feel right to me. Just because she *might* be the person who had stolen my stuff didn't make it all right for me to rifle through her things.

Then I thought I could just ask her to write something down for me. I'd tell her that I was doing a school project – about how to analyze handwriting. No, that was too far-fetched. She'd never believe me.

If only we went to the same school, I could ask her if I could borrow her notes from a certain class. But Hilary goes to a private school. So that was out. I was at a dead end.

Finally, in desperation, I phoned Mallory one night. I had been trying not to take up too much of the club's time with my problem, but after all, Mal was my best friend. If I couldn't ask her for help, who could I ask? I dialled her number.

Somebody answered in a tiny little voice. "Hello?"

"Hi, Claire," I said. "This is Jessi."

"Hi," she replied, breathing into the phone.

"Is Mallory there?" I asked.

"Yes," she said. But she didn't ask if I wanted to speak to her. Kids her age are like that. You have to take everything one step at a time.

"Can I talk to her?" I asked hopefully.

"Okay," said Claire. I heard the phone fall to the floor as she dropped it. Then I heard her footsteps as she ran off to get Mallory. It seemed to take Claire for ever to find her, but I was used to waiting for Mal to come to the phone.

Somebody picked up the receiver a few minutes later, but it wasn't Mal. It was Nicky. "Who's this?" he asked.

I told him who it was. "Hi, Jessi!" he said. "Guess what! There's going to be a pet show, and Frodo's going to be in it!"

I could tell that he was really excited about it – and unlike Becca, he didn't seem to mind that he only had a hamster to enter in the show. We talked for a couple of minutes, and then Mallory picked up the phone in the kitchen.

"Okay, Nicky!" she said. "You can hang up now." We waited for a moment, but Nicky didn't hang up. I heard him breathing on the line. He was probably hoping to listen in on our conversation.

"Come on, Nicky!" said Mal. "I'll give you a dime later on if you'll hang up right now." *Click.* Finally!

"What's up, Jess?" asked Mal.

"I need your help," I said. "I just can't seem to work out how to trap Hilary."

"Okay, let's think," said Mallory. "You can't be too obvious about it. You've got to be like that detective on TV. You know, the one who always makes the suspect feel as if they've got nothing to worry about, and then – *BAM!* – he gets them."

"Well, I don't think Hilary realizes that I suspect her," I said. "I've been trying to act really cool with her, so that she won't guess." It hadn't been that hard. We'd been incredibly busy at rehearsals lately.

"Good," said Mal. "Now, let's look at her personality. There must be some weakness that we can take advantage of."

"You mean, that she's a bit vain?" I asked. I told Mal how Hilary is always looking in the mirror to check on her special French plait.

"Yeah, something like that is good. Now think," said Mal. "How can we use that against her?"

"Maybe I could tell her that I thought she'd make a better Princess Aurora than me," I said, thinking out loud. "She's so vain that she'd probably agree with me, and that would almost prove that she's trying to get rid of me so that she can have the part!" I was excited.

"Jessi," said Mal, "that wouldn't really prove anything, except that she thinks she's a better dancer than you." She was silent for a moment. "No, we've got to come up with something better than that," she said. "Keep thinking."

"What if I just try to catch her off guard with some casual comment?" I asked. "Like 'Hey, thanks for all those notes you sent me!' Then, if she looks upset, that would give her away."

"It might work," said Mallory. "But you'll need witnesses, and that could get complicated. Also, what if she just denies everything? Then you'll have totally blown it."

I had to agree that Mal was right. But I just couldn't come up with any other ideas.

We talked a while longer and then said goodbye, agreeing to talk more the next day.

After dinner that night I helped Aunt Cecelia dry the dishes. I wasn't thinking about anything in particular. Then, out of nowhere, I had this great idea. "That's it!" I said out loud. Aunt Cecelia gave me a funny look.

"*What's* it?" she asked, shaking the soapy water off her hands.

I almost wished I could talk to her about my idea, but I knew it was better not to. I hadn't told her – or my parents – anything about the phantom. It would just make them worry.

"Nothing, Aunt Cecelia," I said. "I was thinking out loud. Is it okay if I go and do my homework now?"

She nodded. "We've just about finished here, Jessica. Thanks for your help." She looked at me carefully, as if she knew there was something I wasn't telling her. It's not easy to fool Aunt Cecelia. She doesn't let much get past her. "Go on, now," she said finally.

I headed up to my room, but I didn't start my homework. I had something more important to think about: my Plan, with a capital P. I just knew it would work. It had to.

Here's what I had worked out: Hilary's weak spot. She was always looking for

Mme Noelle's approval. Of course, everybody in the class was doing the same thing, since we all wanted to please our teacher. But Hilary really seemed to have a need for Mme Noelle to think she was perfect. Maybe it was because of her mother. Mrs Morgan has such high expectations of Hilary.

Anyway, I thought I could somehow use that personality trait to trap Hilary. I just had to make her believe that Mme Noelle wanted her to do something – and then she'd do it without thinking.

I was really concentrating. What could Mme Noelle need from Hilary? Something that she'd have to write, of course, so that I'd know for sure that that special pen really did belong to her. And it would have to be something she'd need in a hurry, so that Hilary wouldn't have time to think about it.

A programme for the performance? No, the programmes were probably being printed professionally, and Hilary would know that. Invitations to our dress rehearsal? Too complicated. I had to keep it simple. What about some kind of sign?

A sign. That was it! Now my mind was racing. I pictured the scene:

Hilary writes something down. Then she realizes that she's been caught. She breaks down and confesses everything, apologizes all over the place, and tries to make me promise not to tell. But I won't. Instead, I march her in to see Mme Noelle, who tells her she's going to have to drop out of dance school. The End!

I knew that the last part of my imagined scene probably wouldn't come true. Most likely, Madame would just give Hilary a warning. But I knew that my plan would work. There was no way it could fail. I practised over and over again how I was going to get Hilary to write something for me, until I felt that it was perfect. I couldn't wait for my next rehearsal.

Once I'd got my plan prepared, I turned to my homework. I couldn't afford to get behind in my classes, no matter how busy I was with rehearsals. But I'd only had my social studies book open for a few minutes when I heard a knock on my door.

"Come in!" I said.

The door opened slowly, and Becca peeped around it. "Can I talk to you for a minute?" she asked.

"Of course, Becca," I said. "What's the matter?" She looked upset about something. I realized suddenly that I hadn't been paying much attention to her lately. I'd been too caught up in solving the mystery of the phantom. I closed my book and told her to sit down.

"It's the pet show," she said, looking at her shoes. "I don't want to go to it."

"Becca, why not?" I asked. "It's going to be so much fun!"

"No it's not," she said. "Not if I can't win a prize."

I frowned. "But who says you won't win one?" I asked. "Misty's a great pet."

She shook her head. "I know. But she's only a hamster! How can she win any prizes? Everybody else has much better pets."

"Like who?" I asked.

"Like Charlotte," she said. "Charlotte is going to enter Carrot in the show, and Carrot can do all kinds of tricks. Did you ever see him say his prayers?"

Charlotte Johanssen is Becca's best friend. She's also one of the kids we sit for regularly. And her dog, Carrot, is pretty clever. When you tell him to say his prayers, he puts his paws on your lap and lays his head down on top of them.

"And David Michael is going to enter Shannon," continued Becca. "I'm sure Shannon will win a prize."

"Becca," I said gently, "there are going to be all kinds of pets in the show. And they all have an equal chance of winning a prize."

She didn't look convinced.

"Misty's brother is going to be in the show," I said. "And Nicky and Margo and Claire and Vanessa aren't worried about whether Frodo will win a prize. They just think the show will be fun."

I wasn't really sure about that, but it didn't hurt to say it. "And guess what Linny Papadakis is entering – a turtle!" I said. "Don't you think that's pretty funny?"

Becca shook her head, refusing to smile. I talked to her for a while, but I couldn't convince her that winning a prize didn't matter. Finally, I just gave her a big hug and told her it was bedtime. Poor Becca. She had her heart set on winning a prize, and Misty wasn't a very impressive pet.

Then, as I was tucking her in, I had an idea. Could it work? I went back to my room and thought it over. Then I went downstairs to the phone in the kitchen. I dialled a number.

"Hello?"

"Kristy!" I said. "This is Jessi. I've just had the *best* idea!"

13th CHAPTER

I told Mallory about my plan for catching Hilary while we ate lunch at school the next day. "Do you think it'll work?" I asked her.

"I don't know. . ." she said. "It sounds as if your timing is going to have to be perfect if you want to catch her alone in the dressing room."

"You're right," I replied. "And I don't want to end up being late for rehearsal, either."

"Maybe you should do it *after* rehearsal," Mal said. "Does Hilary usually take a long time to get changed?"

I told Mal that she did.

"Great! Don't you think that would work better?"

I nodded. It was good to go over my plan with someone else. Mallory and I talked about it for the whole lunch period, polishing every detail until it seemed just right.

"When's your next rehearsal?" she asked, when the lunch bell rang.

I groaned. "Not until Thursday!" I couldn't believe I had to wait that long. It was only Tuesday.

"Don't worry," said Mal. "You've got a great plan, and I'm positive it's going to work."

If only I could be so sure. It was hard not to worry. This was going to be my only chance to trap Hilary. I spent the next days thinking about the plan, going over it in my head, practising what I was going to say, and imagining how Hilary would react.

I'm sure that my parents thought something was wrong with me, but they must have put it down to my being nervous about the performance, which was coming up soon. At dinner I would stare into space, forgetting to eat, while I pictured Hilary's shocked face. At breakfast, I would forget what I was doing and pour the milk into my cereal bowl until it overflowed.

Aunt Cecelia seemed suspicious, too – but she didn't say anything. She just gave me sharp looks as we washed the dishes together. I tried not to show how preoccupied I was, but it was hard.

Becca got the worst of it, I'm sure. She was still upset about the pet show, which was going to be held that weekend. But I was just too distracted to give her any more consolation and advice than I already had. I was happy to hear that she had decided to go to the pet show after all, and that she was going to enter Misty. She was trying to work out how to make her more – "special." Once, I had to stop her from trying to squeeze Misty into one of her Barbie doll's evening dresses.

Squirt was probably the only member of my family who didn't notice that there was something on my mind. Or maybe he did, and he didn't care. As long as I was around to give him "hawssy rides" (horsey rides), he didn't mind my distracted attitude.

On Tuesday night, I had a dream about trapping Hilary. In my dream, she got to her knees on the dressing room floor and begged me to forgive her.

On Wednesday afternoon we had a club meeting. I had hoped to be able to talk over my plan with everybody, but I didn't have a chance. There were too many last-minute preparations to take care of for the pet show.

On Wednesday night, I had another dream. This time, Hilary turned into a fanged monster and leaped at me when I accused her of being the phantom. I woke up with a start. What a nightmare! But I knew that, whatever else happened, there wasn't much chance that Hilary was going to turn into a monster right in front of me.

My classes dragged on Thursday, but finally school was over and it was time for rehearsal. I walked into the dressing room, and saw right away that Hilary wasn't there. I panicked. How was I going to wait a few *more* days to try out my plan? I'd never make it.

But Hilary dashed in just as I'd finished getting dressed. She was out of breath from running up the stairs. "Am I late?" she asked.

"No, but you'd better hurry," I said. "Mme Noelle just gave us the signal that she's ready to start." I almost wished that I had stuck to my original idea. At least the whole thing would be over *before* rehearsal. But it was too late now. In a moment, Mme Noelle would be taking the register.

I grabbed my toe shoes and ran to the stage, with Hilary on my heels. Mme Noelle barely looked up as we took our places.

"We have only four rehearsals left before zee performance, mesdemoiselles," she said. "I osk for your complete concentration." She looked me right in the eye as she said that. I gulped. And I nodded.

But unfortunately, my concentration was terrible that day. While we were doing our warm-up exercises at the *barre*, I lost count and kicked in the wrong direction, almost knocking Lisa over.

"Sorry!" I whispered.

She smiled at me. "That's okay," she whispered back. "I'd be nervous, too, if I were playing Princess Aurora."

Little did she know that my role was the least of my worries. I shook myself and tried to forget about Hilary. If Mme Noelle noticed how distracted I was, she would be furious.

I got through the rest of the rehearsal with no major accidents. As we finished our work for the day, I began to feel more and more nervous. What if Hilary didn't fall for my trick? What if she hadn't brought her special red pen that day? What if. . .

"You are dismissed!" said Mme Noelle, clapping her hands. "Jessica Romsey, please stay for a moment."

Oh, no! She was going to tell me how terribly I'd danced that day. Maybe she was going to take the role away from me. After everyone else had gone, I crossed to where she stood, next to the record player.

"Yes, Madame?" I asked.

"Mademoiselle Romsey, please tell me," she said. "Is everything all right? I am worrying about you." She was looking deeply into my eyes.

For a moment, just for a moment, I considered telling her everything. I'm not sure what stopped me. I suppose I wanted to be able to prove what I suspected before I brought her into it. "I – I'm fine," I said. "I know my dancing hasn't been perfect. I'm sorry."

She smiled at me. "Even Anna Pavlova was not always perfect," she said.

Anna Pavlova is probably the most famous ballerina of all time. Every dancer wants to be "another Pavlova", including me. I smiled back at Mme Noelle. Then, suddenly, I realized that I'd better get going if I wanted to catch Hilary in the dressing room.

"May I go now?" I asked Mme Noelle.

She nodded. "But Jessica, if something is bothering you, please speak to me of it."

"Thank you." I said. She can be so nice sometimes, even though she's a tough teacher. I suppose she just expects a lot of her pupils. I turned and ran off the stage.

When I reached the corridor, I paused to catch my breath. This was it! I was about to unmask the phantom. Could I do it? Go for it, Jessi! I said to myself. Taking a deep breath, I pushed open the door of the dressing room. I looked round. It was empty. I'd blown it.

Then I heard a cough. I spun around and saw Hilary by the mirror.

"Hilary!" I said. "I'm glad you're here!"

She turned and looked at me curiously. "Why?" she asked.

I tried to sound as if I was out of breath from running, which wasn't hard. My heart was pounding like crazy, just from nervousness. "It's – it's Mme Noelle," I said.

"What?" asked Hilary. "Is something wrong? Is she hurt?"

This wasn't going in the right direction. "No, no," I said. "Nothing like that. It's just that she needs a sign." I paused. There was something I was forgetting. "And she wants you to make it," I added, breathlessly. This wasn't going as smoothly as I'd imagined.

Hilary gave me another funny look. Then she went over to her bag and started to rummage through it. "A sign, huh?" she asked. "Okay, no problem. What should it say?"

I could have kicked myself. I'd forgotten an important part of my script! "The caretaker has spilled some cleaning stuff on the stairs," I said. "Mme Noelle is afraid someone will slip on it and hurt themselves before he has a chance to clean it up."

Hilary waited silently.

"So," I finished, "I suppose it should just say something like 'Danger! Slippery Steps!'"

"That sounds simple enough," said Hilary. "I'll make Mme Noelle the best sign she ever saw."

I sighed with relief. Then I saw the pen she had pulled out of her bag. It wasn't red! It was just an ordinary blue ballpoint. "Don't forget," I said. "It has to be highly visible, so everyone can see it."

Hilary glanced at the pen in her hand and shrugged. Then she threw it back into her bag and rummaged around some more. I almost sighed out loud. She certainly wasn't making this easy for me!

Finally, she pulled out a red pen and started to write. From where I stood, I couldn't see what the writing looked like, so I just had to wait patiently. But my heart was racing.

"How does this look?" she asked, holding the sign up for me to see. I walked over and took it from her. One glance told me that the pen she was using was the same one she'd used to write those nasty notes.

"GOTCHA!" I cried.

"What?" she asked, turning white.

"This pen!" I said. "And this writing. *You* sent me all those notes! And now I've caught you."

"What notes?" asked Hilary, narrowing her eyes. "I never sent you any notes. Just try convincing Mme Noelle that I did. It'll be your word against mine, and she'll never believe you. You can't prove anything."

"Oh, yes I can," I said. "For one thing, I've kept every note you sent me. Anyone could see that the writing is the same as the writing on that sign."

"So what?" she asked. "Why would I write you notes?"

"Because you wanted me to get so scared that I'd drop the role of Princess Aurora," I said. "You thought you'd have a chance at it if you could audition again."

"I wasn't the only one who wanted you to drop out," said Hilary.

"You're right," I said. "Katie Beth and Carrie would have liked to get that role, too. But Carrie was absent when I got a note one day, and Katie Beth saved me when you pushed that scenery on to me."

"Scenery!" said Hilary. "I didn't do that! That thing fell by accident, I swear. I didn't want you to get hurt *that* badly." Then she put her hand over her mouth. I could tell that she had realized she'd practically confessed to all her other "crimes".

"Oh, please!" she begged. "Please don't tell Mme Noelle! I couldn't stand it if I got kicked out of dance school. And my mother would be furious."

"That's why you did it in the first place, isn't it?" I asked. "Because of your mother."

Hilary nodded. "It's so important to her for me to be a good dancer. I work really hard to live up to her expectations, but sometimes I just can't. You're a better dancer than me – that's why you got the role. But she doesn't understand."

I looked closely at Hilary. I could tell that she was about to start crying.

"I promise I won't do anything else to you, Jessi!" she said. "No more notes, no more 'accidents'. I'll leave you alone. I'll pay you back for those leotards I ruined. Just please, don't tell Madame!"

I didn't know what to do. I felt sorry for Hilary because of her mother, but I was still angry with her. I thought about it for a minute while she waited, tears in her eyes.

I was still worried that she'd try some nasty trick on me during rehearsals, or even during a performance. But since I had proof of her "crimes", she probably wouldn't. She knew she'd just be in even deeper trouble. And I realized that she had probably already suffered enough by having to deal with her awful mother.

"Okay," I said. "But don't forget that I have proof of what you did." I paused. "You'd better not try anything else, or you know what I'll do!" I tried to sound as threatening as I could, even though I didn't really know exactly what I would do to her.

Hilary was incredibly grateful. She even surrendered her calligraphy pen. "You can have this," she said. "I won't be needing it any more." Then she ran out to meet her mother.

I sat down on the dressing room bench, exhausted but happy. I'd caught the phantom! I just hoped I had done the right thing by letting her off. What if she decided to pull some last-minute trick on opening night? She might do it, just for the pleasure of seeing me look like a fool in front of the huge audience that would fill the civic centre. I tried to put the thought out of my head as I went out to meet my father. I should have been feeling happy, not worried. After all, the mystery had finally been solved!

14th CHAPTER

Saturday

Well, at least we had a nice day for the pet show. Imagine if it had been raining, on top of everything else! I don't know about the rest of you lot, but I really did have a great time today - disasters and all. Still, I don't think we should make this pet show an annual event. We should remember how competitive kids can get sometimes. Jessi, your idea saved the day. Everybody went home happy.

Stacey was sitting for Charlotte Johanssen on the day of the pet show, so they arrived at Dawn and Mary Anne's early on that sunny afternoon, to help set up. Charlotte had brought Carrot with her. He was all spruced up. You could tell straight away that he'd had a bath. And he was wearing a brand-new red collar. The leash that Charlotte was walking him on was also brand-new, and she looked pretty proud as she entered the garden.

The rest of us, except Kristy, who hadn't got there yet, were setting up tables for snacks and for the judges to sit at. Charlotte wanted to help, so Stacey tied Carrot to a tree.

"You be a good dog," said Charlotte. Carrot barked a few times and then curled up and went to sleep while we worked.

We set up a "ring" – a judging area in front of the judges' table – by making a circle of rocks we'd found in the drive. Stacey surveyed it when it was done.

"It's not exactly round," she said, "but it'll have to do." Stacey was going to be one of the judges. We had decided that not every member of the club should be a judge – only those who could never be accused of being partial to one pet or another.

I couldn't be a judge because of Misty.

Kristy couldn't be a judge because Karen, Andrew and David Michael were all going to enter pets.

Mallory couldn't be a judge because of Frodo – and because of the mystery pet that Mallory now thought the triplets were entering.

And we had decided that Mary Anne shouldn't be a judge because she loves her kitten, Tigger, so much that she might be biased towards any cats that were entered.

So that left Stacey, Claud and Dawn as the Official Pet Show Judges.

Just as we'd finished setting up the snack tables, we heard a car horn honking at front of the house. It sounded like Charlie's horn – and it was. In a second, we saw what looked like a parade coming around to the back garden. First came Charlie (with Emily Michelle riding on his shoulders) and Sam. They were going to be spectators. Behind them was Kristy, who was trying to help David Michael control Shannon. Shannon's not used to walking on a leash, and she tends to lunge all over the place.

Then there was Karen, who was proudly carrying the small cage that held Emily Junior, her rat. And next to her walked Andrew, pulling a frightened-looking Midgie (I suppose he doesn't like crowds) behind him.

Stacey looked closely at Emily Junior as Karen put the cage on one of the tables. "What's on her head?" she asked, puzzled.

"Mickey Mouse ears!" said Karen proudly. "They're her costume!"

Sure enough, Karen had cut out a tiny pair of black ears and stuck them on Emily Junior's head. Stacey stifled a laugh. "Very nice, Karen," she said. "And Andrew, this must be Midgie," she said, turning to look at him. "What a nice little dog."

Andrew looked proud. "He is nice," he said. "Even if he can't do any tricks. He's the nicest dog in the world!"

Kristy got Shannon and David Michael settled and came over to talk to the rest of us. "Are you lot ready for this?" she asked, laughing. "You should have seen us on the way over here. The car was like a three-ring circus! First Emily Junior escaped from her cage. Then, just when we'd caught her and put her back, Shannon started trying to jump out of the car at every set of traffic lights. What a mess!"

Just then, another car pulled into the drive. This time it was Mrs Papadakis, who had brought Hannie and Linny with their pets, and also Scott and Timmy Hsu, who looked a little downcast.

Hannie was holding Pat the cat in her arms, and Linny was carrying Myrtle the turtle – whose shell had apparently been repainted just that morning. It looked terrific.

Kristy told Timmy and Scott that they could sit with Sam and Charlie, as spectators. "I'm glad you're here," she said. "We need an audience." They smiled at her, but they still didn't seem very happy. They looked longingly at the other pets that were being paraded around. Stacey told me later that she felt pretty sorry for them – and that she could understand since she'd never been allowed to have pets, either.

The next kids to arrive were the Delaneys, and boy, did they have a surprise for the rest of us. When Mr Delaney pulled his car into the drive, Amanda got out first. She was carrying a perfectly groomed Priscilla, and she was looking very possessive. Obviously, she had decided not to let Max share her pet.

Then Max climbed out of the car, and Stacey got the shock of a lifetime. In his arms was a very calm and happy-looking cat. A big, fat cat. It was Boo-Boo! And he didn't look mean at all. He looked as if he'd be happy to let Max carry him round all day.

Stacey looked at Kristy and raised her eyebrows. "I know," said Kristy. "Isn't it weird? It just seems that Boo-Boo's taken a liking to Max. You should hear him purring when Max pets him." Then she stopped and sniffed the air. "What is that smell?" she asked.

Stacey smelled it, too. "It's like that perfume my mother sometimes wears – Paris Romance, I think it's called." She looked around. "But who would have that on in the middle of the day? My mum only wears it for special occasions."

"It's Priscilla," said Amanda proudly. "Doesn't she smell lovely?" The cat must have been drenched in perfume. You couldn't get too close to her without feeling like you were going to keel over, just from the waves of fragrance that rose from her white fur.

"Lovely," said Stacey, wrinkling her nose.

By then, Dawn and Mary Anne's back garden was really filling up. A lot of barking and meowing was going on as the pets got to know each other. Stacey looked around for Charlotte and saw her standing near the tree where Carrot had been tied up. Carrot was nowhere in sight, and Charlotte looked as if she was about to cry.

Stacey ran over to her. "Don't worry, Char," she said. "We'll find him." They began to walk around the garden, calling for Carrot. He wasn't near the judging circle, or by the snack table. He wasn't playing with Shannon and Midgie. "Carrot!" called Charlotte, in a tearful voice.

"There he is!" said Stacey suddenly. She saw Carrot standing next to Matt and Haley Braddock, whom she hadn't seen arriving. Matt was holding his leash. Charlotte and Stacey ran to him, and when they got closer they saw the sign that Haley was holding.

OFFICIAL HANDLERS, it said. WE'LL LOOK AFTER YOUR PET WHEN YOU NEED SOME TIME OFF.

"That's a good idea," said Stacey. "But you'd better get permission from the owners before you start holding their pets. You had Charlotte a bit worried!"

"I'm sorry," said Haley, after signing to Matt to tell him to hand over Carrot. "We were just trying to help. Carrot looked so lonely, tied up to that tree."

Stacey smiled. "I know, but he was fine. Anyway, I'm glad you thought of a way to be part of the show. Let's go and see if anyone can use your services."

As she was walking with Charlotte and the Braddocks, Stacey saw the Pikes arrive. The triplets were struggling with a large, mysterious bundle. "What's that?" she asked.

"Nothing," said Adam and Byron together.

"We were just going to put it over there," said Jordan, pointing to a large bush by the side of the house.

Stacey shrugged. "Okay," she said. "Hey, what have you got there?" she asked, turning to Nicky. He and Margo and Claire stood huddled together over a small box. Vanessa stood off to the side, looking as if she wanted nothing to do with her younger brothers and sisters.

"It's Frodo," said Nicky.

"And wait till you see what they did to him," added Vanessa. "Show Stacey," she said to Nicky.

Nicky opened the lid of the box. Stacey peered in, then jumped back. "What was that green thing?" she asked.

"That's Frodo," said Nicky proudly.

"They got into the dyes my mum uses for cake icings," said Vanessa, rolling her eyes. "Can you believe it?"

Stacey looked again and laughed. "He looks pretty funny," she said. "But it *is* different, I have to say that!"

"It *is* different," said Becca, who had just appeared next to Nicky. She was looking enviously at Frodo's bright green fur. "I wish I'd thought of that." She held up Misty, who looked like an ordinary hamster – one who had had her hair combed neatly.

"Misty looks nice," said Stacey. Then trying to change the subject, she said, "Look, here come the Barretts, with Pow." Sure enough, there were Suzi and Buddy, walking Pow, who was covered with pink ribbons. He looked a bit silly, but Suzi and Buddy seemed proud.

Stacey barely had a chance to say hello to them before Kristy and Dawn ran up to her, out of breath. "Have you seen Myrtle?" Kristy asked. "He ran off, and Linny is so upset."

A search party was organized. Matt and Haley were given dogs to hold while their owners ran around the garden, looking for the turtle. Linny looked as if he was about to cry as he crawled under some bushes. "Myrtle!" he called. "Where are you?"

Just then there was a shout. Timmy Hsu held up Myrtle as he yelled, "I've found her! I've found her!" Myrtle had been sitting among the rocks in the judging circle, her painted shell blending with the dandelions that spotted the lawn.

"Thanks, Timmy," said Linny. "Listen, you can be Myrtle's part owner, just for today, okay?"

Timmy nodded happily, but his smile faded as he glanced at Scott, who was standing to one side, looking sad. Then Hannie spoke up. "Scott, since you're my husband, I suppose you can be part owner of Pat the cat."

By that time, it looked as if just about everybody had arrived. Gabbie and Myriah were the last to come. They had spent their morning running after Chewy, who had, as usual, pulled his leash right out of their hands.

"I think we're ready to begin the judging," said Kristy loudly. Her voice was barely audible over the noise that all those kids and their pets were making.

The rest of us helped to round up the kids and get them into line for the parade past the judges. After the parade, each pet would be shown briefly in the judging circle. Then the judges would consult with each other and the prizes would be announced.

Everybody went quiet as they led their pets past the judges' table. The tension increased as each pet had its time in the ring. Some pets, like Carrot, did tricks for the judges. Others just sat there, looking – or in Priscilla's case, smelling – pretty.

We'd all forgotten about the triplets' mystery pet until Adam ran to the judges to tell them that there was a late entry. Then he ran back to the bush where the bundle had been left and reappeared, leading – a pony! Jordan and Byron were dressed up as the front and back of a horse, and Adam led them proudly past the judges' table. The pony pranced and bucked and kicked until the kids and the judges were nearly hysterical.

After the judging, Kristy led the pet owners to the snack table while the judges conferred. I saw Becca looking nervous as she ate a piece of cake and waited for the results. But she had nothing to be nervous about. Guess why? Because of my idea. Here's what it was: Every pet in the show would get a prize – not first prize or second prize, just a prize that said something about why that pet was special.

The idea was a total success. I saw a lot of happy faces when the judges announced the prizes, starting with "Most Unusually Coloured Pet", for Frodo, going on to "Best Smelling" (guess which white cat won that) and "Cleverest". (Carrot won that one.)

"Funniest Pet" went to the triplets, while "Largest Pet" was awarded to Shannon. "Nicest Pet" went to Midgie, and Myrtle won "Prettiest Shell". Karen was thrilled when Emily Junior won "Best Costume", and Scott and Hannie looked proud when Pat the cat won "Cutest". Pow won "Shortest Legs".

Gabby and Myriah laughed when Chewy was named "Strongest Pet", and even Matt and Haley got a prize for being "Best Pet Handler". Boo-Boo won for "Best Personality". (*That* was a surprise!) And what did Becca win? Well, I predict that Misty's ribbon will be hanging in Becca's room for a long, long time. Here's what it says: "Best All-Round Pet".

15th CHAPTER

Opening Night. I think that those two words may be the most exciting in the English language. I get a shiver just hearing them. And now it was finally here. Opening Night.

We'd had a pretty good dress rehearsal earlier in the week. A few small problems were ironed out that night. For example, my tutu. I think someone mixed up my measurements with the ones belonging to Jumbo the circus elephant. But that's what dress rehearsal is for. And Aunt Cecelia had no trouble taking it in for me. By opening night, my tutu fitted perfectly.

"Try it on for me one more time!" begged Becca. She loves to see me all dressed up like a 'real' ballerina.

"There's no time," I said. "You'll see me in it when I come onstage. But remember, you have to be quiet while I'm dancing." Once, when Becca was younger and I was dancing in *The Nutcracker*, she'd yelled, "Hi, Jessi!" when I made my entrance. Everybody in the audience laughed, and I almost died of embarrassment.

"I won't," she promised. "Don't forget that you promised to give me your toe shoes after the show."

I was going to autograph them and give them to her as a souvenir. That's what the really famous ballerinas do for their fans. Toe shoes usually can't be worn for more than one or two performances – they just don't last under that kind of use.

"Ready, Jessi?" my mum called up the stairs. "I think your friends are here."

I looked out of the window and saw Charlie's car parked in the street. He was going to drive my friends to the performance. But why were they here? I was going to be driving with my parents.

I ran downstairs and out the door. My friends had got really dressed up for the occasion. "Wow, you all look great!" I said.

"So do you," said Kristy. I was wearing my black velvet dress. I wanted to have something nice to change into after the performance.

Claudia looked extremely cool and exotic, as usual. Her hair was plaited with silver ribbons, and she wore a shimmery dark blue mini-dress. On her feet were silver sandals, with laces up the calves – a bit like toe shoes.

Stacey had on a dinner jacket! That's right, a dinner jacket, just like one a boy would wear. But it was made to fit her perfectly, and she looked great. She must have got it in New York.

Kristy had put on a dress, for once, and it was strange to see her in something other than a poloneck and jeans. She looked really pretty. And Mallory, standing next to her in her best skirt and blouse, looked great, too. Dawn and Mary Anne must have swapped clothes – they do that a lot – because I recognized Mary Anne's new Laura Ashley dress on Dawn, and Dawn's pink jumpsuit on Mary Anne.

"We just came round to wish you luck," said Mallory. "I know you're going to do a great job. We can't wait to see you dance!"

"And don't worry about you-know-who," said Dawn. "I'm sure she won't try anything."

I nodded. But I wasn't so sure. I was still worried about Hilary. It wouldn't take much to ruin my performance and make me look like a fool in front of everybody. She'd only have to give me a shove, or spill something on the stage before I went on. I just didn't trust her.

"Thanks for coming round, you lot," I said. "I'll see you after the show, okay? You're all invited backstage."

"Great!" said Stacey. "Break a—" Then she stopped. "I can't say it," she said.

I was glad. I was worried that if somebody said "break a leg" I really might, especially if Hilary decided to pull one of her tricks. I waved at my friends as they got back into the car. "Have fun!" I yelled, as they drove off. By then, Becca had come out of the house. She grabbed my hand and pulled me over to the car.

"I have a surprise for you," she said. "But I'm not going to tell yet. I promised." I wondered what she was talking about. She looked very excited. She also looked very cute, dressed in her ruffly pink party dress.

I got into the car to wait for Mama and Daddy and Aunt Cecelia, but then I jumped back out. I'd forgotten to say goodbye to Squirt! Logan was going to sit for him so that the rest of my family could come to the ballet.

Mama was just telling Logan about Squirt's bedtime when I burst through the door. Squirt was sitting in his high chair, and I picked him up very carefully after making sure that he didn't have too much food on his face (he was eating creamed spinach). "'Bye, Squirt," I said, kissing him. "Wish me luck!"

"Uck," said Squirt. I laughed.

"Do you think he's wishing me luck, or just telling us what he thinks of creamed spinach?" I asked Mama.

"I don't know," she said, laughing. "But we'd better get going. All right, Logan?"

He nodded.

And then it was time to leave. We piled into the car and drove to the civic centre. In the car park, I said goodbye to my family. Then I went in through the backstage entrance.

Backstage before a performance is an exciting place. People are running round and shouting things like, "Where's the blue filter for the spotlight?" and, "Has anyone seen my tiara?" Some of my classmates had already changed into their costumes and were warming up in the wings. The orchestra was making tootling noises in the pit in front of the stage.

I took a minute to peep around the curtain. The audience looked huge! At first I couldn't find my family. Where were they? Then I spotted them, sitting in the middle of the third row. And my friends were sitting behind them. I waved to Mallory, but I knew she couldn't see me. Then I ran to the dressing room.

I changed into my costume carefully, making sure not to rip out any of Aunt Cecelia's careful stitches. I was wearing a brand-new pair of pink tights, to match my pink tutu. After I'd plaited my hair, I pinned on my headpiece – a crown of roses. Later I'd replace it with a (fake) diamond tiara, but for the Rose Adagio I wore flowers in my hair.

I decided to do my make-up before getting into my toe shoes, so I sat down at the big mirror that ran across the ceiling of the dressing room. As I was putting on some blusher (which I never get to wear in real life), I looked behind myself in the mirror and saw Hilary looking straight at me. She smiled shyly when she caught my eye.

"Good luck," she said. "You look beautiful."

"Thanks," I said cautiously. "So do you." Did she really mean it? Or was she just trying to throw me off?

I finished doing my make-up and then took one last look in the mirror. Suddenly I didn't look like Jessi Ramsey, sixth-grade babysitter any more. I looked like a ballerina. The pink tutu was fluffed out perfectly around my waist. The crown of roses sat elegantly on my head. And my face looked – different. Older, more sophisticated. I hardly recognized myself.

"Five minutes!" called somebody from outside the dressing room door. Oh, my lord! I hadn't even warmed up yet! For a minute I felt totally panicked. Then I remembered. I wasn't even in the first act! I had plenty of time.

I ran to the wings, carrying my toe shoes. All of the dancers who were in the first act were already arranged on the stage. The curtain went up, and the orchestra began to play. I heard applause from the audience. Then the ballet began.

I watched the first act as I put on my toe shoes and did my warming-up exercises. I was beginning to get caught up in the story – the story I'd almost forgotten during those weeks of rehearsal. I'd got totally involved in practising my steps over and over again, and the wonderful fairy tale of the Sleeping Beauty had become less important. But now it was coming to life.

On the stage, the king and queen sat on thrones while each fairy danced a special dance as she presented a gift to the baby princess. Then, just as the Lilac Fairy was about to present her gift, the bad fairy, Carabosse, appeared in a coach drawn by four giant rats. (The rats were dancers from the beginner's classes.) She shrieked and cackled as she danced, screaming at the king and queen because they hadn't invited her to the baby's christening.

The king and queen begged her forgiveness, but she wouldn't listen. Instead, she put a curse on the baby princess – that she would one day prick her finger on a spindle and die.

All the dancers fell back when Carabosse cursed the baby – except for the Lilac Fairy. Lisa looked beautiful in her costume as she stepped forward with her wand held high, driving Carabosse back and trying to remove the curse. The Lilac Fairy couldn't take the curse off, but she did manage to change it, so that instead of dying, the princess would only sleep – for a hundred years, until a handsome prince woke her up.

I was completely caught up in the story by the time the first act ended and the "fairies" came rushing off the stage. Then I heard the music that was my cue. I took a deep breath and walked on to the stage. I hoped I looked like a real princess – like Princess Aurora, on her sixteenth birthday.

The Rose Adagio began, and almost immediately, I was swept into the dance so completely that my nervousness fell away. I didn't worry about Hilary. I didn't worry about whether Becca was going to call my name. And I didn't worry about whether my friends were having a good time. I just danced.

At the end of the second act, Carabosse came back onstage. She tempted me with her spindle, and when I took it I pricked my finger and collapsed into my hundred-year sleep. The rest of the dancers put me into a bed, and the "magic forest" grew up around me as I slept.

Next, I danced for the prince who had come looking for me one hundred years later. Of course, I was only supposed to be a vision – a dream. He kept trying to dance with me, but I kept escaping from his embrace.

Then I had a rest, as the prince journeyed to find me, led by the Lilac Fairy. And then he found me and kissed me. I didn't giggle at all. (My friends probably did.) I woke up and danced with all the fairy-tale creatures, including Carrie as the Bluebird of Happiness. That part was especially fun.

Then, at the end, I danced with the prince, who was now my husband. The dancer who played him was from another class. I think he's an eighth-grader. He's a good dancer, and very strong. That's important in this dance, because he keeps having to lift me up in the air.

The music in that part is so pretty that I could have danced for ever. But finally, the music ended and the performance was over. Carrie hugged me as soon as the curtain came down.

"You were *great*!" she said.

"So were you," I answered. "Do you think they liked us?" I listened to the applause. It had started immediately, and it didn't stop as we took our first curtain call.

"I think they did!" she said to me, as the curtain went down again.

When we took our second curtain call, she pushed me out in front of the line of dancers. I'd almost forgotten that I was supposed to curtsy by myself. When I did, the applause swelled, and I heard Kristy's whistle. My dad was yelling "Bravo!" I smiled, and looked to my right. There, in the wings, was Mme Noelle. She smiled back at me. She looked proud.

Then I looked back at the audience. People were starting to stand up – but they weren't leaving. They were still clapping. A standing ovation! I'd never got one before. I felt the tears come to my eyes. And then I saw Becca, her arms full of pink roses, climbing the stairs to the stage.

She walked across the stage and handed them to me, smiling. "Surprise!" she whispered. I took the roses and gave her a huge hug. She'd kept that secret very well. When I let her go, I looked up to see Mallory standing there with another bouquet of roses – white ones. (I think she knew how I felt about red roses!) "These are from everybody in the club," she said, handing them to me. "You were wonderful!"

I was speechless. I stood with my arms full of roses, smiling out at the audience, until the curtain fell again. I will never forget that moment!

Then the show was really over. It was time to get out of my costume, wash the make-up off my face, and go back to being Jessi.

I headed for the dressing room and ran into Hilary in the hall. "Jessi, you were fantastic!" she said.

"So were you. So was everybody," I answered. "Wasn't it fun?" I'd almost forgotten that I'd ever been worried about Hilary and her dirty tricks.

"I want to apologize again," she said. "I'm really sorry for what I did. And you know what? After this, I'm giving up dance."

I was shocked. "You're kidding!" I said.

"Nope," she answered. "I never really loved it. Not like you do. I mainly did it for my mother. And I just wasn't that good at it."

"But you are good," I said. I didn't like to hear her put herself down.

"Not good enough for my mother," Hilary replied. "And I realized that things had got out of hand that day when you confronted me in the dressing room. I must have been crazy to do the things I did to you."

"How does your mother feel about your giving up?" I asked.

She frowned. "I haven't told her yet. But it's my life, and I have to do what I want."

I gave her a hug. "Good luck," I said. "I'll miss you in class." And as soon as I said it, I knew it was true. I would miss her. Hilary's okay. And maybe once she gives up dance her mother will be easier on her.

When I walked into the dressing room, I saw my friends from the BSC waiting for me. They rushed over to hug me and tell me how wonderful the ballet had been.

"Anybody up for ice cream?" I asked, after I'd thanked them for the flowers. My dad had said that I could invite my friends out for a celebration after the performance.

"Sounds great!" said Mallory, and everyone else agreed. After I'd changed, we walked out of the theatre together to meet my family. Becca threw herself at me, and I gave her the toe shoes I'd worn in the show.

"Did you autograph them?" she asked.

"Certainly did," I said, smiling at Mama and Daddy and Aunt Cecelia, who were standing nearby, waiting their turn to hug me. "See? Right there."

I pointed to my left shoe, where I'd written (in red ink, with the calligraphy pen that no longer cursed me), "For Becca, with love from Princess Aurora".

The Babysitters Club

Need a babysitter? Then call the Babysitters Club. Kristy Thomas and her friends are all experienced sitters. They can tackle any job from rampaging toddlers to a pandemonium of pets. To find out all about them, read on!

1 Kristy's Great Idea
2 Claudia and the Phantom Phone Calls
3 The Truth About Stacey
4 Mary Anne Saves the Day
5 Dawn and the Impossible Three
6 Kristy's Big Day
7 Claudia and Mean Janine
8 Boy-Crazy Stacey
9 The Ghost at Dawn's House
10 Logan Likes Mary Anne!
11 Kristy and the Snobs
12 Claudia and the New Girl
13 Goodbye Stacey, Goodbye
14 Hello, Mallory
15 Little Miss Stoneybrook . . . and Dawn
16 Jessi's Secret Language
17 Mary Anne's Bad-Luck Mystery
18 Stacey's Mistake
19 Claudia and the Bad Joke
20 Kristy and the Walking Disaster
21 Mallory and the Trouble with Twins
22 Jessi Ramsey, Petsitter
23 Dawn On The Coast
24 Kristy and the Mother's Day Surprise
25 Mary Anne and the Search for Tigger
26 Claudia and the Sad Goodbye
27 Jessi and the Superbrat
28 Welcome Back, Stacey!
29 Mallory and the Mystery Diary
30 Mary Anne and the Great Romance
31 Dawn's Wicked Stepsister
32 Kristy and the Secret Of Susan
33 Claudia and the Great Search
34 Mary Anne and Too Many Boys
35 Stacey and the Mystery Of Stoneybrook
36 Jessi's Babysitter
37 Dawn and the Older Boy
38 Kristy's Mystery Admirer
39 Poor Mallory!

40 Claudia and the Middle School Mystery
41 Mary Anne Vs. Logan
42 Jessi and the Dance School Phantom
43 Stacey's Emergency
44 Dawn and the Big Sleepover
45 Kristy and the Baby Parade
46 Mary Anne Misses Logan
47 Mallory On Strike
48 Jessi's Wish
49 Claudia and the Genius of Elm Street
50 Dawn's Big Date
51 Stacey's Ex-Best Friend
52 Mary Anne and Too Many Babies
53 Kristy For President
54 Mallory and the Dream Horse
55 Jessi's Gold Medal
56 Keep Out, Claudia!
57 Dawn Saves the Planet
58 Stacey's Choice
59 Mallory Hates Boys (and Gym)
60 Mary Anne's Makeover
61 Jessi and the Awful Secret
62 Kristy and the Worst Kid Ever
63 Claudia's Friend
64 Dawn's Family Feud
65 Stacey's Big Crush
66 Maid Mary Anne
67 Dawn's Big Move
68 Jessi and the Bad Babysitter
69 Get Well Soon, Mallory!
70 Stacey and the Cheerleaders
71 Claudia and the Perfect Boy
72 Dawn and the We Love Kids Club
73 Mary Anne and Miss Priss
74 Kristy and the Copycat
75 Jessi's Horrible Prank
76 Stacey's Lie
77 Dawn and Whitney, Friends For Ever
78 Claudia and Crazy Peaches
79 Mary Anne Breaks the Rules
80 Mallory Pike, No1 Fan
81 Kristy and Mr Mum
82 Jessi and the Troublemaker
83 Stacey Vs. the BSC
84 Dawn and the School Spirit War
85 Claudia Kishi, Live on Air
86 Mary Anne and Camp BSC
87 Stacey and the Bad Girls
88 Farewell Dawn

Goosebumps

R.L.Stine

Reader beware – you're in for a scare!

These terrifying tales will send shivers up your spine:

1 Welcome to Dead House
2 Say Cheese and Die!
3 Stay Out of the Basement
4 The Curse of the Mummy's Tomb
5 Monster Blood
6 Let's Get Invisible!
7 Night of the Living Dummy
8 The Girl Who Cried Monster
9 Welcome to Camp Nightmare
10 The Ghost Next Door
11 The Haunted Mask
12 Piano Lessons Can Be Murder
13 Be Careful What You Wish For
14 The Werewolf of Fever Swamp
15 You Can't Scare Me!
16 One Day at HorrorLand
17 Why I'm Afraid of Bees
18 Monster Blood II
19 Deep Trouble
20 Go Eat Worms
21 Return of the Mummy
22 The Scarecrow Walks at Midnight
23 Attack of the Mutant
24 My Hairiest Adventure
25 A Night in Terror Tower
26 The Cuckoo Clock of Doom
27 Monster Blood III
28 Ghost Beach
29 Phantom of the Auditorium

Goosebumps

30	It Came From Beneath the Sink!
31	Night of the Living Dummy II
32	The Barking Ghost
33	The Horror at Camp Jellyjam
34	Revenge of the Garden Gnomes
35	A Shocker on Shock Street
36	The Haunted Mask II
37	The Headless Ghost
38	The Abominable Snowman of Pasadena
39	How I Got My Shrunken Head
40	Night of the Living Dummy III
41	Bad Hare Day
42	Egg Monsters From Mars
43	The Beast From the East
44	Say Cheese and Die – Again!
45	Ghost Camp
46	How to Kill a Monster
47	Legend of the Lost Legend
48	Attack of the Jack-O'-Lanterns
49	Vampire Breath
50	Calling All Creeps!
51	Beware, the Snowman
52	How I Learned to Fly
53	Chicken Chicken
54	Don't Go To Sleep!
55	The Blob That Ate Everyone
56	The Curse of Camp Cold Lake
57	My Best Friend is Invisible
58	Deep Trouble II
59	The Haunted School
60	Werewolf Skin
61	I Live in Your Basement
62	Monster Blood IV

GOOSEBUMPS

Reader beware – here's THREE TIMES the scare!

Look out for these bumper GOOSEBUMPS editions. With three spine-tingling stories by R.L. Stine in each book, get ready for three times the thrill ... three times the scare ... three times the GOOSEBUMPS!

COLLECTION 1
Welcome to Dead House
Say Cheese and Die
Stay Out of the Basement

COLLECTION 2
The Curse of the Mummy's Tomb
Let's Get Invisible!
Night of the Living Dummy

COLLECTION 3
The Girl Who Cried Monster
Welcome to Camp Nightmare
The Ghost Next Door

COLLECTION 4
The Haunted Mask
Piano Lessons Can Be Murder
Be Careful What You Wish For

COLLECTION 5
The Werewolf of Fever Swamp
You Can't Scare Me!
One Day at HorrorLand

COLLECTION 6
Why I'm Afraid of Bees
Deep Trouble
Go Eat Worms

COLLECTION 7
Return of the Mummy
The Scarecrow Walks at Midnight
Attack of the Mutant

COLLECTION 8
My Hairiest Adventure
A Night in Terror Tower
The Cuckoo Clock of Doom

COLLECTION 9
Ghost Beach
Phantom of the Auditorium
It Came From Beneath the Sink!

Creatures

The Series With Bite!

Everyone loves animals. The birds in the trees. The dogs running in the park. That cute little kitten.

But don't get too close. Not until you're sure. Are they ordinary animals – or are they creatures?

1. Once I Caught a Fish Alive
Paul's special new fish is causing problems. He wants to get rid of it, but the fish has other ideas...

2. If You Go Down to the Woods
Alex is having serious problems with the school play costumes. Did that fur coat just move?

3. See How They Run
Jon's next-door neighbour is very weird. In fact, Jon isn't sure that Frankie is completely human...

4. Who's Been Sitting in My Chair?
Rhoda's cat Opal seems to be terrified ... of a chair! But then this chair belongs to a very strange cat...

Look out for these new creatures...

5. Atishoo! Atishoo! All Fall Down!
Chocky the mynah bird is a great school pet. But now he's turning nasty. And you'd better do what he says...

6. Give a Dog a Bone
A statue of a faithful dog sounds really cute. But this dog is faithful unto death. And beyond...

Creatures – you have been warned!